FINANCIAL AND MANAGEMENT ACCOUNTING

Financial and Management Accounting

Second Revised Edition

By
Madhu Vij

ANMOL PUBLICATIONS PVT. LTD.
NEW DELHI - 110 002 (INDIA)

ANMOL PUBLICATIONS PVT. LTD.
Regd. Office: 4360/4, Ansari Road, Daryaganj,
New Delhi-110002 (India)
Tel.: 23278000, 23261597, 23286875, 23255577
Fax: 91-11-23280289
Email: anmolpub@gmail.com
Visit us at: www.anmolpublications.com

Branch Office: No. 1015, Ist Main Road, BSK IIIrd Stage
IIIrd Phase, IIIrd Block, Bangalore-560 085 (India)
Tel.: 080-41723429 • Fax: 080-26723604
Email: anmolpublicationsbangalore@gmail.com

Financial and Management Accounting

Second Revised Edition, 2001

Reprint, 2004, 2008, 2010

PRINTED IN INDIA

Printed at Mehra Offset Press, Delhi.

Contents

Preface vii

Acknowledgements x

Part I - An Accounting Overview

1. The Accounting Environment 1
2. Processing Accounting Information 8
3. Special Aspects in the Measurement of Business Income: Depreciation Methods 52
4. Special Aspects in the Measurement of Business Income: Inventory Valuation 73

Part II - Analysis of Financial Statements

5. Statement of Changes in Financial Position: Funds Flow Analysis 94
6. Statement of Cash Flows 113
7. Financial Statement Analysis 132
8. How to Read a Financial Statement 187

Part III - Cost Behaviour, Planning and Decision-Making

9. Basic Cost Concepts for Planning and Control 193
10. Cost-Volume-Profit Relationships 201
11. Short-term Decisions 242
12. The Budgeting Process 256

Part IV - Control and Performance Evaluation

13. Standard Costing and Variance Analysis 271

14. Management Control Systems and Responsibility Accounting 312

15. Transfer Pricing 332

Part V - Special Topics in Accounting

16. Human Resource Accounting and Inflation Accounting 356

17. International Accounting 371

18. Accounting Systems and Computers 385

Appendix-I: Format of a Balance Sheet and an Income Statement 398

Preface

This book is designed to provide a thorough understanding of the financial and management accounting technique as an essential part of the decision-making process in the total business information system. A careful and thorough presentation of the various dimensions and uses of accounting, is the underlying theme of the book.

The book is appropriate as a core text for an introductory course in accounting. It presupposes no prior knowledge of accounting. It presents in a very clear and understandable manner, the important topics that all students of accounting should study. The book is also oriented towards non-accounting financial managers who should have an understanding of the financial implication of business decisions.

Plan of the Book

The book is organised in five major parts. Part I tries to prepare the necessary background by giving an accounting overview and consists of four chapters that help in acquiring a clear and firm grasp of the basic nature of accounting and the environment in which it is developed and used. The generally accepted accounting principles and the balance sheet, as a basic financial statement, are discussed. Special aspects in the measurement of business income viz. depreciation methods and inventory valuation are also discussed.

Part II, concentrates on methods for analysing and interpreting the information contained in the financial statements. Financial statement analysis is a useful tool for understanding the firm's performance and helps us in comparing a company's present financial position with its past position or the company's performance with that of other companies in the industry. Ratio analysis is a technique commonly used for this purpose.

Part III provides an appraisal of the dynamics of cost behaviour and consists of four chapters. An understanding of the cost behaviour is essential if a manager has to develop successful business strategies and make rational decisions. Cost volume-profit analysis is discussed in this section, which is a valuable tool in planning and helps in making a wide variety of business decisions, analysing results and incorporating new information into plans. Budgeting, which provides the foundation for the managerial functions of planning and control, is also discussed in this section. A budget specially provides a means for monitoring whether activities are going as per the plan or not. Special aspects of budgeting like performance budgeting and zero-base budgeting are also discussed.

Part IV, integrates the management functions of control and performance evaluation. To perform these functions more effectively, managers use the technique of standard costing and responsibility accounting. Both the techniques are important for managers to achieve control over business operation. To evaluate performance of setting transfer prices is also discussed.

Finally, Part V, covers special topics in accounting like Human Resource Accounting, Inflation Accounting, International Accounting and Accounting and Computers.

The book will be of immense value to students pursuing the MBA, Commerce and other courses at various universities and professional institutes. It can be used as an introductory course at both the undergraduate programmes. The book can also be used in various Management Development Programmes as a non technical accounting reference for non-accounting financial managers in business and other organizations.

Changes in the Second Edition

All chapters have been revised to incorporate the most up-to-date information available.

Various concepts, tools and techniques of financial and management accounting have been illustrated with suitable examples. Wherever necessary solved problems and also unsolved problems at the end of chapter have been added to provide the students with a more exhaustive coverage.

The text of the revised Accounting Standards as issued by the Council of Institute of Chartered Accountants of India for 'Depreciation Accounting' and 'Valuation of Inventories' has been included.

In the chapter on Financial Statement Analysis we have increased the coverage by adding new problems and case studies.

The chapter on Cost-Volume-Profit Analysis (Chapter 10) has been revised to include both more illustrative problems and unsolved problems at the end of the chapter.

Several new points have been added in chapter 14 and 15 to increase the coverage of these two chapters. A number of problems, both solved and unsolved have also been added to help the students understand the concept of Responsibility Accounting and Transfer Pricing in detail.

Acknowledgements

I would like to acknowledge the contribution of a number of students who assisted me with the second edition of this book. My sincere thanks to all of them. A special thanks is also due to my husband and children--Anupriya and Arjun. Without their influence and moral support, this text-book would not have been possible.

I would like to express my deep sense of gratitude to Prof. V.K. Bhalla who was a constant source of inspiration and help in completing the present work. I would also like to express my sincere thanks to Prof. B.S. Sharma, Vice-Chancellor, Kota Open University, Prof. A.S. Narang, Dean, Faculty of Management Studies, Prof. R.K. Lele, Delhi School of Economics, Prof. M.P. Gupta, Faculty of Management Studies, Ms. Anupama Vohra, Faculty of Management Studies, Ms. Tanuja Agarwala, Faculty of Management Studies.

I owe a lot to my father, Prof. M.C. Kapoor who helped me in more than one way complete the present work. But for his constant encouragement and guidance the book could never have been completed. Finally, I am sincerely grateful to the members of Anmol Publications Pvt. Ltd., New Delhi for the meticulous care taken by them in publishing the present book.

1

The Accounting Environment

Accounting is a dynamic discipline. It is designed to provide financial information regarding the economic activities of an organisation for decision making managers. Business executives use the financial information provided by an accounting system to help them plan and control the activities of the business.

Accounting Defined

Accounting is the 'language of business' and the accounting function is vital to every segment of our society. Accounting terms provide a basic means of communication within and between organisations. Specifically accounting can be defined as "the process of identifying measuring and communicating economic information to permit informed judgements and decisions by the users of the information[1]. This information is primarily financial in nature and is generally stated in money terms.

The American Institute of Certified Public Accountants has defined accounting as "the art of recording, classifying and summarizing in a significant manner and in terms of money transactions and events which are, in part at least, of a financial character and interpreting the results thereof."

Today, the accountant is an indispensable part of the organization and is viewed as a decision maker and an advisor whose decisions and actions determine the success or failure of an organization. Accountants supply management with significant financial and economic data that are useful for decision making.

Keeping the above dimensions in mind, the introductory chapter deals with the nature of accounting and the relationship between accounting and management. The two areas of accounting viz. Financial Accounting and Management Accounting are related and both deal with economic events. But they differ also in many ways. The chapter also discusses the process of planning and control as used by managers in a business.

Objectives of Accounting

The main objectives of accounting are:

1. To maintain a complete and systematic record of all financial transactions in the organization.
2. To present a true and fair financial position of the affairs of the business.
3. To calculate the net profit or net loss of the business.
4. To help in decision making. Managers use accounting information to set goals for their organization, to evaluate the progress towards those goals and to take corrective action if necessary.
5. To provide information to the various parties who are interested in the affairs of the business like investors, creditors, etc.

Financial Accounting and Management Accounting

Accounting is often divided into two categories - Financial Accounting and Management Accounting.

Financial Accounting

Financial accounting information is designed primarily for use by persons outside the firm, such as creditors, stockholders, owners, governmental agencies and the general public.

Most companies publish the financial accounting data through a set of general purpose statements known as the company's annual report. These statements provide most of the information needed by external users. Specialized needs of specific users are satisfied through supplementary reports which are published at various intervals.

Financial accounting provides information that covers relatively long periods of times. In addition, financial accounting information is historical in nature and the financial accounting reports concentrate more on the results of past decisions.

Financial accounting is governed by the generally accepted accounting principles that are subject to ever-changing rules and regulations and also disputed interpretations. Financial accounting reports are developed from the basic accounting system, which is designed to highlight the data about completed transactions.

Management Accounting

Management accounting is primarily concerned with man agers of a company and provides information meant for internal use. Managers gather this data and analyze, process, interpret and communicate the results so that this information can be used for making sound internal decisions, e.g., financial decisions, marketing decisions, production decisions, resource allocation decisions and so on.

Management accounting helps the different departments in an organization to work in a successful coordinated manner by acting as a communication link between various departments.

Managerial accounting reports are usually designed for a specific decision and provide information for relatively short periods of time. They are not governed by any set of principles and are not required by law.

Since management accounting is not required by law, the reports prepared by management accountants are subject to a cost-benefit analysis, i.e., the perceived benefits of the report should exceed the costs. Also, since no external standards are imposed on information provided to internal users, management accounting reports run the risk of being subjective.

In summary, both management and financial accounting deal with economic events. Both are concerned with revenues and expenses, assets, liabilities and cash flows. Also, both require quantifying the results of economic activity. In actual practice, it is difficult to classify an information as being either exclusively financial or managerial. The two accounting systems are part of the total business system and hence they normally overlap. For example, much of the future planning data associated with management accounting is based on the historical information which is retained for financial accounting purposes[2].

The distinction between management accounting and financial accounting is as given below:

Financial Accounting	Management Accounting
1. Provides information to external users.	1. Provides information to internal users.
2. Required by law. Is governed by Generally Accepted Accounting Principles.	2. Not required by law. It not governed by any set of rules.
3. Reports and statements are prepared for relatively long period of time.	3. Reports and statements are prepared for relatively short period of time.
4. Reports prepared are general purpose reports.	4. Reports prepared are specifically designed for a particular user or a particular decision.
5. Reports are historical	5. Reports mainly are concerned with future or outline future plans.
6. Objective data is emphasized and used.	6. Allows use of subjective data also.
7. Statements are for relatively long period of time.	7. Statements are for very short period of time.

Functions of Management

The job of the manager is to get things done through people. The actions of many managers are combined for the smooth functioning of an organization. Managers at the higher level work in coordination with the lower levels of management to achieve the various objectives of the company.

Two important functions of management are planning and control. The planning decision is the process by which managers decide what tasks are needed and how they should be achieved. However, planning by itself is not enough. There must be a complete follow-up to check whether the plans are being carried out as intended.

Controlling ensures that the tasks are properly completed, i.e. the results agree with the plans. Actual performance is compared with the planned performance in controlling. If there are significant deviations from plans, efforts are made by the management to either revise the plans or to direct activities along the original plan. The original plan is adjusted / revised if the management decides to direct activities along a different course from that originally contemplated due to changed circumstances. Also, implicit in control is performance evaluation i.e. Managers reviewing the achievements of the subordinates and comparing them against standards.

Planning

Planning consists of two basic activities: (1) setting goal and (2) selecting a way to achieve these goals. Management often make a distinction between long-term planning and short-term planning. Long-term planning emphasizes the goals that the organization expects to achieve over several years and the activities that will help the organization to achieve these goals. Short-term planning is made in the light of the organization's long-range goals. Short-term goals are more specific than long-range goals and they emphasize the current situation, i.e., they are statements of what management plans to achieve next year. Thus, short-range plans support the long-raange plans and emphasize on specific activities to be undertaken in the near future to move the organization towards long-term goals.

The planning process uses an important mathematical technique—the study of break-even point. The break-even charts, the 'cost-volume-profit' analysis, and the product-mix decisions are some of the widely discussed techniques that help management in the planning process.

Control

Control reports provide feedback to managers to help determine where attention might be required. Managers use such reports to determine whether some aspects of their areas of responsibility require corrective action. The essence of cost control is actually a control over the people who incur the cost. When the costs are identified with the persons responsible for their occurrence, it is called responsibility accounting.

Management places the notion of responsibility accounting at the very centre of the management control system. A responsibility accounting system identifies every expenditure and makes everyy expenditure the responsibility of some manager. This system conforms to the classical principles of management which emphasizes lines of authority and responsibility.

The techniques practised under the responsibility accounting system are mainly two: budgeting and variance analysis. The use of standard costs and/or budgets to quantify plans for responsibility centres, and the measurement of performance in terms of variance therefrom is the main technique of managerial control in organization.

Limitations of Accounting

1. Accounting records only those transactions which are of a financial nature. Facts and events of a non-financial nature that affect the functioning of the business are not recorded. For example skilled human personnel, the location of the business etc. These facts, though important, are not recorded in the books of accounts.
2. The recording of the transaction in accounting is made on the basis of the historical concept. All assets and

liabilities are recorded at historical cost and current values are not taken into consideration. Appreciation or depreciation in the value of certain assets and liabilities is not recorded in the books of accounts. For example building, land etc. may have appreciated in value over time but the accounting records continue to show them at their historical cost figures.

Notes

1. American Accounting Association: A Statement of Basic Accounting Theory (Ivanston, III) 1966, p. 1.

2. Edmonds, McKinron, McGary, "Principles of Accounting", Dame Publishing Inc., Houston, Texas, p. 10.

Questions

(i) Why is accounting considered an information system ?

(ii) Distinguish between management accounting and financial accounting.

(iii) In what way does a planning decision differ from a control decision?

(iv) Briefly explain the role of accounting in the decision-making process.

(v) What broad management objectives are facilitated through the use of accounting information ?

(vi) Explain the scope and limitation of Management accounting.

2

Processing Accounting Information

Generally Accepted Accounting Principles (GAAP) are the accounting standards and concepts developed over a long span of years by the accounting profession. These are the "ground rules" developed for internal use by management and also for external use by persons outside the business, such as owners, creditors, bankers, government agencies, etc. Preparation of financial statements in conformity with GAAP ensures fairly reliable inter- and intra-company comparisons over a period of time.

The chapter discusses these principles, i.e. the GAAP which govern the recording of the business transactions. The contents of the basic Financial Statements viz. the Balance Sheet and the Income Statement are then explained including how these statements are developed.

BASIC CONCEPTS

The Business Entity Concept

An accounting entity is a specific unit for which the accountant wants to measure and report accounting information. The business entity concept assumes that each business is separate and distinct from its owners, creditors, managers, employees, other interested parties and from other businesses. For each business, there is a separate set of accounting records and a separate set of financial statements. The financial statements of a firm identify the accounting entity and report the financial information for that entity only.

For example, X starts a business as a stationery merchant. For maintaining accounting records, the businessman X and individual X are assumed to have a separate legal entity. If X follows the entity concept, he will account for the money generated by the business separately from the money generated by the sale of an item belonging to himself. This separation makes it possible to analyze the financial position of the business clearly. Thus business transactions and personal transactions should not be accounted together. They should be evaluated separately.

The Going Concern Concept

Unless strong evidence exists to the contrary, the accounting system assumes that the business will continue to operate for an indefinitely long period of time. This assumption is referred to as the going concern assumption. Keeping in view this concept, the assets are carried in the books of accounts at their cost, less depreciation value and are not adjusted to liquidation values. Similarly, liabilities reflect what the business owes and not the values for which the creditors would settle in case of liquidation.

Money Measurement Concept

Accounting records only those transaction can be expressed in monetary terms. This concept permits the summarization and analysis of accounting information through mathematical manipulation. Money serves as a common denominator in which various items can be expressed meaningfully. Items like competence and motivation of human resources, howsoever important for the survival of the business are not recorded in the books of accounts as they cannot be translated into monetary terms. Accordingly, accountants try and measure activity in monetary units, whenever possible.

The Cost Concept

Assets (such as land, buildings, equipment etc.) and liabilities are recorded in the accounting records at their historical cost, i.e. the price paid to originally acquired the asset or the liability. As time passes, this amount may be very different from what we would have to pay today to replace the asset or the liability. But the accounting records continue to show the amount when the exchange occured. For example, a business buys a building worth Rs. 1,00,000 in cash. In the accounting records, the value of the building will be entered at its cost price, i.e. Rs. 1,00,000. After four years, the value of the building goes up to Rs. 5,00,000. However, the accounting records would continue to show the value of the building at the cost price of Rs. 1,00,000 less depreciation.

Historical cost is verifiable. It represents the cost that was objectively agreed upon the buyer and the seller. Hence the basic objective of the cost principle is the measurement of accurate and reliable profits and losses for a business over a period of time. However, some accountants have argued that in todays inflationary environment, the relevance of historical cost is lost. Their arguments are gaining popularity, as is evidenced by many large companies, who now prepare supplementary information after taking into account the changes in the purchasing power. Nevertheless, historical cost continues to be used for the preparation of the primary financial statements.

The Conservation Concept

The concept states 'Anticipate no profits but provide for all possible losses'. The accountants normally take a conservative position in the application of accounting principles. For example, if the assets are worth more than their costs, the accountants will rarely take note of this in his books of account; but if he has evidence that assets may be realized at even less than cost, then he is more inclined to accept this in recording of the transaction.

This concept is somewhat illogical and the account must recognize the persons can be misled by understatement as well as by overstatements of the accounting records.

The Consistency Concept

An accounting method or procedure once chosen should be followed consistently from year to year. Consistency in accounting records is necessary for the purposes of comparison over a period of time. For example, inventories may be accounted for on a first-in, first-out basis, a last-in, first-out basis, or by some other method. The method of accounting chosen for pricing of inventories should be followed consistently over a period of time. The choice of a particular method will have an influence on the reported profits as well as on the inventory cost for the balance sheet.

However, consistency does not imply rigidity. Desirable changes should be made and improved accounting techniques should be introduced if the firm has a good reason to do so.

The Dual Aspect Concept

This is the basic and the most fundamental concept of accounting. There are always at least two items to be considered in each transaction. A business transaction does not affect just one item alone. In every transaction something is given and something is received. The dual aspect of each transaction forms the basis of the double-entry accounting. In double-entry accounting, it is recognized that no asset can exist without someone having a claim to it.

Assets are things of value to the firm. They are the resources owned by the firm. Equities are the claims of various parties against the assets. Equities are of two types: Owners' Equity and liabilities. Owners' Equity represents the claims of the owners while liabilities represents the claims of the creditors against the firm. Since the assets of a business are equal to its Equity, the fundamental accounting equality is:

ASSETS = EQUITIES

or ASSETS = OWNERS' EQUITY + LIABILITIES

Both the assets and the equities are accounted for at the time the transactions are recorded. Let us consider an example.

Y starts a business with a capital of Rs. 1,00,000. The accounting records of the business will be shown as follows after the first transaction:

Owners' Equity	Rs. 1,00,000	Cash	Rs. 1,00,000.

In the example given above, if the business purchases land worth Rs. 40,000, then the accounting records after the second transaction will be shown as:

Owners' Equity	Rs. 1,00,000	Cash	60,000
		Land	40,000

Hence, the double-entry system is designed to maintain the logical equality of the acconting equation, i.e., sum of the assets must always be equal to the total equities.

The Realization Concept

According to this concept, revenues are not recognized unless they are realized. The point at which the revenue is realised will vary depending upon circumstances. For example, revenue is realised when goods are delivered to customers and not when the contract is signed to deliver the goods.

Matching Concept

Expenses incurred for a period are matched to the revenues for the same period to arrive at a reasonably correct measurement of the net income or the net loss. For every accounting period, if expenses are not properly offset against revenue for the same period, the resulting net income or net loss will be reported incorrectly. In some situations matching must be done on an estimated basis. For example, an equipment/ fixed asset with a useful life of more than one year. Here, the cost of the equipment will be matched agaisnt the revenues of the future fiscal periods that will benefit from its use. The portion of the cost that has to be deferred and matched against the revenues of any given year depends upon the useful life and salvage value of the asset.

The Matching concept is accomplished through the earnings statement. The difference between revenues and expenses is a measure of how effectively management has utilized the firm's resources. Investment and financing decisions are largely dependent on the ability of the management to utilize the invested capital effectively. For this reason, the matching principle is regarded as one of the most important concept in accounting theory.

The Accounting Period Concept

The accounting period used by business for preparing its Financial Statements is usually one year. The Income Statement and the Balance Sheet are prepared by the business at the end of each accounting period. The Income Statement discloses the operating results of a business by matching the revenues earned during the accounting period with the expenses incurred in obtaining that revenue. The Balance Sheet shows the financial position of the company at the end of the accounting period.

Materiality Concept

Accountants should record only events or material that are important and overlook materially insignificant events. Choice of material and inmatrerial events is left to the discretion of the accountant.

THE ACCOUNTING EQUATION

For accounting purposes, all business prepare financial statements that describe the business activity. These statements cannot be prepared until the accountant has recorded, analyzed, and summarized all the financial information in a relevant manner. All financial statements can be expressed in the form of the basic accounting equation.

The Basic Accounting Equation is often expressed as

Assets = Liabilities + Owner's Equity

The accounting equation shows the relationship among assets, liabilities and owner's Equity.

An economic entity employs a certain amount of capital. This fund of capital can be described in two different ways: *First,* as to the form of its investment or the things that were purchased with the fund and *second* as to the source of the fund of capital. For example, if a business is using Rs. 1,00,000 of capital, an investigation will show the various properties or assets in which the Rs. 1,00,000 is invested—land, buildings, machinery, materials, etc. Then, we can find an answer to the question where did it come from, or who furnished the Rs. 1,00,000 of capital. Part of the capital could have been furnished by the owner or the stockholders, part could be borrowed from the bank, partly by employees and so on. And since a certain total of invested capital is merely being viewed in its two aspects, it follows that the totals of the two groups of items must be equal.

Assets

Assets are things of value. They are economic resources which are owned by a business and that can be measured objectively in terms of money. Cash, Accounts Receivable Inventory, land, building, machinery are examples of assets. Assets can be classified into 2 main categories - Fixed Assets and Current Assets. Some of the most commonly used assets are listed below:

Current Assets

Current assets are those assets that can be converted into cash within an operating cycle of the firm. The time required to complete an operating cycle depends upon the nature of the business though it usually does not extend beyond a year. Examples of Current Assets are Cash, Accounts Receivable Inventory, etc. Assets such as building, machinery, etc. used in conducting the business will not be converted into cash in the normal course of operations and hence are classified as fixed assets.

Cash denotes funds readily available with the firm either in currency form or as bank balance.

Accounts Receivable: They are also known as Debtors and are amounts due from customers of a business for goods and services sold "on account".

Inventories consist of stocks of raw materials, work-in-progress, finsihed goods and stores and spares.

Prepaid Insurance refers to Insurance premiums paid or payable which are applicable to the future.

Fixed Assets: These assets are used in business operations over a relatively long period of time and it is not expected that the assets will be sold or converted into cash. Examples of fixed assets are land, buildings, machinery equipment. These assets are generally expressed at their acquisition cost less depreciation. As per conventional accounting principles, accounting does not measure economic values—for example, land and buildings may have appreciated in value and their current market value may be high, but accounting principles require that a portion of their future benefit be depreciated each year.

Investment are financial securities owned by the firm. Some investments may be short-term in nature and may be classified under current assets. Some investment may be held for a longer period of time for example equity shares of other firms.

Miscellaneous Expenditure and Losses

Two items constitute this category: *(i)* Miscellaneous expenditure and *(ii)* Losses. Items like preliminary expenses which have not been written off are included in Miscellaneous expenditures. Losses are shown on the asset side of the balance sheet mainly to keep the share capital in tact. As per Company Law requirements, the Share Capital (also referred to as Owner's Equity) cannot be reduced when a loss occurs.

Liabilities

Liabilities are claims of the outsiders. These outside parties are called creditors. "Insider Claims" are called 'Owners' Equity' or Capital. These are claims held by the owners of the business. An owners has a claims to the entity's assets because of his investment in the business.

Current Liabilities: Liabilities are obligations arising from business operations that have to be normally paid within one year. Examples of current liabilities are accounts payable, creditors taxes payable, wages payable, advance payment received etc.

Long-term liabilities are obligations that will mature in more than one year from the Balance-Sheet date. Examples listed under this heading include long-term loans, bonds, debentures, fixed-deposits etc.

Owner's Equity in a company generally arises from two sources: the amount the shareholders paid for their shares when it was originally issued, and of the amount of Retained Earnings (Reserves & Surplus).

Share Capital is of two types: Equity capital and Preference capital. Equity capital represents the contribution of the equity shareholders who are theoretically the owners of the organisation. The rate of Dividend on the Equity Share Capital is not fixed. Preference capital represents the contribution of preference shareholders and the dividend rate here is normally fixed.

Reserves and Surplus: They are also known as retained earnings i.e. the earnings which have been retained by the firm and have not been distributed to the shareholders. Reserves are held in various forms: General Reserve, Capital Reserve, Investment Reserve, Capital Redemption Reserve and so on.

Debits & Credits

Accounts: An account may be defined as a record of increases, decreases and balances in an individual item of Asset, Liability, Capital, Revenue or Expenses. The simple form of an account is the 'T' Account as it resembles the capital letter 'T' and may appear somewhat as shown below:

Name of the account	
Debit	Credit

An account has three parts—(1) name of the account, (2) Left side of the account known as *debit* side, and (3) Right side of the account known as *credit* side. It is a common practice to abbreviate the terms debit and credit with the initials "Dr." and

"Cr." respectivelyy. Increases in accounts are entered on one side and decreases on the other side of the account. The balance is inserted near the last figure on the side within the last larger amount.

The act of recording a debit entry is called *debiting* the account; recording a credit entry is called *crediting* the amount. Accountants use the term debit and credit simply to refer to the two sides of an account, without any hidden or subtle implication. Many non-accountants seem to think that debit means something unfavourable and credit means something favourable. This is not the case. The words merely refer to the both sides of an account.

Whether an increase in a given item is debited or credit depends on category of the item.

ANY ASSET A/C

Dr.	Cr.
+	-
Increases	Decreases

ANY LIABILITY OR OWNER'S EQUITY A/C

Dr.	Cr.
-	+
Decreases	Increases

The rules to be followed for debiting and crediting accounts are arbitrarily defined but are logically consistent. For example, a debit means an increase in any asset, but a debit will also decrease any liability or owner's equity account.

An account will have a debit balance when the sum of its debit exceeds the sum of its credit; it has a credit balance when the sum of the credits is larger. Hence, the balance of the account is the difference between the sum of the items on both sides of the account.

Double-Entry Accounting—the Equality of Debits & Credits

The rules for debits and credits are designed in a manner that the accounting equation will always hold true so that debits will always equal the credits. Hence Assets will always equal Equities; i.e. the sum total of debits will always equal the sum total of credit.

Hence, till now, two fundamental requirements of the double-entry accounting have been discussed. First is the equality of the basic accounting equation (i.e. Assets = Equities) which must be maintained, and second is total debits must equal total credits. To maintain these two equalities, the recording scheme to be followed will now be discussed.

Recording Transactions: Given below are a few transactions which are recorded with the help of 'T' account. The transaction number is used as a recording reference.

1. X starts business with a capital of Rs. 2,00,000.
2. Land was purchased for cash at a cost of Rs. 40,000.
3. Equipment was purchased for Rs. 20,000 on credit.
4. Part of the land was sold for Rs. 15,000 on credit.

Cash

Dr.	Cr.
(1) 2,00,000	(2) 40,000

Capital

Dr.	Cr.
	(1) 2,00,000

Land

Dr.	Cr.
(2) 40,000	(4) 15,000

Equipment

Dr.	Cr.
(3) 20,000	

Creditors or Accounts Payable

Dr.	Cr.
	(3) 20,000

Accounts Receivable

Dr.	Cr.
(4) 15,000	

Each transaction can be traced in terms of debits and credits to the respective accounts. The detailed recording of each transaction takes place with the help of the various books which are described below:

I. The Journal is the book of original entry for accounting data. The transactions are entered in a chronological order in the journal. The simplest journal consists of a book with a column for dates at the left, a wide column for description of the account titles and two columns for entering monetary amounts. The first column is called the debt column, and the second is called the credit column. A simple journal of this type is called a *general journal*. The process of recording transactions in the journal is known as journalizing. The format of a general journal is as given below:

General Journal

Date 1999	Description	Debit (Rs.)	Credit (Rs.)
January 1	Cash	2,00,000	
	To		
	Capital		2,00,000
	(Invested cash in the business)		

After journalizing the data is posted to the ledger, the book of subsequent or secondary entry.

II. Ledgers: A ledger is a group of 'T' accounts. It is a means of accumulating all the information in one place about changes in a specific asset, a liability, or owner's equity. For example, a ledger account for cash records the amount of cash receipts, cash payments and the current cash balance. This record of cash can help management in planning operations in advance regarding the availability of cash.

III. The Trial Balance: The process of transferring information from the journal to the ledger for the purpose of summarizing the data is called posting. After the posting has been completed, the ledger account balances can be computed. A list of the balance of the general ledger accounts is called a trial balance. Thus, a trial balance is a list of ledger account titles and their respective balances.

As every transaction results in an equal amount of debits and credits in the ledger, the total of all debit entries in the ledger ought to equal the total of all credit entries. At the end of the accounting period, we check this equality by preparing a trial balance.

The procedure for preparing a trial balance is as under:

1. Record the debit and credit balances of each account.
2. Add the columns and record the total.
3. Compare the totals.

If the totals agree, i.e. Debit = Credit, then the trial balance is in balace. However, trial balance indicataes only arithmetical accuracy of the records. It is quite possible that an incorrect amount has been included both as a debit and as a credit or the transaction has been left out entirely or a compensating error has been committed.

The Trial Balance will appear as given below:

Arjun Ltd.
Trial Balance as on June 30, 19×1

Particulars	Dr.	Cr.
Cash	10,000	
Accounts Receivable	5,000	
Land	6,000	
Accounts Payable		3,000
Sales		25,000
Buildings	7,000	
Purchases	10,000	
Capital		10,000
Total	38,000	38,000

Hence, a trial balance should be prepared whenever the accountant feels that it would be useful to test the equality of debits and credits. The needs of the company dictate the accounting policy and a trial balance should be drawn whenever it is beneficial to do so.

The Adjustment Entries

After the trial balance has been prepared, several adjustment entries have to be made so that the financial statements will be as accurate as possible. These adjustments usually refer to the economic events that have taken place during the period but have not been recorded earlier.

Adjustment can be classified under the following heads:

1. The depreciation adjustment
2. Provision for bad debts
3. Provision of dividends and income taxes
4. Accrual Adjustments—for example, expenses that increase with the passage of time must be recorded, whether paid or not; and the liability for unpaid expenses must also be recognised. Similarly, revenues that increase with the passage of time must be recorded, whether collected or not; and the asset representing the amount due must be recognised.
5. Prepayment Adjustment—If a company pays Rs. 300 as insurance for two years, then the prepaid insurance remaining is shown on the asset side of the balance sheet to the extent of Rs. 150. The balance Rs. 150 is shown as insurance expense in the income statement of the current year.

Preparation of Financial Statements

After the trial balance has been prepared and all adjustment entries made, we then proceed to the preparation of final accounts. Final accounts are prepared with the help of two statements:

1. Trading and Profit and Loss Account for the Year

This statement matches against the income, the corresponding costs for a specified period. If revenues exceed costs, there is a net profit for the business; if not, there is a net loss. The Trading and Profit and Loss Account first calculates the Gross Profit for the company after taking into account all manufacturing cost for the year. From this Gross Profit, all administrative and other remaining costs are deducted to arrive at a figure of Net Profit.

2. Balance Sheet

A Balance sheet is a statement of the financial affairs of the firm at a given point of time. It tells us nothing of how the firm has arrived at this situation.

The Balance sheet contains two parts—assets and liabilities and owner's equity. *Assets* are resources owned by the company acquired at a measurable money cost. They are of two types—current assets and fixed assets. Examples of current assets are cash, accounts receivable, prepaid expenses, inventories, etc. Examples of fixed assets are land, building, machinery, etc.

Liabilities are amount owed to outsiders e.g. accounts payable.

Capital or Owner's Equity is the interest of the owners in an organization.

The format of a Balance Sheet is as follows:

Liability & Owner's Equity	**Assets**
— Share Capital	— Fixed Assets
— Reserves and Surplus	— Investments
— Secured Loans	— Current Assets, Loans and Advances
— Unsecured Loans	— Miscellaneous Expenditures and Losses
— Current Liabilities and Provisions	

By definition, the two sides of the Balance Sheet must always be equal.

A detailed and exact format of the Income Statement and the Balance Sheet as prescribed by the Indian Companies Act, 1956 are contained in Appendix I. The appendix also contains a Financial Statement Analysis of the given Income Statement and the Balance Sheet.

Illustrative Problems

I. Journalise the transactions given below in the books of X :

Jan. 1 X starts business with Rs. 20,000.

Jan. 2	X purchases furniture Rs. 850 and typewriter Rs. 1,500 payment made by cheque.
Jan. 3	Goods purchased on credit from Y, Rs. 5,000.
Jan. 4	Goods purchased for cash from X, Rs. 1,000.
Jan. 5	Goods sold on credit to M, Rs. 2,000.
Jan. 6	Goods sold for cash to L, Rs. 1,000.
Jan. 7	Paid rent for Jan. Rs. 200.
Jan. 8	Paid for Postage Stamps, Rs. 100.
Jan. 9	Received cash from M, Rs. 1,900.
Jan. 10	Issued cheque to Y, Rs. 5,000.
Jan. 11	Deposited Rs. 1,000 in Bank.
Jan. 12	Paid Insurance Premium, Rs. 450 by cheque.

II. R was carrying on business as a cloth dealer. On 1st July, his assets were furniture and office equipment Rs. 2,500, stock Rs. 25,000, cash in hand Rs. 600, Bank balance Rs. 8,500, amount due from B Rs. 1,200, amount due from G Rs. 1,500. On that date he owed Rs. 2,000 to M and Rs. 1,450 to N. His transactions during the month of July were:

July 2	Sold cloth on credit to X,	Rs. 500
July 3	Purchase cloth from Y on credit,	Rs. 2,000
July 4	Paid rent for July by cheque,	Rs. 800
July 5	Purchases of cloth (paid by cheque),	Rs. 2,000
July 7	Cash Sales,	Rs. 450
July 8	Received cheque from B,	Rs. 1,180
Allowed him discount (for July 1 transaction)		Rs. 20
July 9	Paid for Stationery and Postage.	Rs. 50
July 10	Drawn cash for private use.	Rs. 250
July 11	Purchased goods on credit from M.	Rs. 2,500
July 12	Sent cheque to M in full settlement (for July 1 transaction).	Rs. 1,950
July 13	Sold goods on credit to G.	Rs. 1,800

July 14	Paid Telephone charges.	Rs. 80
July 15	Cash Sales.	Rs. 300
July 18	Paid for advertising.	Rs. 350
July 19	Cash purchases.	Rs. 600
July 30	Paid salaries for the month.	Rs. 800

Solution I:

Date	Particulars	Dr. Rs.	Cr. Rs.
Jan. 1	Cash	20,000	
	To Capital		20,000
Jan. 2	Furniture	850	
	Typewriter	1,500	
	To Bank		2,350
Jan. 3	Purchases		
	To Y		5,000
Jan. 4	Purchases		
	To Cash		1,000
Jan. 5	M	2,000	
	To Sales		2,000
Jan. 6	Cash	1,000	
	To Sales		1,000
Jan. 7	Rent	200	
	To Cash		200
Jan. 8	Postage Stamps	100	
	To Cash		100
Jan. 9	Cash	1,900	
	Discount allowed	100	
	To M		2,000
Jan. 10	Y	5,000	
	To Bank		5,000
Jan. 11	Bank	1,000	
	To Cash		1,000
Jan. 12	Insurance Premium		450
	To Bank	450	

Solution II:

July 1	Furniture and office equipment Dr.	2,500
	Stock Dr.	25,000

Date	Particulars	Dr.	Rs.
	Cash in Hand Dr.		600
	Cash at Bank Dr.		8,500
	B Dr.		1,200
	G Dr.		1,500
	To		
	M		2,000
	N		1,450
	Capital (Balancing figure)		33,850
July 2	X	500	
	To Sales		500
July 3	Purchases	2,000	
	To Y		2,000
July 4	Rent	800	
	To Bank		800
July 5	Purchases	2,000	
	To Bank		2,000
July 7	Cash	450	
	To Sales		450
July 8	Bank	1180	
	To B		1,200
July 9	Stationery & Postage	50	
	To Cash		50
July 10	Drawings	250	
	To Cash		250
July 11	Purchases	2,500	
	To M	2,500	
July 12	M	2,000	
	To Bank		1950
	To Discount received		50
July 13	G	1,800	
	To Sales		1,800
July 14	Telephone charges	80	
	To Cash		80
July 15	Cash	300	
	To Sales		300
July 18	Advertising	350	
	To Cash		350

July 19	Purchases	600	
	To Cash		600
July 30	Salaries	800	
	To Cash		800

III: At the end of the current fiscal year, the following was the trial balance of the ABC Ltd.

ABC Ltd.
Trial Balance
June 30, 1999

	Rs.	
Cash	31,800	
Accounts Receivable	18,544	
Prepaid Insurance	19,600	
Opening Stock	4,370	
Land	20,000	
Building	3,60,600	
Furnishings	3,05,000	
Office Equipment	16,040	
Accounts Payable		45,506
Debentures		41,900
Mortgage Payable		300,000
Capital		312,648
(Drawing)	60,000	
Sales		456,600
Purchase	157,000	
Office Wage Expense	24,000	
Debtors	112,700	
Interest Expense	27,000	
	11,56,654	11,56,654

The following adjustments are required:

1. Closing Stock is Rs. 11,000.
2. Provision on Debtors is 5% and Reserve on Debtors is 5%.
3. Accurred but unpaid wages is Rs. 500.

4. Estimated depreciation on the building is Rs. 14,000.
5. Estimated depreciation on the furnishings is Rs. 36,000.
6. Estimated depreciation on the office equipments is Rs. 3,100.

Prepare an Income Statement and a Balance Sheet for ABC Ltd.

Solution III:

Trading and Profit & Loss A/c for the year ended June 30, 1999.

	Dr.		Cr.
To Opening Stock	Rs. 4,370	Sales	Rs. 4,56,600
Purchases	1,57,000	Closing	11,000
Outstanding Wages	500		
Gross Profit	3,05,730		
(Balancing figure)			
	Rs. 4,67,600		Rs. 4,67,600
To Prepaid Insurance	Rs. 19,600	To Gross Profit	Rs. 3,05,730
Office Wage Expenses	24,000		
Interest Expense	27,000		
To Depreciation:			
Building	14,000		
Furnishings	36,000		
Office Equipment	3,100		
To Provision on Debtors (5%)	5,635		
Reserve on Debtors	5,353		
Net Profit	1,71,042		
(Balancing figure)			
	Rs. 3,05,730		Rs. 3,05,730

Balance Sheet as on June 30, 1999

Liabilities		Assets		
Capital	Rs. 3,12,648	Cash		Rs. 31,800
Less Drawings	60,000	Accounts Receivable		18,544
	2,52,648	Land		20,000
Add net profit	1,71,042	Building	3,60,600	
	4,23,690	Less depreciation	14,000	3,46,600
Debentures	41,900	Furnishing	3,05,000	
Mortgage payable	3,00,000	Less depreciation	36,000	2,69,000
Accounts Payable	45,506	Office Equipment	16,040	
Wages outstanding	500	Less depreciation	3,100	12,940
		Debtors	1,12,700	
		Less provision (5%)	5,635	
			1,07,065	
		Less Reserve (5%)	5,353	1,01,712
		Closing Stock		11,000
	Rs. 8,11,596			Rs. 8,11,596

IV. Prepare Trading and Profit & Loss Account and Balance Sheet of Mr. X as on December 31, 19×9.

	Rs.	Rs.
Capital		3,600
Machinery	800	
Sales		8,300
Sales Returns	200	
Stock Jan. 1	1,000	
Drawings	400	
Wages	800	
Carriage Inwards	150	
Salaries	600	
General Expenses	300	
Rent	500	
Purchases	4,000	
Purchases Returns		50
Debtors	3,000	
Cash	500	
Carriage Outwards	100	
Advertising	200	
Creditors		600
	12,550	12,550

The following adjustments are required:

1. The closing stock was valued at Rs. 2,000.
2. The depreciation on machinery was Rs. 100.
3. Salaries outstanding for the year were Rs. 200.
4. Rent prepaid amounts to Rs. 300.

Solution IV.

Trading and Profit & Loss A/c for the year ended 31st Dec. 19×9

Opening Stock		Rs. 1,000	Sales	Rs. 8,300	
Wages		800	Less Sales return	200	
Carriage Inward		150		8,100	
Purchases	4,000				
Less Purchases returns	50	3,950	Closing stock	2,000	
Gross Profit c/d		4,200			
		10,100		10,100	

Carriage Outward		100	By G.P. b/d	4,200
General Expenses		300		
Salaries	600			
Add outstanding	200	800		
Depreciation on Machinery		100		
Rent	500			
Less Prepaid	300	200		
Advertising		200		
To Net Profit transferred to Profit & Loss A/c		2,500		
		4,200		4,200

Balance Sheet as on Dec. 31, 19×9

Liabilities			Assets		
Capital	Rs. 3,600		Machinery	800	
Less Drawings	400		Less depreciation	100	Rs. 700
		3,200	Debtors		3,000
Add Net Profit		2,500	Cash		500
		5,700	Rent prepaid		300
Creditors		600	C.S.		2,000
Salaries outstanding		200			
		Rs. 6,500			Rs. 6,500

V. From the following Trial Balance prepare the Final Accounts for the Company for the year ended 31st December, 19×9.

	Rs.
Stock at the beginning	11,000
Bills Receivable	4,450
Purchases	39,000
Salaries and Wages	2,500
Insurance	700
Debtors	30,000
Carriage Inwards	800
Commission (Debts)	800
Interest on Capital	700
Stationery	450
Returns Inwards	1,300
Returns Outwards	500
Trade Expenses	200

Office Fixtures	1,000
Cash in Hand	6,850
Rents and Taxes	1,100
Carriage Outwards	1,450
Sales	60,000
Bills Payable	3,700
Creditors	18,650
Capital	17,900
The Stock at the close was	25,000

The following adjustments are necessary:

(i) Rs. 150 are due for rent outstanding.

(ii) Rs. 350 are due for salaries unpaid.

(iii) Write off the office fixtures by 5 per cent.

(iv) Make a reserve for bad and doubtful debts @5 per cent.

Solution V:

Trading & Profit and Loss A/c for the year ended 30th June, 19×9

Opening stock		Rs. 11,000	Sales	Rs. 60,000	
Purchases	3,900		Less Return		
Less Return Inward		37,700	outwards	500	59,500
Carriage Inwards	1,300	800	Closing Stock		25,000
Trade expenses		200			
Gross profit c/d		34,800			
		Rs. 84,500			Rs. 84,500
Carriage outward		1,450	By Gross Profit b/d		34,800
Rent & Taxes	1,100				
Add outstanding	150	1,250			
Stationery		450			
Salaries & Wages	2,500				
Add outstanding	350				
		2,850			
Insurance		700			
Reserve on debtors		1,500			
Commission		800			
Interest on capital		700			
Depreciation of Office fixtures		50			
Net Profit Transferred to Balance Sheet		25,050			
		Rs. 34,800			Rs. 34,800

Balance Sheet as on June 30th, 19×9

Liabilities (Rs.)			Assets (Rs.)		
Capital	17,900		Bills Receivable		Rs. 4,500
Add Net Profit	25,050				
		42,950			
Credit on		18,650	Debtors	30,000	
			Less Reserve	1,500	28,500
Bills Payable		3,700	Office fixtures	1,000	
			Less Depreciation	50	
					950
Salaries outstanding		350	Cash in hand		5,250
Rent outstanding		150	Closing stock		25,000
		Rs. 65,800			Rs. 65,800

VI. From the following Trial Balance, prepare the Final Accounts of the Company for the year ended 31st December, 19×6:

Trial Balance

	Dr.	Cr.
Share Capital		Rs. 1,00,000
Reserves		50,000
Loans @ 6%		40,000
Creditors		50,000
Goodwill	Rs. 4,000	
Land & Buildings	100,000	
Plant & Machinery	40,000	
Investments	20,000	
Loose Tools	2,000	
Stock	10,000	
Debtors	14,000	
Cash	45,000	
Commission paid	2,000	
Rent	8,000	
Purchases	40,000	
Sales		80,000
Insurance	4,000	
Prepaid Expenses	4,000	
Advertisement	2,000	
Bad Debts	10,000	
Interest Paid	10,000	
Power & Fuel	5,000	
	Rs. 3,20,000	Rs. 3,20,000

The following adjustments are required:

1. Closing stock was valued at Rs. 20,000.
2. Provide for outstanding liabilities:

   Rent is Rs. 1,000

   Insurance is Rs. 200
3. Provide 5% on Debtors against Bad Debts and 2% against Discount.
4. Depreciate Plant and Machinery and Loose Tools at the rate of 5%.
5. Collection of Debtors is Rs. 1,000.
6. Payment of Creditors is Rs. 2,000.

Solution VI:

Trading and Profit & Loss Account for the year ended 19×6

To Opening Stock	Rs. 10,000	By Sales	Rs. 80,000
Purchases	40,000	By Closing Stock	30,000
Power & Fuel	5,000		
To Gross Profit c/d (balancing figure)	55,000		
	Rs. 110,000		Rs. 110,000
To Provision on Debtors	650	By Gross Profit c/d	55,000
Discount on Debtors	247		
Bad Debts	10,000		
Interest Paid	10,000		
Commission paid	2,000		
Rent	8,000		
Add outstanding	1,000		
Insurance	4,000		
Add outstanding	200		
Prepaid expenses	4,000		
Advertisement	2,000		
Depreciation:			
Plant & Machinery	2,000		
Loose Tools	100		
Net Profit transferred to Balance Sheet (Balancing figure)	10,803		
	Rs. 55,000		Rs. 55,000

Balance Sheet
as on 31st Dec. 19×6

Liabilities:			Assets:		
			Land & Buildings		Rs. 100,000
Share Capital		100,000	Plant & Machinery	40,000	
Reserves		Rs. 50,000	Less Depreciation	2,000	38,000
Add net profit	10,803		Investments		20,000
	60,803		Lose Tools	2,000	
Less			Less depreciation	100	1,900
Drawings	4,000	56,803			
			Debtors	14,000	
			Less Collection	1,000	
				13,000	
			Less Provision	650	
			(5% on 13,000)	12,350	
Loans @ 6%		40,000	Less Discount	247	12,103
			(2% on 12,350)		
Creditors	50,000				
Less Payment					
to Creditors	2,000		Cash	45,000	
		48,000	Add collection from	1,000	
Rent outstanding		1,000	debtors	46,000	
Insurance outstanding		200	Less payment		
			to Creditors	2,000	44,000
			Closing stock		30,000
		Rs. 246,003			Rs. 246,003

Questions

1. "The ledger is the major book of original entry because it is more essential than the journal". Do you agree Elucidiate?
2. What are GAAP? Why are they important to the readers and users of financial statements?
3. How is the income statement related to the balance sheet?
4. Why is the balance sheet sometimes called the statement of financial position?
5. "Debits are bad, credits are good". Comment on this statement.
6. What is the meaning of the statement, "The bank account has a debit balance of Rs. 700" ?
7. What is the relationship between the journal and the ledger?
8. Briefly explain the following concepts with examples:
   - (i) Business entity concept.
   - (ii) Going concern concept.
   - (iii) Dual aspect.
   - (iv) Matching concept.
9. Give examples of the types of transactions that *(a)* increase assets, and *(b)* increase liabilities.
10. "A trial balance assumes that the amounts in the financial statements are correct." Do you agree? Explain.
11. What is the accounting equation? Why must it always balance ?
12. Why is the entity concept so important to accountants?

Problems

1. During the month of June, AV Company had the following transactions:

   a. Paid salaries for April, Rs. 5,400.

   b. Purchased equipment on credit from M, Rs. 9,000.

   c. Purchased goods with cash, Rs. 2,300.

   d. Additional investment by owner, Rs. 12,000.

   e. Sale of goods, Rs. 1,800.

   f. Made partial payment on equipment purchased in transaction b, Rs. 3,000.

   g. Sold goods on credit to B, Rs. 4,800.

   h. Cash withdrawal by owner, Rs. 4,500.

   i. Received payment from customers in transaction g, Rs. 900.

   j. Received cash for goods sold, Rs. 210.

   Journalise the above transactions in the books of AV Company.

2. For each of the following categories, describe a transaction that would have the required effect on the elements of the accounting equation:

   a. Increase one asset and decrease another asset.

   b. Decrease an asset and decrease a liability.

   c. Increase an asset and increase a liability.

   d. Increase an asset and increase owner's equity.

   e. Decrease an asset and decrease owner's equity.

3. The total assets and liabilities at the beginning and end of the year for XYZ Company are given below:

	Assets	Liabilities
Beginning of the year	Rs. 110,000	Rs. 45,000
End of the year	200,000	120,000

Determine XYZ Company's net income for the year under each of the following alternatives:

a. The owner made no investments in or withdrawals from the business during the year.

b. The owner made no investments in the business, but the owner withdrew Rs. 20,000 during the year.

c. The owner made an investment of Rs. 10,000 but made no withdrawals during the year.

d. The owner made an investment of Rs.10,000 in the business and withdrew Rs. 20,000 during the year.

4. Indicate below whether each of the following accounts is an asset (A), a liability (L), or a part of owner's equity (OE):

   a. Cash, b. Salaries Payable, c. Accounts Receivable, d. Capital, e. Land, f. Accounts Payable, g. Bank, h. Debt.

5. Arjun Ltd. started a sole proprietorship. In the first weeks of operation, he completed the following transactions:

   a. Deposited Rs. 20,000 in an account in the name of the company to start the business.

   b. Paid the current month's rent, Rs. 1,500.

   c. Purchased equipment on credit from Y, Rs. 10,000.

   d. Purchases for cash, Rs. 5,200.

   e. Sales, Rs. 2,800.

   f. Sold goods on credit to X, Rs. 2,500.

   g. Paid utility expense, Rs. 750.

   h. Received payment from customers in transaction, Rs. 1,000.

i. Made payment on store equipment purchased in transaction c, Rs. 5,000.

j. Withdrew cash for personal expenses, Rs. 1,000.

Journalise the transaction and prepare ledger accounts.

6. At the end of his first month of operation, AB Ltd. has the following account balances: Cash Rs. 5,800, Accounts Receivable Rs. 2,800, Office Supplies Rs. 540, Office Equipment Rs. 8,400, Account Payable Rs. 3,800 and Capital Rs. 13,740. Soon thereafter, the following transactions were completed:

a. Paid current month's rent, Rs. 800.

b. Made payment toward accounts payable, Rs. 900.

c, Billed clients for services performed, Rs. 1,600.

d. Received payment from clients billed last month, Rs. 2,000.

e. Purchased office supplies for cash, Rs. 160.

f. Paid Secretary's salary, Rs. 1,000.

g. Paid advertising expense, Rs. 180.

h. Paid telephone expense, Rs. 100.

i. Purchased additional office equipment for cash, Rs. 800.

j. Received cash from clients for services performed, Rs. 2,000.

k. Withdrew cash for personal use, Rs. 1,800.

Journal the above transactions, prepare Ledger accounts, and also prepare a Trial Balance.

7. LML Copying Service began operations and engaged in the following transactions during August 19×1.

a. Investment by owner, Rs. 20,000.

b. Paid current month's rent, Rs. 900.

c. Purchased copier for cash, Rs. 5,000.

d. Copying job payments received in cash, Rs. 1,800.

e. Copying job billed to major customer, Rs. 1,500.

f. Paid cash for paper and other copier supplies, Rs. 350.

g. Paid wages to part-time employees, Rs. 750.

h. Purchased additional copier supplies on credit, Rs. 200.

i. Received partial payment from customer in transaction e, Rs. 600.

j. Paid current month's bill, Rs. 200.

k. Made partial payment on supplies purchased in transaction h, Rs. 130.

l. Withdrew cash for personal use, Rs. 1,560.

Journalise the above transactions, prepare Ledger accounts and also prepare a Trial Balance.

8. HL Ltd. is a compute firm. The following are the transactions for the month of June, 19×5.

a. Deposited Rs. 300,000 in the bank to start the business and purchased a systems library with an additional investment of Rs. 20,000.

b. Paid current month's rent on an office, Rs. 2,000.

c. Purchased a minicomputer for cash, Rs. 20,000.

d. Purchased computer supplies on credit, Rs. 5,000.

e. Received revenue from a client, Rs. 4,500.

f. Billed a client on completion of a short project, Rs. 10,000.

g. Paid Wages, Rs. 2,500.

h. Received a partial payment from the client billed in transaction f, Rs. 6,240.

i. Withdrew cash for personal expenses, Rs. 3,500.

j. Made a partial payment on the computer supplies purchased in transaction d, Rs. 2,500.

Journalise the above transactions and prepare a Trial Balance.

9. On October 1, The MN Transport Company completed the following transactions:

a. Deposited Rs. 200,000 in a new bank account to establish the Transport Company.

b. Purchased two trucks for cash, Rs. 90,000.

c. Purchased equipment on credit, Rs. 20,000.

d. Sold goods to a customer for Rs. 5,000.

e. Received cash for goods sold, Rs. 6,250.

f. Received cash payment from the customer billed in transaction d, Rs. 3,250.

g. Made a payment on the equipment purchased in transaction c, Rs. 15,000.

h. Paid expenses in cash, Rs. 3,500.

i. Withdrew cash from the business for personal use, Rs. 2,400.

10. On May 1, 19×1, RS Taxi Service began operation and engaged in the following transactions during May:

a. Investment by owner, Rs. 10,00,000.

b. Purchase of taxi for cash, Rs. 2,13,000.

c. Purchase of uniforms on credit, Rs. 10,000.

d. Taxi fares received in cash, Rs. 30,000.

e. Paid wages to part-time drivers, Rs.15,000.

f. Purchased petrol during month for cash, Rs. 50,500.

g. Purchased car washes during month on credit, Rs. 8,900.

h. Further investment by owner, Rs. 5,50,000.

i. Paid part of the amount owed for the uniforms purchased in transaction c, Rs. 5,500.

j. Billed major client for fares, Rs. 12,560.

k. Paid for automobile repairs, Rs. 9,260.

l. Withdrew cash from business for personal use, Rs. 8,000.

Require: Journalise the transactions & prepare a Trial Balance. Aloso prepare an Income Statement and a Balance Sheet.

11. Indicate the account that should be debited and the account that should be credited to record the following transactions:

    a. Purchased building for cash, Rs. 2,50,000.

    b. Purchased inventory on account, Rs. 30,000.

    c. Received Rs. 2,000 rent for an office in the building.

    d. Purchased land costing Rs. 2,000,000.

    e. Invested an additional Rs. 60,000 cash in the business.

    f. Paid wages Rs. 6,000.

    g. Sold inventory for Rs. 17,500 in cash.

    h. Paid electricity charges amounting to Rs. 5,000.

    i. Withdrew Rs. 1,500 for personal use.

12. During the month of October, XYZ Ltd. completed the following transactions:

    Oct. 3 Began his business with equipment valued at Rs. 12,500 and placed Rs. 35,000 in a bank account.

Oct. 5	Purchased a used truck costing Rs. 13,800. Paid Rs. 10,000 in cash and signed a note for the balance.
Oct. 7	Purchased on account for Rs. 12,240.
Oct. 8	Sales, Rs. 11,000.
Oct. 10	Received Rs. 1000 in cash for services performed.
Oct. 12	Purchases for Rs. 11,200 in cash.
Oct. 13	Received a Rs. 8,240 cheque from the customer billed on October 8.
Oct. 14	Paid Rs. 800 for an insurance policy for eighteen months' coverage.
Oct. 16	Sales to M, Rs. 1,200.
Oct. 18	Paid Salaries, Rs. 7,000.
Oct. 19	Paid Rs. 80 for buying an equipment.
Oct. 20	Paid for the supplies purchased on October 7.
Oct. 21	Purchased a new equipment for Rs. 1700 on account.
Oct. 23	Received a telephone bill for Rs. 620, due next month.
Oct. 24	Received Rs. 660 in cash from the customer.
Oct. 25	Transferred Rs. 600 to a personal account.
Oct. 26	Sales Rs. 720 in cash.
Oct. 28	Paid Rs. 400 on the note signed for the truck.
Oct. 29	Salaries paid, Rs. 7000.

Required: 1 Prepare journal entries to record these transactions in the general journal.

2. Prepare a Trial Balance for XYZ Ltd. as of October 31, 19×1.

13. Sagar started a consulting service and during the first month of operations completed the following selected transactions:

Jan. 1	Sagar started the business with an investment of Rs.30,000 cash and a building valued at Rs. 120,000.
Jan. 3	Borrowed Rs. 60,000 from the bank on account.
Jan. 5	Purchased office supplies on account, Rs. 2,600.
Jan. 6	Paid Rs. 36,000 for office furniture.
Jan. 10	Paid salary Rs. 4,400.
Jan. 12	Paid Rs. 1,600 of the accounts payable due on Jan. 5.
Jan. 15	Performed consulting service on account, Rs.4,200.
Jan. 20	Performed consulting service and received cash Rs. 3,200.
Jan. 25	Receive cash on account, Rs. 2,400.
Jan. 28	Paid Rent, Rs. 1,400.
Jan. 29	Paid Advertising expense, Rs. 1,000.
Jan. 30	Withdrew Rs. 17,000 for personal use.
Required:	Record each transaction, prepare Ledger accounts and also a Trial Balance for the month of January.

14. The account balances for Anu Ltd. at the end of March are presented in the Trial Balance below:

Anu Ltd.
Trial Balance
for the year ended March 31, 19×1

Cash	Rs. 6,200	
Accounts Receivable	440	
Purchases	920	
Prepaid Insurance	800	
Equipment	8,800	
Accounts Payable		Rs. 7,400
Capital		8,400
Drawings	840	
Sales		2,980
Lease Expenses	580	
Other Expenses	200	
	Rs. 18,780	Rs. 18,780

During April, Anu Ltd. completed the following transactions:

April 3 Paid for purchases on credit last month, Rs. 300.

April 5 Billed customers for services, Rs. 400.

April 6 Paid Rs. 400.

April 8 Received cash from customers not previously billed, Rs. 580.

April 9 Purchased new equipment from a Manufacturing Company on account, Rs. 8,000.

April 11 Received a bill for Rs. 300.

April 13 Returns inwards, Rs. 70.

April 14 Received payments from customers previously billed, Rs. 380.

April 16 Paid the bill received on March 11.

April 18 Took cash from the business for personal use, Rs. 220.

April 21 Billed customers for services, Rs. 300.

April 24 Received payments from customers previously billed, Rs. 900.

April 30 Made a payment to reduce the principal of the note payable, Rs. 1,200.

Required: Record each transaction and also prepare a Trial Balance for the month of April.

15. Trial Balance for the year ended December 31, 19×1.

Trial Balance
December 31, 19×

	Debit	Credit
Cash	Rs. 1,380	
Accounts Receivable	1,940	
Investment	238	
Prepaid Insurance	720	
Mach.	24,000	
Commission received		Rs. 10,000
Accounts Payable		940
Capital		15,780
Withdrawals	14,400	
Rentals		91,090
Wages Expenses	46,800	
Insurance Expense	1,440	
Supplies Expense	530	
Depreciation Expense, Mach.	4,800	
Other Expenses	21,562	
	Rs. 117,810	Rs. 117,810

Required: Prepare a Trading and Profit & Loss Account and a Balance Sheet as on December 31, 19×1.

16. The Trial Balance below was taken from the Ledger of XYZ Ltd. at the end of the company's fiscal year.

XYZ Ltd.
Trial Balance
Dec. 31, 19×1

	Debit	Credit
Cash	Rs. 32,428	
Accounts Receivable	14,776	
Purchases	2,608	
Prepaid Insurance	3,600	
Prepaid Advertising	1,800	
Land	10,000	
Building	200,000	
Creditors		Rs. 88,400
Equipment	250,000	
Accounts Payable		30,088
Notes Payable		140,000
Commission received		5,000
Capital		121,626
Withdrawals	48,000	
Sales		1,232,526
Wages Expense	754,228	
Advertising Expense	28,600	
Rent expense	84,400	
Maintenance Expense	168,200	
Opening Stock	19,000	
	Rs. 1,617,640	Rs. 1,617,640

Required: Prepare a Trading and Profit Loss and Balance Sheet for XYZ Ltd. after completing the work sheet using the following information.

a. Closing stock was Rs. 25,000.

b. Expired insurance, Rs. 3,000.

c. Expired advertising Rs. 1,800.

d. Estimated depreciation on building, Rs. 10,000.

e. Estimated depreciation on equipment, Rs. 20,000.

f. Accrued but unpaid wages, Rs. 8,000.

17. The Balance Sheet of the Anu Mills Company as on June 30, 19×6, was as follows:

Anu Mills Company
Balance Sheet
June 30, 19×6

Assets	
Cash	Rs. 10,000
Accounts receivable	50,000
Land	1,50,000
Total Assets	Rs. 2,10,000
Liabilities and Owner's Equity	
Liabilities:	
Accounts payable	Rs. 36,000
Owner's equity:	
Capital	1,64,000
Total Liabilities and owner's equity	Rs. 2,10,000

Summarised, the transactions for the month of July 19×6 were as follows:

Transactions:

1. The owner invested an additional Rs. 60,000 cash in the business.
2. Collected Rs. 30,000 on accounts receivable.
3. Paid Rs. 20,000 on accounts payable.
4. Sold land costing Rs. 50,000 for Rs. 75,000 cash. The gain of Rs. 25,000 increases owner's equity and is shown as a revenue in the income statement.
5. Services were rendered to customers for cash, Rs. 40,000; and on account, Rs. 30,000.
6. Employee services and other operating costs were incurred: for cash, Rs. 15,000; and on account, Rs. 40,000.
7. The owner withdrew Rs. 6,000 cash.

Required: (a) Prepare a summary of transactions using column headings for items appearing in the above Balance Sheet. Enter the balances shown in the June

30, 19×6, balance sheet as beginning balances in the summary of transactions. Determine balances after each transactions.

(b) Prepare an income statement for the month of June 30, 19×6.

(c) Prepare a Balance Sheet as of June 30, 19×6.

18. From the following Trial Balance prepare an income statement and a Balance Sheet as on Dec. 31, 19×6.

Trial Balance
Dec. 31, 19×6

	Dr.	Cr.
Cash	Rs. 7,300	
Accounts Receivable	5,800	
Furniture	8,400	
Supplies	400	
Rent	1,800	
Accumulated depreciation		Rs. 1,750
Accounts payable		1,725
Capital		19,325
Drawings	2,000	
Retained earnings		4,375
Salary	1,200	
Advertising expense	275	
Total	Rs. 27,175	Rs. 27,175

The following adjustments are required:

a. Unexpired rent, Rs. 800.

b. Salary outstanding, Rs. 400.

c. Depreciation on furniture @ 5%.

19. Following is the Trial Balance of Neha Ltd. as on December 31, 19×1

Neha Ltd.
Trial Balance
Dec. 31, 19×1

Particulars	Dr.	Cr.
Cash	Rs. 18,138	
Accounts Receivable	82,425	
Inventory, beginning	1,09,807	
Land	2,00,000	
Building	85,400	
Accounts Payable		Rs. 30,975
Taxes Payable		24,345
Retained Earning		1,10,500
Sales		6,70,000
Purchases	4,25,000	
Salaries	1,20,500	
Wages	86,250	
Insurance Expenses	4,500	
Equity Capital		3,00,000
Advertising	3,800	
	Rs. 11,35,820	Rs. 11,35,820

The following adjustments are required:

1. The closing stock was valaued at Rs. 1,60,000.
2. Depreciation on land and building is at 5% per annum.
3. Salaries earned but not paid are Rs. 35,000.
4. Interest outstanding during the year was Rs. 700.

From the above information prepare an Income Statement and a Balance Sheet as on Dec. 31, 19×1.

20. From the following Trial Balance, prepare the Final Accounts of the Company for the year ended 31st December, 19×6 :

Trial Balance
Dec. 31, 19×6

	Dr.	Cr.
Share Capital		Rs. 1,00,000
Reserves		50,000
Loans @ 6%		40,000
Creditors		50,000
Goodwill	Rs. 4,000	
Land & Building	1,00,000	
Plant & Machinery	40,000	
Investments	20,000	
Loose Tools	2,000	
Stock	10,000	
Debtors	14,000	
Cash	45,000	
Commission paid	2,000	
Rent	8,000	
Purchases	40,000	
Sales		80,000
Insurance	4,000	
Prepaid Expenses	4,000	
Advertisement	2,000	
Bad Debts	10,000	
Interest Paid	10,000	
Power & Fuel	5,000	
	Rs. 3,20,000	Rs. 3,20,000

The following adjustements are required:

1. Closing stock was valued at Rs. 20,000.
2. Provide for outstanding liabilities:
   Rent is Rs. 1,000.
   Insurance is Rs. 200.
3. Provide 5% on Debtors against Bad Debts and 2% against Discount.
4. Depreciate Plant and Machinery and Loose Tools at the rate of 5%.
5. Collection of Debtors is Rs. 1,000.
6. Payment of Creditors is Rs. 2,000.

21. Business Decision Problem:

Analysis of the transactions of R Ltd. for the month of November 1996, discloses the following:

Revenue received from main business		Rs. 35,000
Rent expenses	Rs. 6,000	
Advertising expenses paid	Rs. 9,000	
Revenue received from other business		Rs. 6,000
Wages expenses	Rs. 8,000	
Salaries expenses	Rs. 5,000	
Other expenses	Rs. 2,000	

The Asset and Liability of R Ltd. as of November 1996 include the following:

Cash	— Rs. 50,000
Land	— Rs. 10,000
Accounts Payable	— Rs. 11,000

The Capital Account of R Ltd. had a balance of Rs. 37,000 as on November 1, 1996.

Required:

a. Prepare an Income Statement for the month of November 1996.

b. Prepare a Balance Sheet as of November 30, 1996.

c. Was the month of November a beneficial month for the Company?

3

Special Aspects in the Measurement of Business Income: Depreciation Methods

Depreciation is a systematic procedure for allocating the acquisition cost of a capital asset over its useful life. Capital assets such as building, machinery and equipment are of use to a company for a limited number of years. The entire cost of a capital asset is not charged to any one year as an expense; rather the cost is spread over the useful life of the asset. Thus, the cost of the asset is charged as an expense to the periods that benefit from the use of the asset. That part of the cost which is charged to operation during an accounting period is known as depreciation. Hence, the objective of depreciation is to achieve the maching principle i.e. offset the costs of the goods and services being consumed in an accounting period with the revenue of the same period so as to arrive at the profit or loss made by the business.

The various factors affecting the amount of depreciation are: cost of the asset, estimated useful life of the asset and the estimated scrap value (or salvage value) of the asset at the end of its useful life.

The next two chapters explain the problems in the measurement of business income in relation to depreciation and inventory valuation. The alternative methods of charging depreciation are discussed alongwith the various aspects which managers should take into account while selecting a method for their organization.

Definition of Depreciation

According to the Institute of Cost and Management Accountants "Depreciation is the diminution in the intrinsic value of an asset due to use and/or lapse of time."

According to the International Accounting Standards Committee "Depreciation is the allocation of the depreciable amount of an asset over its estimated useful life."

Measuring Depreciation

To measure the depreciation of an asset we must know its cost, its estimated residual value and its estimated useful life. *Cost of a Asset.* The purchase price of the asset plus all other expenses paid to acquire the asset so that it is ready for use are included in the cost of the asset. *Estimated residual value* is known as the salvage value or scrap value. This is the expected cash value of the asset at the end of its useful life. In calculating depreciation, estimated residual value is not depreciated because the business expects to receive this amount from selling off the asset. The cost of the asset minus its residual value is called the depreciable cost of the asset. The depreciable cost is allocated over the useful life of the asset. However if the asset is expected to have no residual value, the total cost of the asset is depreciated. *Estimated useful life* is the number of years of service the business expects to get from the asset.

Causes of Depreciation

The causes of depreciation are physical deterioration and obsolescence.

Physical deterioration: Assets decrease in their value due to constant use and wear and tear. All assets have a useful life and every machine eventually reaches a point when it must be discarded, however good the repair policy of the organization is.

Obsolescence: An asset may become obsolete because of better designs, new inventions or simply changed fashions. This may result in the asset being discarded even though it is still useful and in excellent physical condition.

Depreciation is a Process of Cost Allocation not of Valuation

Depreciation is allocated over the useful life of the asset on the basis of book value of the asset originally entered in the books of accounts. The market value of the asset may increase or decrease during the useful life of the asset. However, the allocation of depreciation in each accounting period continues on the basis of the book value without regard to such temporary changes. Also, depreciation expense is merely a book entry and represents a "non cash" expense. It is a non cash expense since no cash payment is involved in the depreciation of fixed assets unlike other normal operating expenses which are paid in cash. Depreciation is charged as an expense in the income statement and is subtracted from the value of the asset in the balance sheet. Thus depreciation is a process of cost allocation, not a process of valuation.

METHODS

The various methods of charging depreciation are as under:

1. Straight-Line Method

This method is most appropriate when the cost assigned to each year is the same. This is the simplest and the most widely used method for calculating depreciation. The depreciation expense in this method is calculated as follows:

$$\text{Depreciation} = \frac{\text{Cost of the asset} - \text{Residual value}}{\text{Number of years of useful life}}$$

It is advantageous to use the straight line method when the usage of asset in all the years is fairly uniform. To illustrate, assume that the cost of the asset is Rs. 50,000 with a useful life of 10 years. The depreciation expense for each year will be as follows:

$$\frac{50,000}{10} = \text{Rs. } 5,000$$

In the above example, the depreciation rate can also be specified in terms of a percentage. A 10-year life indicates a depreciation rate of 1/10 or 10%. Also, since the asset had an estimated useful life of 10 years, the depreciation expense each year was 1/10 of the depreciable amount. In actual practice, when it becomes difficult to estimate the residual value or the calculation of residual value is not material, depreciation can be calculated by simply dividing the cost of the asset by the number of years of estimated useful life.

2. Accelerated Depreciation Methods

Accelerated depreciation methods charge relatively greater amounts of depreciation in the early years in the life of the asset and smaller amounts in the later years. These methods can be defended as being logical, because plants and equipments are most efficient when new and hence provide better services in the early years of useful life. If the benefits gained from the asset are maximum when the asset is relatively new, then the amount to be allocated as depreciation expense should be the greatest in these same early years. This is also consistent with the basic accounting concept of matching costs against the resulting revenues.

The commonly used method under Accelerated Deprecia-tion Methods are:

(a) *Diminishing balance method:* This method is also known as the written down value (WDV) method. Under this method, depreciation is charged on the book value of the asset, and the amount of depreciation goes on decreasing every year. To illustrate, if the cost of an asset is Rs. 50,000 and the depreciation rate is 10%, then the depreciation expense in the first year will amount to Rs. 5,000. In the second year, the depreciation expense would drop to Rs. 4,500, computed at 10% of the remaining book value of Rs. 45,000 (i.e. Rs. 50,000 - Rs. 5,000). In the third year, the depreciation will be Rs. 4,050, in the fourth year Rs. 3,645 and so on. The following table shows the calculations of the depreciation expense by the diminishing balance method for the first four years:

Year	Computation	Depreciation Expense	Book Value
			50,000
1.	(10% of Rs. 50,000)	5,000	45,000
2.	(10% of Rs. 45,000)	4,500	40,500
3.	(10% of Rs. 40,500)	4,050	36,450
4.	(10% of Rs. 36,450)	3,645	32,805

(b) *Sum-of-the-years-digits method (SYD method):* The depreciation expense under this method is calculated by adding up the number of years of the useful economic life (i.e. if the asset has 5 years economic useful life, the numbers 1, 2, 3, 4 and 5 are added up. The resulting sum 15 becomes the denominator while the numerator is the number of remaining years of the useful economic life of the asset. This method calculates the depreciation expense with the help of the following formula:

$$\frac{\text{Remaining years of useful life of the asset (including the beginning of the year)} \times \text{Original cost of the asset}}{\text{Sum of the digits of the years of useful life}}$$

The depreciation so determined constitutes the depreciation expense to be charged every year.

For example, if the cost of an asset is Rs. 15,000, with a useful life of 5 years, and a zero salvage value then the depreciation for each year will appear as follows:

Depreciation schedule: sum-of-the-year digits method

Year	Cost subject to	Allocating Fraction	Depreciation
	Rs.		
1.	15,000	x 415	= Rs. 5,000
2.	15,000	x 4/15	= Rs. 4,000
3.	15,000	x 3/15	= Rs. 3,000
4.	15,000	x 2/15	= Rs. 2,000
5.	15,000	x 1/15	= Rs. 1,000

(c) *Double-declining balance method:* This method uses a rate that is twice the straight-line depreciation rate. This doubled rate is applied to the underpreciated book value of the asset each year. No allowance is made for the scrap value of the asset in making the calculation. This is because this method provides an "automatic residual value" as the asset is never entirely written off.

To illustrate, if the cost of the asset is Rs. 50,000 and it is depreciated by the double-rate method at 20 per cent, then the depreciation for each year would be computed as follows:

Depreciation schedule: Deouble-declining balance method

Year	Computation	Depreciation Expense	Accumulated Dep.	Book Value
				Rs. 50,000
1.	(20% of 50,000)	10,000	Rs. 10,000	40,000
2.	(20% of 40,000)	8,000	Rs. 18,000	32,000
3.	(20% of 32,000)	6,400	Rs. 24,400	25,600
4.	(20% of 25,600)	5,120	Rs. 29,520	20,480

Management Viewpoint

It is the responsibility of the management to select an appropriate method to depreciate company assets. For purposes of annual reporting to investors, management may select the straight line method. For income tax purposes, it is quite possible for a company to use an accelerated depreciation method. In selecting a particular method, various aspects which should be taken into account by the management are:-

Income Taxes: Income tax rules are an important factor to be considered in the formulation of a suitable depreciation policy. Many companies use accelerted depreciation method because this enables them to retain more resources in the early years. A rupee saved today is more valuable and can be reinvested to generate immediate returns.

The Principle of Consistency: The Principle of Consistency in the context of depreciation means that a company should not change every year the method used in calculation the depreciation expense for an asset. Consistency here does not imply rigidity. The management may adopt a new method if it is convinced that the change is in the best interest of the company.

Estimating correctly the net income: While selecting a depreciation method, management must ensure that the method gives a true and fair picture of the company's profit or loss for the concerned period. The useful life and the residual value of the asset should be estimated correctly by the management after taking into account the company's past experience, current circumstances and future plans. If the estimates are reasonable, the amount of net income reported for each period will also be correct.

Straight Line Method (SLM) Vs. Written Down Value (WDV) Method

The two methods common in India for financial reporting purposes are the SLM and WDV method. For determining the amount of depreciation, the rates of depreciation both for SLM and WDV methods for different kinds of assets have been prescribed by the Indian Companies Act 1956.

In the WDV method, since higher amounts of depreciation are charged in the earlier years, profit reported is low in these years. However in the SLM reported profits are relatively higher and value of the assets shown in the Balance Sheet is also higher.

Some Companies are also known to change the method of depreciation during the life time of the asset. Many Companies in India are believed to have reduced their depreciation expense and have shown better profits by changing the method of charging depreciation from the WDV to the SLM.

Disclosure in Financial Statements

The methods used to depreciate assets must be disclosed by the Company in the notes to its financial statements. For example, the accelerated depreciation methods transfer the costs of assets to expenses more quickly than the straight line method. An investor analysing the Balance Sheet of such a company will be able to infer that the company uses a more conservative approach in balance sheet valuation of assets and measurement of net income.

Change in Estimated Useful Lives

If, after using the asset for a few years, management decides a that the asset is actually going to last for a significantly shorter or longer period than was originally estimated, then the management should prepare a revised estimate of the useful life and increase or decrease the depreciation accordingly. This correction in the depreciation amount would affect only the current and future periods. The functional statements of the past will not be affected.

For example, a company acquires an asset for Rs. 20,000 with a 20-year useful life and no residual value under the straight line method, the depreciation expense every year is Rs. 1,000. At the beginning of the tenth year the management decides that the assets will last for only five more years. The revised estimate of useful life is therefore, a total of 15 years. The changed depreciation expenses for the eleventh year and for each of the remaining years will be Rs. 2,000 calculated as follows:

Undepreciated cost at the end of tenth year	Rs. 10,000
Revised estimate of remaining years useful life	5 years
Revised amount of annual depreciation	Rs. 2,000

Illustrative Problems

(i) R Company purchased an equipment for Rs. 14,500. The equipment has a residual value of Rs. 1,000 and a useful life of 5 years. Compute the depreciation expense for the next 2 years assuming the following methods:

a. Straight Line.

b. Sum of the year's digit.

c. Double declining method.

Solution:

Depreciation expense:

(a) Straight line method

(14,500-1,000) / 5 = Rs. 2,700

Depreciation will be Rs. 2,700 for the next five years.

(b) Sum of the years digit method:

$$\text{First year} = (14,500-1,000)\times\frac{5}{15} = \text{Rs. } 4,500$$

$$\text{Second year} = (14,500-1,000)\times\frac{4}{15} = \text{Rs. } 3,600$$

(c) Double declining balance method:

2 x Book Value ÷ N where N refers to the number of years of useful life.

First year 2 x 14,500 ÷ 5 = Rs. 5,800.

Second year 2 x (14,500-5,800) ÷ 5 = Rs. 3,480.

Questions

1. Is the purpose of depreciation to determine the value of equipment? Elucidiate with examples.

2. Contrast the assumptions underlying the straight line depreciation method with the assumptions underlying the diminishing balance depreciation method.

3. 'Depreciation is a process of allocation and not of valuation.' Elecidiate with examples.

4. The valid basis for choice among alternative depreciation methods is their capacity to allocate the value of

the assets over their useful life. Elucidiate giving the managements view point in his regard.

5. 'Accelerated depreciation methods are more realistic in todays world.' Give examples to illustrate your answer.
6. What factors should management take into account in selecting an appropriate methods to depreciate company assets?
7. How does depreciation affect income taxes? Elucidiate with examples.
8. Which depreciation method is best for income tax purposes? Explain with examples.

Problems

1. ABC Ltd. purchased a piece of equipment on Jan. 1, 1999. The following information is available for the purchase:

Purchase Price -	Rs. 900,000
Transportation -	Rs. 100,000
Installation -	Rs. 130,000
Salvage Value -	Rs. 50,000
Useful Life -	4 years

Required:

(a) Compute the cost of the Fixed Asset that should be capitalised.

(b) What will be the depreciation expense for the year ended Dec. 31, 1999, assuming the company uses each of the following: (a) Straight line method, (b) Sum-of-the-years' digit method, (c) Double declining method.

2. Neha and Company acquired an equipment on January 15, 19×1, at a cash cost of Rs. 140,000. Transportation charges amounted to Rs. 2,000 and installation costs totalled Rs. 3,000. The equipment was damaged while being installed, and the cost of repairing the damage was Rs. 500.

The equipment was estimated to have a useful life of 10 years and a salvage value of Rs. 5,500 at the end of its life. It was further estimated that the equipment would be used in the production of 800,000 units of product during its life. During 19×6, 150,000 units of product were produced.

Required: Compute the depreciation for 19×6 and 19×7. If the company used (a) Straight line method, (b) The Sum-of-the-years' digit method, (c) The Double declining method.

3. A company purchased office furniture on March 12, 19×1 for Rs. 41,000. The company expects it to remain useful for 8 years and to have a residual value of Rs. 1,000. Prepare a schedule of depreciation expense for 8 years under the four depreciation methods. Also identify the depreciation method that would be most advantageous from an income tax perspective.

4. Neha Industries purchased a piece of equipment on January 1, 19x1. The following information is available for this purchase:

Purchase Price	Rs. 900,000
Transportation	Rs. 100,000
Installation	Rs. 130,000
Salvage Value	Rs. 50,000
Useful Life	4 Years

Required:

a. Compute the cost of the fixed asset that should be capitalized.

b. Find the depreciation as per the following methods:

   1. Sum-of-the-years-digits depreciation method.

   2. Double-declining-balance depreciation method

   3. Straight-line depreciation method.

APPENDIX

ACCOUNTING STANDARD 6 (REVISED)*

DEPRECIATION ACCOUNTING

The following is the text of the revised Accounting Standard (AS) 6. Depreciation Accounting, issued by the Institute of Charatered Accountants of India.

Introduction

1. This Statement deals with depreciation accounting and applies to all depreciable assets, except the following items to which special considerations apply:—

(i) forests, plantations and similar regenerative natural resources;

(ii) wasting assets including expenditure on the exploration for and extraction of minerals, oils, natural gas and similar non-regenerative resources;

(iii) expenditure on research and development;

(iv) goodwill;

(v) live-stock.

This statement also does not apply to land unless it has a limited useful life for the enterprise.

2. Different accounting policies for depreciation are adopted by different enterprises. Disclosure of accounting policies for depreciation followed by an enterprise is necessary to appreciate the view presented in the financial statements of the enterprise.

Definitions

3. The following terms are used in the statement with the meanings specified :

3.1. **'Depreciation'** *is a measure of the wearing out, consumption or other loss of value of a depreciable asset arising from use,*

---

* Originally issued in 1982. Revised in August 1994. Mandatory in respect of accounts for periods commencing on after 1.4.1995.

effluxion of time or obsolescence through technology and market changes. Depreciation is allocated so as to charge a fair proportion of the depreciable amount in each accounting period during the expected useful life of the asset. Depreciation includes amoritisation of assets whose useful life is predetermined.

3.2. **'Depreciable assets'** are assets which

(i) *are expected to be used during more than one accounting period; and*

(ii) *have a limited useful life; and*

(iii) *are held by an enterprise for use in the production or supply of goods and services, for rental to others, or for administrative purposes and not for the purpose of sale in the ordinary course of business.*

3.3. **'Useful life'** *is either (i) the period over which a depreciable asset is expected to be used by the enterprise; or (ii) the number of production or similar units expected to be obtained from the use of the asset by the enterprise.*

3.4. **'Depreciable amount'** *of a depreciable asset is its historical cost, or other amount substituted for historical cost*[1] *in the financial statements, less the estimated residual value.*

Explanation

4. Depreciation has a significant effect in determining and presenting the financial position and results of operations of an enterprise. Depreciation is charged in each accounting period by reference to the extent of the depreciable amount, irrespective of an increase in the market value of the assets.

5. Assessment of depreciation and the amount to be charged in respect thereof in an accounting period are usually based on the following three factors:

(i) historical cost or other amount substituted for the historical cost of the depreciable asset when the asset had been revalued;

---

1 This statement does not deal with the treatment of the revaluation difference which may arise when historical costs are substituted by revaluations.

(ii) expected useful life of the depreciable asset; and

(iii) estimated residual value of the depreciable asset.

6. Historical cost of a depreciable asset represents its money outlay or its equivalent in connection with its acquisition, installation and commissioning as well as for additions to or improvement thereof. The historical cost of a depreciable asset may undergo subsequent changes arising as a result of increase or decrease in long term liability on account of exchange fluctuations, price adjustments, changes in duties or similar factors.

7. The useful life of a depreciable asset is shorter than its physical life and is:

(i) pre-determined by legal or contractual limits, such as the expiry dates of related leases;

(ii) directly governed by extraction or consumption;

(iii) dependent on the extent of use and physical deterioration on account of wear and tear which again depends on operational factors, such as, the number of shifts for which the asset is to be used, repair and maintenance policy of the enterprise etc; and

(iv) reduced by obsolescence arising from such factors as:

(a) technological changes;

(b) improvement in production methods;

(c) change in market demand for the product or service output of the asset;

or

(d) legal or other restrictions.

8. Determination of the useful life of a depreciable asset is a matter of estimation and is normally based on various factors including experience with similar types of assets. Such estimation is more difficult for an asset using new technology or used

in the production of a new product or in the provision of a new service but is nevertheless required on some reasonable basis.

9. Any addition or extension to an existing asset which is of a capital nature and which becomes an integral part of the existing asset is depreciated over the remaining useful life of that asset. As a practical measure, however, depreciation is sometimes provided on such addition or extension at the rate which is applied to an existing asset. Any addition or extension which retains a separate identity and is capable of being used after the existing asset is disposed of, is depreciated independently on the basis of an estimate of its own useful life.

10. Determination of residual value of an asset is normally a difficult matter. If such value is considered as insignificant, it is normally regarded as nil. On the contrary, if the residual value is likely to be significant, it is estimated at the time of acquisition/installation, or at the time of subsequent revaluation of the asset. One of the basis for determining the residual value would be the realisable value of similar assets which have reached the end of their useful lives and have operated under conditions similar to those in which the asset will be used.

11. The quantum of depreciation to be provided in an accounting period involves the exercise of judgement by management in the light of technical, commercial, accounting and legal requirements and accordingly may need periodical review. If it is considered that the original estimate useful life of an asset requires any revision, the unamortised depreciable amount of the asset is charged to revenue over the revised remaining useful life.

12. There are several methods of allocating depreciation over the useful life of the assets. Those most commonly employed in industrial and commercial enterprises are the straightline method and the reducing balance method. The management of a business selects the most appropriate method(s) based on various important factors e.g. (i) type of asset, (ii) the nature of the use of such asset and (iii) circumstances prevailing in the business. A combination of more than one method is

sometimes used. In respect of depreciable assets which do not have material value depreciation is often allocated fully in the accounting period in which they are acquired.

13. The statute governing an enterprise may provide the basis for computation of the depreciation. For example, the Companies Act, 1956 lays down the rates of depreciation in respect of various assets. Where the management's estimate of the useful life of an asset of the enterprise is shorter than that envisaged under the provision of the relevant statute, the depreciation provision is appropriately computed by applying a higher rate. If the management's estimate of the useful life of the asset is longer than that envisaged under the statute, depreciation rate lower than that envisaged by the statute can be applied only in accordance with requirements of the statute.

14. Where depreciable assets are disposed of, discarded, demolished or destroyed, the net surplus or deficiency, if material, is disclosed separately.

15. The method of depreciation is applied consistently to provide comparability of the results of the operations of the enterprise from period to period. A change from one method or providing depreciation to another is made only if the adoption of the new method is required by statute or for compliance with an accounting standard or if it is considered that the change would result in a more appropriate preparation or presentation of the financial statements of the enterprise. When such a change in the method of depreciation is made, depreciation is recalculated in accordance with the new method from the date of the asset coming into use. The deficiency or surplus arising from retrospective recomputation of depreciation in accordance with the new method is adjusted in the accounts in the year in which the method of depreciation is changed. In case the change in the method results in deficiency in depreciation in respect of past years, the deficiency is charged in the statement of profit and loss. In case the change in the method results in surplus, the surplus is credited to the statement of profit and loss. Such a change is treated as a change in accounting policy and its effect is quantified and disclosed.

16. Where the historical cost of an asset has undergone a change due to specific circumstances, the depreciation on the revised unamortised depreciable amount is provided prospectively over the residual useful life of the asset.

17. The depreciation methods used, the total depreciation for the period for each class of assets, the gross amount of each class of depreciable assets and the related accumulated depreciation are disclosed in the financial statement along with the disclosure of other accounting policies. The depreciation rates or the useful lives of the assets are disclosed only if they are different from the principal rates specified in the statute governing the enterprise.

18. In case the depreciable assets are revalued, the provision for depreciation is based on the revalued amount on the estimate of the remaining useful life of such assets. In case the revaluation has a material effect on the amount of depreciation, the same is disclosed separately in the year in which revaluation is carried out.

19. A change in the method of depreciation is treated as a change in an accounting policy and is disclosed accordingly.[2]

Accounting Standard

(*The Accounting Standard comprises paragraphs 20-29 of this Statement. The Standard should be read in the context of paragraphs 1-19 of this Statement and of the Preface to the Statement of Accounting Standards.)*

20. The depreciable amount of a depreciable asset should be allocated on a systematic basis to each accounting period during the useful life of the asset.

21. The depreciation method selected should be applied consistently from period to period. A change from one method of providing depreciation to another should be made only if the adoption of the new method is required by statute or for

2. Refer to AS 5, "Prior Period and Extra-ordinary Items and Changes in Accounting Policies."

compliance with an accounting standard or if it is considered that the change would result in a more appropriate preparation or presentation of the financial statements of the enterprise. When such a change in the method of depreciation is made, depreciation should be recalculated in accordance with the new method from the date of the asset coming into use. The deficiency or surplus arising from retrospective recomputation of depreciation in accordance with the new method should be adjusted in the accounts in the year in which the method of depreciation is changed. In case the change in the method results in deficiency in depreciation in respect of past years, the deficiency should be charged in the statement of profit and loss. In case the change in the method results in surplus, the surplus should be created to the statement of profit and loss. Such a change should be treated as a change in accounting policy and its effect should be quantified and disclosed.

22. The useful life of a depreciable asset should be estimated after considering the following factors:

(i) expected physical wear and tear;

(ii) obsolescence;

(iii) legal or other limits on the use of the asset.

23. The useful lives of a major depreciable assets or classes of depreciable assets may be reviewed periodically. Where there is a revision of the estimated useful life of an asset, the unamortised depreciable amount should be charged over the revised remaining useful life.

24. Any addition or extension which becomes an integral part of the existing asset should be depreciated over the remaining useful life of that asset. The depreciation on such addition or extension may also be provided at the rate applied to the existing asset. Where an addition or extension retains a separate identity and is capable of being used after the existing asset is disposed of, depreciation should be provided independently on the basis of an estimate of its own useful life.

25. Where the historical cost of a depreciable asset has undergone a change due to increase or decrease in long term liability on account of exchange fluctuations, price adjustments, changes in duties or similar factors, the depreciation on the revised anamortised depreciable amount should be provided prospectively over the residual useful life of the asset.

26. Where the depreciable assets are revalued, the provision for depreciation should be based on the revalued amount and on the estimate of the remaining useful lives of such assets. In case the revaluation has a material effect on the amount of depreciation, the same should be disclosed separately in the year in which revaluation is carried out.

27. If any depreciable asset is disposed of, discarded, demolished or destroyed, the net surplus or deficiency, if material, should be disclosed separately.

28. The following information should be disclosed in the financial statements:

(i) the historical cost or other amount substituted for historical cost of each class of depreciable assets;

(ii) total depreciation for the period for each class of assets; and

(iii) the related accumulated depreciation.

29. The following information should also be disclosed in the financial statements alongwith the disclosure of other accounting policies:

(i) depreciation methods used; and

(ii) depreciation rates or the useful lives of the assets, if they are different from the principal rates specified in the statute governing the enterprise.

Depreciation in the Indian Context

In India, 'Section 350' of 'The Companies Act of 1956' deals with depreciation. It states that:

'The amount of depreciation to be deducted in pursuance of clause (k) of sub-section (4) of section 349 shall be the amount calculated with reference to the written down value of the assets as shown by the books of the company at the end of the financial year expiring at the commencement of this Act or immediately thereafter and at the end of each subsequent financial year at the rate specified in Schedule XIV:

Provided that if any asset is sold, discarded, demolished or destroyed for any reason before depreciation has been provided for in full, the excess if any, of the written down value, shall be written off in the financial year in which the asset is sold, discarded, demolished or destroyed'.

Section 205 of the Act dealing with dividends also provides for depreciation before paying dividends. It is done in accordance with sub-section (2) of Section 205. It states that:

Depreciation shall be provided either:

(a) to the extent specified in Section 350; or

(b) in respect of each item of the depreciable asset, for such an amount as is arrived at by dividing ninety five per cent, of the original cost thereof to the company specified by the period in respect of such asset ; or

(c) on, any other basis approved by the central government which has the effect of writing off by way of depreciation ninety-five per cent of the original cost to the company of each such depreciable asset on the expiry of the specified period; or

(d) as regards any other depreciable asset for which no rate of depreciation has been laid down by this act or the rules made thereunder on such basis as may be approved by the Central Government by any general order published in the Official Gazette or by any special order in any particular case.'

Rates of Depreciation

Nature of Assets	Single Shift		Double Shift		Triple Shift	
	WDV	SLM	WDV	SLM	WDV	SLM
Buildings (other than factory buildings) NESD	5%	1.63%				
Factory buildings	10%	3.34%				
Purely Temporary structures	100%	100%				
Plant and Machinery	15%	5.15%	22.5%	8.09%	30%	11.31%
Cycles (NESD)	20%	7.07%				
Glass Melting Furnaces	20%	7.07%	30%	11.31%	40%	16.21%
Aeroplanes - Aircraft, aerial photographic apparatus (NESD)	30%	11.31%				
Dies and Moulds (NESD)	30%	11.31%				
Shoes and Leather goods factories	30%	11.31%	45%	18.96%	60%	29.05%
Data Processing Machines including computers (NESD)	40%	16.21%				
Motor Vehicles used in business on run on hire. (NESD)	40%	16.21%				
Iron and Steel Industries - Rolling Mill rolls	100%	100%				
Equipment used in Mines and Quarries	100%	100%				
Furniture and Fittings (NESD)	10%	3.34%				
F&F in commercial use (NESD)	15%	5.15%				

4

Special Aspects in the Measurement of Business Income: Inventory Valuation

Inventory consists of all unconsumed and all goods held for sale in the ordinary course of business. In the case of a manufacturing concern, there are three types of inventory: raw materials, goods-in-process and finished goods. Inventory listed in the balance sheet under the heading current assets, includes all the three types of inventories. However, in the case of a trading concern, inventory mainly consists of finished goods.

Accurate inventory valuation is an important aspect which is taken into account by most companies in preparing their balance sheet. Inventory valuation also has a significant effect upon reported net income. The three main items listed under the head current assets are cash, accounts receivable and inventory. Of these three, inventory is the most significant because of its relatively large size. An error in inventory valuation will significantly affect other key figures like cost of goods sold, gross profit, net income, etc.

Hence, proper determination of income by matching appropriate costs with corresponding revenues is a major objective of inventory valuation.

Methods of Inventory Valuation

There are various methods to value inventory. Four main methods that will be considered here are:

1. First-in-First-out (FIFO) Method

2. Last-in-First-out (LIFO) Method
3. Specific Identification Method
4. Weighted Average Method.

The following example gives a comparative assessment of the three inventory methods—LIFO, FIFO and Weighted Average. As can be seen from the example, the choice of an inventory method significantly affects the closing stock and gross profit (and hence net income).

Example: Following is the record of purchases and sales made throughout the year. Prepare a comparative statement of Gross Profit for the year ended Dec. 31 using FIFO, LIFO and Weighted average inventory methods:

Jan.	Opening stock	200 units @ Rs. 3/-	Rs. 600
Feb.	Receipts	50 units @ Rs. 4/-	Rs. 200
March	Issues	100 units	
May	Receipts	100 units @ Rs. 5/-	Rs. 500
July	Issues	120 units	
Other	Receipts	80 units @ Rs. 6/-	Rs. 480
December	Issues	80 units	

It is further given that the sales were made at the following prices:

March	100 units at Rs. 5/-
July	120 units at Rs. 8/-
December	50 units at Rs. 10/-

1. First-in-First-out-Method: This method assumes that the inventory acquired first is also the first to be sold or used up. According to this method, inventory acquired earliest is deemed to have been the first inventory sold, without regard to the physical flow of the goods. The ending inventory under the FIFO method, therefore, consists of the most recent purchases made while the cost of the beginning inventory and the cost of goods sold are made up of the earliest purchases in the year.

The value of closing stock under the FIFO Method is Rs. 730 while the Gross Profit is Rs. 910.

2. *Last-in-First-out Method:* This method, commonly referred to as LIFO, assumes that the inventory purchased last are the first to be issued or sold. As the most recently acquired goods were sold first, the ending inventory is very outdated as it consists of the earliest purchases. LIFO method is also a method for inventory costing under the generally accepted accounting principles. The physical movement of inventory does not conform to either the FIFO or LIFO assumption.

The Gross Profit under the LIFO method is Rs. 570 and the value of closing stock is Rs. 390. Both the values under the LIFO method are less than those under the FIFO method.

3. *Specific Identification Method:* This method is specifically used when each unit of inventory is unique, different from all others and has a different cost. For relatively expensive goods like jewellery, valuable paintings, etc., the specific identification method is the only logical choice. This is the only method where the inventory costing is exactly same as the physical flow of goods.

4. *Weighted Average Method:* Under this method of inventory costing, all goods available for sale are priced on the basis of a weighted average cost. Weighted cost is calculated by dividing the total cost of goods available for sale by the number of units available for sale. Till a fresh purchase of materials is made the weighted average cost remains the same.

This method shows a gross profit of Rs. 786 which is somewhere between that obtained under the FIFO and LIFO methods. Similarly, the value of ending inventory is Rs. 606 (compared with Rs. 730 and Rs. 390).

COMPARISON OF THE METHODS

FIFO vs LIFO

The two most widely used methods are FIFO and LIFO. Both the methods have their merits and demerits and accountants tend to follow both the methods depending upon the company and their applicability in each situation. However, a recent survey of large corporations shows that the LIFO is the most widely used of all inventory methods[1].

LIFO method is generally preferred for Income Tax considerations. In a period of rising prices (e.g. during inflation) LIFO assigns the most recent inventory cost to the cost of goods sold. The most recent cost are also the highest cost, and hence the LIFO method usually results in reporting lower taxable income. This results in paying less income tax and less cash dividends. Hence most companies prefer the LIFO method as it helps them to conserve cash and reduce their income tax liability.

In a period of rising prices, the FIFO method "overstates" profits and "understates" the cost of goods sold. This results in the reported net income by companies being higher, resulting in higher Income Tax and more cash being distributed to shareholders as cash dividends.

The effect on the Balance Sheet and Income Statement by following the LIFO and FIFO methods can also be examined. Under the FIFO method, the value of clsoing stock consists of the most recently acquired stock while under the LIFO method, the ending inventory consists of goods acquired in the earliest purchases. And as closing stock appears on the asset side of the balance sheet, accountants and managers feel that the balance sheet is more realistic when the company follows the FIFO method.

The Income statement is however more realistic under the LIFO method as current costs are charged to current revenues. The FIFO method, as mentioned earlier, charges 'older' costs and hence, in periods of rising prices, may overstate profits.

An argument is favour of FIFO given by managers is that this approach corresponds most closely to the actual physical flow of goods and avoids spoilage, obsolescence etc.

Thus, both LIFO and FIFO are popular methods used by companies in various situations of inventory costing.

1. American Institute of Certified Public Accounts, Accounting Trends and Techniques, (New York: 1987), p. 126.

Solution :

Comparison of Inventory Methods

		FIFO	LIFO	W.A.
January	Opening Stock 200 @ 3/- = Rs. 600			
February Receipt	50 @ 4/- = Rs. 200			
March Issue	100 units	100 @ 3/- = 300	50 @ 4/- = 200 50 @ 3/- = 150 350	100 @ 3.20 = 320/-
May Receipt	100 @ 5/- = Rs. 500			
June Issue	120 units	100 @ 3/- = 300 20 @ 4/- = 80 380	100 @ 5/- = 500 20 @ 3/- = 60 560	120 @ 3.37 = 444/-
November Receipts	80 @ 6/- = Rs. 480			
December Issue	80 units	30 @ 4/- = 120 50 @ 5/- = 250 370	80 @ 6/- = 480 = 410/-	80 @ 5.13 = 410/-

Calculation of Cost of Goods Sold	**FIFO**	**LIFO**	**W.A.**
Opening stock	600	600	600
Add purchases (200+500+480)	1180	1180	1180
	1780	1780	1780
Less closing stock (130 units)	730	390	606
Cost of goods sold	1050	1390	1174
Sales	Rs. 1960	Rs. 1960	Rs. 1960
Less cost of goods sold	1050	1390	1174
Gross profit	Rs. 910	Rs. 570	Rs. 786

Regarding the choice between the two methods, no specific generalization can be made regarding the superiority of one method over the other. The effect of the two methods on the income statement and balance sheet can be very substantial. In a period of rising prices, LIFO tends to give a more realistic picture of the income statements but not of the balance sheet while FIFO method gives a more realistic picture of the balance sheet but a less realistic position of the Income statement.

Further, in periods of rising prices, LIFO offers substantial income tax advantages and hence may be preferred by accountants and managers. Many companies adopt the LIFO method as it is acceptable for income tax purposes.

Hence, both LIFO and FIFO have their own advantages and disadvantages and depending upon the situation, a choice between the two methods can be made.

Consistency Principle in Evaluation of Inventory

The principle of consistency means that once the business has adopted a particular accounting method, it should follow the same method and procedures from period to period. Switching of from one method to the other makes it difficult to compare a company's financial statements from one period to the other. For example when a company changes its inventory method from LIFO to FIFO, its net income increases significantly only as a result of the change in inventory method.

However, the principle of consistency does not mean that a company can never change its method of pricing inventory. If a change is made, the company must disclose the reasons for the change, as also the effect of the change on the net income of the company.

Illustrative Problems

1. Using the information given below for the year end Dec. 31, 19×6, prepare a comparative statement of net income using FIFO, LIFO and weighted average inventory methods? Assume that other expenses are Rs. 1,500 and the Income Tax rate is 50%.

Solution I.

Comparison of Inventory methods for the year ended Dec. 31, 19×6

		FIFO		LIFO	Weighted Average
Sales 480 units		5,760		5,760	5,760
Cost of goods sold:					
Beginning Inventory 200 @ Rs. 5		1,000		1,000	1,000
Purchases 510 Units		3,550		3,550	3,550
		4.550		4.550	4.550
Available for Sale, 710 units ending inventory, 230 units					
150 @ Rs. 8	1,200				
			1000		
80 @ Rs. 7	560	1,760	180	1,180	1472
or					
200 @ Rs. 5					
30 @ Rs. 6					
or					
230 @ 6.4					
Cost of goods sold, 480 units		2,790		3,370	3,078
Gross Profit		2970		2390	2682
Other expenses		1,500		1,500	1,500
Income before taxes		1,470		890	1,182
Income taxes at 50%		735		445	591
Net Income		735		445	591

	Balance	Purchases	Sales
Dec. 31, 19×6	200 @ Rs. 5 = Rs. 1,000		
Jan. 28		170 @ Rs. 6 = Rs. 1,020	
Feb. 20			150*
April 25		190 @ Rs. 7 = Rs. 1,330	
June 15			230*
July 16		150 @ Rs. 8 = Rs. 1,200	
Dec. 29			100*
Total	510	3,550	480

*Selling prices were Rs. 10, Rs. 12, and Rs. 15 respectively.

150 @ Rs. 10 = Rs. 1,500
230 @ Rs. 12 = Rs. 2,760
100 @ Rs. 15 = Rs. 1,500
Total Sales 480 = Rs. 5,760

II. The following data relates to the opening stock and purchases of a given product for a Company for the year 19×6:

Inventory January 1	5,000	@ Rs. 2.00
February 28	4,000	@ Rs. 2.10
April 3	7,000	@ Rs. 2.25
June 15	5,000	@ Rs. 2.40
November 20	3,000	@ Rs. 2.60
	24,000	

During the year 21,000 units were sold. Calculate the ending inventory under each of the following method:

a. FIFO

b. LIFO

c. Weighted Average

Solution II.

The ending inventory consists of 3,000 units (24,000-21,000):

a. Ending inventory under FIFO:

Purchased	Units	Unit Cost	Total Cost
November 20	3,000	Rs. 2.60	Rs. 7,800
	3,000		Rs. 7,800

b. Ending inventory under LIFO:

	Units	Unit Cost	Total Cost
Inventory, January 1	3,000	Rs. 2.00	Rs. 6,000

c. Ending inventory under weighted average:

Purchased	Units	Unit Cost	Total Cost
Inventory, Jan. 1	5,000	Rs. 2.00	Rs. 10,000
February 28	4,000	2.10	8,400
April 3	7,000	2.25	15,750
June 15	5,000	2.40	12,000
November 20	3,000	2.60	7,800
	24,000		53,950

Weighted Average Unit cost is Rs. 53,950 ÷ 24,000 = Rs. 2.25.

Ending inventory cost is Rs. 2.25 × 3,000 = Rs. 6,750.

Questions

1. What are the main advantages from the use of FIFO and LIFO?

2. How can a company manipulate its net income if it uses LIFO? Is the same opportunity available under FIFO? Why or why not?

3. If the beginning inventory is Rs. 20,000, purchases total Rs. 1,50,000 and ending inventory is Rs. 25,000 how much is the cost of goods sold.

4. Briefly discuss the four generally accepted inventory methods. Which method is preferred during a period of rising prices? Which method produces the highest reported net income?

5. What are the chief drawbacks of the LIFO and the weighted average method?

6. Which methods of inventory valuation are more popular in practice? Elucidiate with examples.

7. Why is there a need for valuation of Inventories? What are the objectives of Inventory Valuation?

8. A company reported the following information:

Balance Sheet	**19×6**	**19×7**
Closing Stock	Rs. 80,250	Rs. 95,380
Income Statement		
Net purchases	Rs. 4,10,000	Rs. 5,35,000
Cost of goods sold	3,85,000	5,40,000

Calculate the cost of goods sold for 19×7 under LIFO and FIFO which method shows a higher reported net income?

Problems

1. The beginning inventory, purchases, and sales of Product MNO for May and June are presented below. The company closes its books at the end of each month:

July 1	Beginning Inventory	60 units @ Rs. 147
July 9	Sales	30 units
July 12	Purchases	100 units @ Rs. 156
July 25	Sales	60 units
August 5	Purchases	120 units @ Rs. 160

August 9	Sales	100 units
August 14	Purchases	50 units @ Rs. 170
August 19	Sales	80 units
August 24	Purchases	100 units @ Rs. 175
August 28	Sales	100 units

Required: Calculate the value of closing stock as per the following methods: (1) FIFO, (2) LIFO, (3) Simple Average Method, (4) Weighted Average Method.

2. The beginning inventory of Product M and data on purchases and sales for a two-month period follow. The company closes its books at the end of each month:

November 1 Inventory	50 units @ Rs. 200
November 9 Sale	25 units
November 15 Purchase	100 units @ Rs. 220
November 20 Sale	60 units
December 4 Purchase	100 units @ Rs. 230
December 10 Sale	100 units
December 16 Purchase	50 units @ Rs. 234
December 20 Sale	40 units
December 23 Purchase	60 units @ Rs. 240
December 25 Sale	30 units
December 31 Sale	10 units

Required: Compute the value of the ending inventory of Product M on November 30 and December 31 on a FIFO and LIFO basis. In addition, determine cost of goods sold for November and December.

3. The data for X Ltd. for the month of July is given below:

Inventory data, July 31

July 1	Inventory	50 units	@ Rs. 10 = Rs. 500
July 8	Purchased	50 units	@ Rs. 11 = Rs. 550
July 15	Purchased	150 units	@ Rs. 12 = Rs. 1,800
July 23	Purchased	100 units	@ Rs. 13 = Rs. 1,300
July 26	Purchased	150 units	@ Rs. 14 = Rs. 2,100
Goods available for sale		500 units	500 units Rs. 6,250
Sales		280 units	
Stock on hand, July 31		220 units	

Required: Calculate the cost of goods sold by the following four methods: FIFO, LIFO, Average Cost Method and Specific Identification Method.

4. The records of Sunny Ltd. for the current year are given below:

	Inventory			
Jan. 1	Balance 800 units	@Rs. 8.50	=	Rs. 6,400
	Purchases			
Jan 15	300 units	@Rs. 8.50	=	Rs. 2,550
March 13	900 units	@Rs. 9.00	=	Rs. 8,100
June 15	6,500 units	@Rs. 9.50	=	Rs. 61,750
July 27	400 units	@Rs. 10.00	=	Rs. 4,000
Dec. 30	200 units	@Rs. 10.00	=	Rs. 2,000
Dec. 31	Balance			Rs. 78,400
	Sales Revenue			
Feb. 27	1,000 units	@Rs. 11/-	=	Rs. 11,000
April 3	500 units	@Rs. 15/-	=	Rs. 7,500
July 16	4,500 units	@Rs. 15.00	=	Rs. 13,950
October 5	1,200 units	@Rs. 17.00	=	Rs. 20,400
November 20	400 units	@Rs. 17.50	=	Rs. 7,000

a. Calculate the closing stock and cost of goods sold during the year.

b. Prepare a partial income statement under the FIFO, LIFO and weighted average method.

5. N.K. Industries entered into the following transactions during 1999 involving inventory:

Date	Purchases	
July Beginning Inventory	10 units	@Rs. 15
1.7.99	12 units	@Rs. 15.5
3.7.99	20 units	@Rs. 20
7.7.99	25 units	@Rs. 20

8.7.99	10 units	@Rs. 25
12.7.99	20 units	@Rs. 30
30.7.99	10 units	@Rs. 40
Sales		
3.7.99	20 units	
20.7.99	25 units	
25.7.99	15 units	
27.7.99	10 units	

Calculate the ending inventory under each of the following methods:

a. LIFO

b. FIFO

c. Weighted Average Method.

6. A.Company began business in 19×1. Inventory units purchased and sold for the first six months are given below:

	Units Furchased	Costs Per Unit	Units (all in the month of May) Sold
Jan.	10,000	Rs. 10	Rs. 6,000
Feb.	12,000	25	10,000
Feb.	25,000	25	2,000
March	20,000	20	10,000
April	8.000	20	20,000

Required:

a. Compute the cost of goods sold, if the company uses the following methods:

   1. LIFO cost flow assumption,

   2. FIFO cost flow assumption, and

   3. Weighted average method

b. Does the choice of a cost flow assumption affect total net income over the life of a business? Explain your answer.

c. **If the choice of a cost flow assumption does not affect net income over the life of a business, how does the choice of a cost flow assumption give rise to a tax benefit?**

7. (Different inventory methods and cost flow assumptions) Company XYZ had 15,000 units of inventory on hand as of January 1, 19×1 and each unit had a cost of Rs. 5. The following information was extracted from the inventory records of XYZ for 19 ×1

Inventory Purchases

2nd Feb.	10,000 units @ Rs. 10 per unit
10th May	15,000 units @ Rs. 15 per unit
15th June	10,000 units @ Rs. 20 per unit
16th July	30,000 units @ Rs. 25 per unit
29th Dec.	15,000 units @ Rs. 30 per unit

Inventory Sales

15th May	15,000 units
30th Aug.	10,000 units
3rd Sept.	25,000 units
30th Dec.	25,000 units

Compute cost of goods sold and the value of ending inventory by each of the 3 methods - LIFU, FIFO, W.A.

8. The purchase schedule of a company is given below:

Date	**Items purchased**	**Cost per Item**
March 15	5,000	Rs. 3
July 30	8,000	Rs. 4
December 17	9,000	Rs. 5
Total	22,000	

The inventory balance as of the beginning of the year was Rs. 20,000 (10000 units @ Rs. 2/-) and an inventory count at year-end indicated that 10,000 items were on hand. The sales made were on April 15 (8000 units), July 16 (10000 units) November 20 (4000 units). The Selling Prices were Rs. 10, 11, 12 respecively. Sales and expenses (excluding Cost of Goods Sold) totalled Rs.

55,000 and Rs. 15,000 respectively. The income tax rate is 50 Percent.

Required:

a. Prepare three income statements one under each of the assumptions: FIFO, LIFO and weighted average method.

b. How many rupees would be saved by using LIFO instead of FIFO?

APPENDIX

Accounting Standard 2 (Revised)

Values of Inventories

The following is the text of the revised Accounting Standard (AS) 2, 'Valuation of Inventories', issued by the Council of the Institute of Chartered Accountants of India. This revised Standard supersedes Accounting Standard (AS) 2, Valuation of Inventories, issued in June, 1981. The revised standard comes into effect in the respect of accounting periods commencing on or after April 1, 1999 and is mondatory in nature.[1]

Objective

A primary issue is accounting for inventories is the determination of the value at which inventories are carried in the financial statements until the related revenues are recognised. This Statement deals with the determination of such value, including the ascertainment of cost of inventories and any write-down thereof to net realisable value.

Scope

1. This Statement should be applied in accounting for inventories other than :

---

1. This implies that, while discharging their attest function, it will be the duty of the members of the Institute to examine whether this Accounting Standard is complied with in the presentation of financial statements covered by their audit. In the event of any deviation from this Accounting Standard, it will be their duty to make adequate disclosures in their audit reports so that the users of financial statements may be aware of such deviations.

(a) work-in-progress arising under construction contracts, including directly related service contracts (see Accounting Standard (AS) 7, Accounting for Construction Contractrs);

(b) work-in-progress arising in the ordinary course of business of service providers;

(c) shares, debentures and other financial instruments held as stock-in-trades; and

(d) producers' inventories of livestock, agricultural and forest products, and mineral oils, ores and gases to the extent that they are measured at net realisable value in accordance with well established practices in those industries.

2. The inventories referred to in paragraph 1(d) are measured at net realisable value at certain stages of production. This occurs, for example, when agricultural crops have been harvested or mineral oils, ores and gases have been extracted and sale is assured under a forward contract or a government guarantee, or when a homogenous market exists and there is a negligible risk of failure to sell. These inventories are excluded from the scope of this Statement.

Definitions

3. The following terms are used in this Statement with the meanings specified : **inventories** are assets :

(a) held for sale in the ordinary course of business;

(b) in the process of production for such sale; or

(c) in the form of materials or supplies to be consumed in the production process or in the rendering of services.

Net realisable value is the estimated selling price in the ordinary course of business less the estimated costs of completion and the estimated costs necessary to make the sale.

4. Inventories encompass goods purchased and held for resale, for example, merchandise purchased by a retailer and

held for resale, computer software held for resale, or land and other property held for resale. Inventories also encompass finished goods produced, or work-in-progress being produced, by the enterprise and include materials, maintenance supplies, consumables and loose tools awaiting use in the production process. Inventories do not include machinery spares which can be used only in connection with an item of fixed asset and whose use in expected to be irregular, such machinery spares are accounted for in accordance with Accounting Standard (AS) 10, *Accounting for Fixed Assets.*

Meaurements of Inventories

5. Inventories should be valued at the lower of cost and net realisable value.

Cost of Inventories

6. The cost of inventories should comprise all costs of purchase, costs of conversion and other costs incurred in bringing the inventories to their present location and condition.

Costs of Purchase

7. The costs of purchase consist of the purchase price including duties and taxes (other than those subsequently recoverable by the enterprise from the taxing authorities), freight inwards and other expenditure directly attributable to the acquisition. Trade discounts, rebates, duty drawbacks and other similar items are deducted in determining the costs of purchase.

Costs of Conversion

8. The costs of conversion of inventories include costs directly related to the units of production, such as direct labour. They also include a systematic allocation of fixed and variable production overheads that are incurred in converting materials into finsihed goods. Fixed produciton overheads are those indirect costs of production that remain relatively constant regardless of the volume of production, such as depreciation and maintenance of factory buildings and the cost of factory management and administration. Variable production over-

heads are those indirect costs of produciton that vary directly, or nearly directly, with the volume of production, such as indirect materials and indirect labour.

9. The allocation of fixed production overheads for the purpose of their inclusion in the costs of conversion is based on the normal capacity of the production facilities. Normal capacity is the production expected to be achieved on an average over a number of periods or seasons under normal circumstances, taking into account the loss of capacity resulting from planned maintenance. The actual level of production may be used if it approximate normal capacity. The amount of fixed production overheads allocated to each unit of production is not increased as a consequence of low production or idel plant. Unallocated overheads are recognised as an expense in the period in which they are incurred. In periods of abnormally high production, the amount of fixed production overheads allocated to each unit of production is decreased so that inventories are not measured above cost. Variable production overheads are assigned to each unit of production on the basis of the actual use of the production facilities.

10. A production process may result in more than one product being produced simultaneously. This is the case, for example, when joint products are produced or when there is a main product and a by-product. When the costs of conversion of each product are not separately identifiable, they are allocated between the products on a rational and consistent basis. The allocation may be based, for example, on the relative sales value of each product either at the stage in the production process when the products become separately identifiable, or at the completion of production. Most by-products as well as scrap or waste materials, by their nature, are immaterial. When this is a case, they are often measured at net realisable value and this value is deducted from the cost of the main product. As a result, the carrying amount of the main product is not materially different from its cost.

Other Costs

11. Other costs are included in the cost of inventories only

to the extent that they are incurred in bringing the inventories to their present location and condition. For exampoe, it may be appropriate to include overheads other than production overheads or the costs of designing products for specific customers in the cost of inventories.

12. Interest and other borrowing costs are usually considered as not relating to bringing the inventories to their present location and condition and are, therefore, usually not included in the cost of inventories.

Exclusions from the Cost of Inventories

13. In determining the cost of inventories in accordance with paragraph 6, it is appropriate to exclude certain costs and recognise them as expenses in the period in which they are incurred. Examples of such costs are :

(a) abnormal amounts of wasted materails, labour, or other production costs;

(b) storage costs, unless those costs are necessary in the production process prior to a further production stage;

(c) adminstrative overheads that do not contribute to bringing the inventories to their present location and condition; and

(d) selling and distribution costs.

Cost Formulas

14. The cost of inventories of items that are not ordinarily interchangeable and goods or services produced and segregated for specific projectrs should be assigned by specific identification of their individual costs.

15. Specific identification of cost means that specific costs are attributed to identified items of inventory. This is an appropriate treatment for items that are segregated for a specific project, regardless of whether they have been purchased or produced. However, when there are large numbers of items of inventory which are ordinarily interchangeable, specific iden-

tification of costs is inappropriate since, in such circumstances, an enterprise could obtain predetermined effects on the net profit or loss for the period by selecting a particular method of ascertaining the items that remain in inventories.

16. The cost of inventories, other than those deals with in paragarph 14, should be assigned by using the first-in, first-out (FIFO), or weighted average cost formala. The formula used should reflect the fairest possible approximation to the cost incurred in bringing the items of inventory to their present location and condition.

17. A variety of costs formulas is used to determine the cost of inventories other than those for which specific identification of individual costs is appropriate. The formula used in determining the cost of an item of inventory needs to be selected with a view to providing the fairest possible approximation to the cost incurred in bringing the item to its present location and condition. The FIDO formula assumes that the items of inventory which were purchased for produced first are consumed or sold first, and consequently the items remaining in inventory at the end of the period are those most recently purchased or produced. Under the weighted average cost formula, the cost of each item is determined from the weighted average of the cost of similar items at the beginning of a period and cost of similar items purchased or produced during the period. The average may be calculated on a periodic basis, or as each additional shipment is received, depending upon the circumstances of the enterprise.

Techniques for the Meausrement of Cost

18. The techniques for the measurement of the cost of inventories, such as the standard cost method or the retail method, may be used for convenience if the results approximate the actual cost. Standard costs take into account normal levels of consumption of materials and supplies, labour, efficiency and capacity utilisation. They are regularly reviewed and, if necessary, revised in the light of current conditions.

19. The retail method is often used in the retail trade for measuring inventories of large numbers of rapidly changing

items that have similar margins and for which it is impracticable to use other costing methods. The cost of the inventory is determined by reducing from the sales value of the inventory the appropriate percentage gross margin. The percentage used takes into consideration inventory which has been marked down to below its original selling price. An average percentage for each retail department is often used.

Net Realisable Value

20. The cost of inventories may not be recoverable if those inventories are damaged, if they have become wholly or partially obsolete, or if their selling prices have declined. The cost of inventories may also not be recoverable if the estimated costs of completion or the estimated costs necessary to make the sale have increased. The practice of writing down inventories below cost of net realisable value is consistent with the veiw that assets should not be carried in excess of amounts expected to be realised from their sale or use.

21. Inventories are usually written down to net realisable value of an item-by-item basis. In some circumstances, however, it may be appropriate to group similar or related items. This may be the case with items of inventory relating to the same product line that have similar purposes or end uses and are produced and marketed in the same geographical area and cannot be practicably evaluated separately from other items in that product line. It isnot appropriate to write down inventories based on a classification of inventory, for example, finished goods, or all the inventories in a particular business segment.

22. Estimates of net realisable value are based on the most reliable evidence available at the time the estimates are made as to the amount the inventories are expected to realise. These estimates take into consideration fluctuations of price or cost directly relating to events occurring after the balance sheet date to the extent that such events confirm the conditions existing at the balance sheet date.

23. Estimates of net realisable value also take into consideration the purpose for which the inventory is held. For ex-

ample, the net realisable value of the quantity of inventory held to satisfy firm sales or service contracts is based on the contract price. If the sales contracts are for less than the inventory quantities held, the net realisable value of the excess inventory is based on general selling prices. Contingent losses on firm sales contracts in excess of inventory quantities held and contingent losses on firm purchase contracts are dealt with in accordance with the principles enunciated in Accounting Standard (AS) 4, *Contingents And Events Occurring After The Balance Sheet Date.*

24. Materials and other supplies held for use in the production of inventories are not written down below cost if the finished products in which they will be incorporated are expected tobe sold at or above cost. However, when there has been a decl'ne in the price of materials and it is estimated that the cost of the finished products will exceed net realiable value, the materials are written down to net realisable value. In such circumstances, the replacement cost of the materials may be the best available measure of their net realisable value.

25. An assessment is made of net realisable value as at each balance sheet date.

Disclosure

26. The financial statements should disclose:

(a) the accounting policies adopted in measuring inventoıies, including the cost formula used; and

(b) the total carrying amount of inventories and its classification appropriate to the enterprise.

27. Information about the carrying amounts held in different classifications of inventories and the extent of the changes in these assets is useful to financial statement users. Common classifications of inventories are raw materials and components, work-in-progress, finished goods, stores and spares, and loose tools.

5

Funds Flow Analysis

In accounting, three major financial statements are usually prepared from the accumulated financial data. The balance sheet is the first of the three major financial statements which is prepared. The balance sheet shows the financial position of a firm as on the last day of the accounting period. The second major financial statement is the income statement also known as the profit-and-loss statement. The income statement shows the results of operation for a company during a given accounting period. The income statement restricts itself to transactions that pertain to rendering goods or services to customers.

The third important financial statement is the statement of changes in financial position also known as the funds flow statement[1]. This statement measures the changes that have taken place in the financial position of a firm between two balance sheet dates. It shows where the financial resources (funds) have come from and where they have gone. The statement of changes in financial position summaries the long-term financing and investing activities of an enterprise. The change in financial position could refer to different concepts of the word "funds". Two most commonly used measures of the term

1. Beginning in 1988, the FASB has stated that all companies should discontinue the preparation of the funds flow statement and instead prepare a new statement known as the 'statement of cash flows.' The new guidelines have been specifically issued by the FASB because of alternative definitions of the world 'funds' adopted by various companies. This makes comparison by the investors very difficult. The new Cash Flow Statement is discussed in Chapter-6.

funds are 'cash' and 'working capital'. Thus, two statements are prepared i.e., the statement of changes in the working capital (also known as the flow of funds statement or the sources and uses of funds statement) and the statement of changes in cash (also known as the cash flow statement). This chapter aims to illustrate and explain the technique of preparing a funds flow statement.

Concept of Funds

The term 'Funds' in the context of the preparation of funds flow statement refers to net working capital i.e. the difference between current assets and current liabilities. The net working capital view is widely accepted by financial analysts and business executives for logical reasons.

The term 'Flow' means movement or change. Thus the term 'Flow of Funds' means change in funds. Viewed from the perspective of the working capital concept of funds the flow of funds means changes in working capital. This means that transactions exclusively between working capital accounts do not change the net working capital and hence do not involve a 'flow of funds'. Flow of funds takes place when a transaction affects one current account and the other non-current account and vice versa. Hence changes in working capital involves inflow and outflow of funds.

Funds Flow Statement

The basic purpose of the funds flow statement is to provide information about the inflow and outflow of funds in an organization. The funds flow statement is basically concerned with explaining why a firm's net working capital (current assets less current liabilities) increased or decreased during an accounting period. The effective use of working capital by the management is shown by the funds flow statement. In addition, it also helps the analyst in finding out how a firm has financed its activities and acts as an instrument for allocation of resources.

Importance of Funds Flow Statement

Some of the significant advantages of a funds flow statement are as follows:

1. It helps us to know from where a firm has acquired its funds and the uses which the firm has made of these funds.
2. It helps the firm in allocating its resources in a scientific manner.
3. It provides a meaningful link between two successive balance sheets of the organization.
4. The statement helps the financial analyst to know about the strengths and weaknesses of the organization, enabling the business to take suitable corrective action.
5. It helps the firm in planning its financial activities for the future.

Preparation of A Funds Flow Statement

A fund flow statement can be prepared from comparative balance sheets, income statement and additional data. The statement can be prepared in three steps as follows:

1. Sources and Applications of Funds.
2. Schedule of changes in Working Capital.
3. Funds from Operations.

Each of these three statements are explained briefly first, after which a comprehencive illustration is discussed which highlights the preparation of a Funds Flow Statement.

I. Sources and Applications of Funds

The various sources of funds are:-

1. *Issue of Share capital*: An issue of equity shares or preference shares results in an inflow of working capital because the firm receives funds.
2. *Long-term borrowing*: When a firm borrows by issuing debentures or obtaining loans from the financial institutions, the working capital of the company increases because of cash inflow.
3. *Sale of fixed assets*: Sale of fixed assets such as plant and machinery, equipment, land and building etc. consti-

tute an important source of working capital. The total inflow of cash on the sale of fixed assets is shown as a source of working capital.

4. *Funds from operations*: The most important source of funds is funds from operations. This is the only internal source of funds. These funds come from the daily business of the firm, i.e. the net profit of the firm. The net profit from operations as shown in the profit and loss account of the firm contains certain items which do not affect working capital. Thus, appropriate adjustments are required to the figure of net profit to find out the real funds from operations. Table 1 gives the list of items to be added or substracted to the reported net income after taxes to arrive at the figure of funds from operation. The format of the sources and application is of funds is given below:

Sources and Applications of Funds

Sources of Funds	**Application of Funds**
Funds from Operations	Purchase of Fixed Assets
Issue of Share Capital	Payment of Cash Dividends
Long-term borrowings	Redemption of Debentures
Sale of Fixed Assets	Redemption of Preference Shares
Decrease in Working Capital	Payment of long-term loans.
	Loans from Operations
	Increase in Working Capital
Total	Total

Use of Funds/Application of Funds

Funds may be applied by the firm in a number of areas. Some of the more common uses of funds are:-

1. *Payment of Dividend*: Payment of cash dividend results in a cash outflow, and thus is a use of funds.

2. *Repayment of Liabilities*: This involves a cash outflow and hence is a use of funds.

3. *Purchase of Fixed Assets*: A firm pays cash when plant, equipment or land is purchased. This is a use of funds.

4. Payment of Dividend.
5. Redemption of debentures.
6. Redemption of preference shares.

II. Schedule of Changes in Working Capital

The schedule of changes in working capital is prepared by comparing the current assets and current liabilities of two periods. The format of a schedule of changes in working capital is as shown below:

Item	Increase	Decrease
Current Assets		
Cash		
Bank		
Accounts Receivable		
Closing stock		
Debtors		
Current Liabilities		
Accounts Payable		
Creditors		
Bank overdraft	-----------	-----------
Net Increase or Decrease in Working Capital		

Funds from operation - The format of the funds from operation statement is shown in Table 1.

Table 1

Net Income (or loss) after taxes

Add the following items as they do not result in outflow of funds:

- Depreciation
- Interest expenses
- Loss on sale of Fixed Assets
- Preliminary Expenses or goodwill written off

Deduct the following items as they do not increase funds:

- Profit on Sale of fixed assets
- Profit on revaluation of fixed assets
- Dividend received
- Rent received
- Funds from operations

Illustration

Prepare a Funds Flow Statement from the given Balance Sheet & Income Statement for the XYZ Company.

Balance Sheet as on Dec. 31, 19x2

	X1	X2		X1	X2
Share Capital	Rs. 3,50,000	Rs. 5,00,000	Current Assets		
Reserves & Surplus	1,50,000	2,00,000	Cash	Rs. 40,000	80,000
Long-term debt	50,000	1,00,000	Accounts receivable	20,000	40,000
	5,50,000	8,00,000	Debtors	80,000	1,20,000
Current Liabilities			Investors	2,00,000	2,50,000
Creditors	60,000	1,00,000		3,40,000	4,90,000
Accounts Payable	50,000	90,000	Fixed Assets		
			Plant & Equipment	1,20,000	2,50,000
			Investment	50,000	50,000
			Land	1,50,000	2,00,000
	Rs. 6,60,000	Rs. 9,90,000		Rs. 6,60,000	Rs. 9,90,000

Income Statement of XYZ Company for the year ending Dec. 31, 19×2.

Net Sales		7,50,000
Less		
Cost of goods sold	4,40,000	
Operating Eξpenses	60,000	
excluding depreciation		
Depreciation	30,000	
Interest	20,000	
	5,50,000	5,50,000
Net income before tax		2,00,000
Tax		1,50,000
Net profit after tax		50,000

Solution

Schedule of changes in Working Capital

Item	Increase	Decrease
Cash	40,000	
Accounts Receivable	20,000	
Debtors	40,000	
Inventories	50,000	
Creditors		40,000
Accounts Payable		40,000
Net increase in Working Capital		70,000
		(balancing figure)
	1,50,000	1,50,000

Funds Flow Statement of XYZ Company for the year ended Dec. 31, 19×2

Use of Funds		Sources of Funds	
Purchase of Plant & Equipment	1,60,000	Issue of Share Capital	1,50,000
Purchase of land	50,000	Issue of L.T. debt	50,000
Net Increase in working capital	70,000	Funds from operations	80,000
	2,80,000		2,80,000

Working Notes

(1) Funds from operations

Net profit after tax	50,000
Add Depreciation	30,000
	80,000

(2) Plant and Equipment A/c

To balance b/f	1,20,000	By Depreciation	30,000
To purchases (balancing figure)	1,60,000	By balance c/d	2,50,000
	2,80,000		2,80,000

Difference between Funds Flow Statement and Cash Flow Statement

(i) The funds flow statement is useful to the firm in long-term planning whereas a cash flow analysis helps management to make short-run predictions. The firm needs cash to meet its day-to-day requirements and hence a cash flow statement only makes reliable projections of cash receipts and disbursements in the near future. A funds flow statement helps management to plan for a long-term period, say for 5 to 7 or 10 years. The management can plan the repayment of long-term loans, purchase of fixed assets, payment of cash dividend, etc. with the help of a funds flow statement.

(ii) A cash flow statement only measures the inflows and outflows of cash while a funds flow statement measures the changes in the working capital position between two balance sheet dates.

Solved Problems

Illustration I

From the following details, calculate the funds from operations:

Profit and Loss Account

	Rs.		Rs.
To Rent	25,000	By Gross Profit	1,60,000
To Goodwill written off	3,800	By Profit on Sale of Plant	4,500
To Loss on Sale of Machinery	12,300		
To Salaraies	45,000		
To Depreciation on Machinery	4,800		
To Provision for Tax	700		
To General Reserve	5,000		
To Interim Dividend paid	7,200		
To Net Profit	55,000		
	1,65,100		1,65,100

Solution I

Calculation of Funds from Operation

Net Profit		Rs. 55,000
Add items which do not decrease funds from operation:		
Provision for tax	Rs. 7,000	
Goodwill written off	3,800	
Loss on Sale of Machinery	12,300	
Depreciation	4,800	
Transfer to General Reserve	5,000	
Interim Dividend paid	7,200	
	40,100	40,100
	95,100	95,100
Add items which do not decrease funds from operation:		
Profit on Sale of Plant	4,500	
Funds from operation	90,600	90,600

Illustration II

	1st Jan.	31st Dec.		1st Jan.	31st Dec.
Equity share capital	1,00,000	1,43,000	Land and Building	50,200	4,10,300
Share Premium	2,000	22,000	Machinery	40,300	55,200

Reserve	7,000	12,000	Furniture &		
Net Profit	4,000	9,000	Fittings	3,200	3,500
8% Debentures	5,000	6,000	Stock	35,000	39,000
Creditors	33,500	38,800	Sundry		
			Debtors	24,600	30,200
Provision for taxation	8,000	10,900	Bank	23,200	15,500
Proposed dividend	15,000	12,000			
	1,76,500	2,53,700		1,76,500	2,53,700

Depreciation written off during the year

Machinery	15,000
Furniture and fittings	800

Solution II

Schedule of Changes in Working Capital

	Increase (Rs.)	Decrease (Rs.)
Stock	4,000	
Debtors	5,600	
Bank		7,700
Creditors		3,300
Net Decrease in working capital (balancing figure)	1,400	
	11,000	11,000

Funds Flow Statement

Sources	Rs.	**Applications**	Rs.
Share capital issued	43,000	Purchase of Land & Building	60,100
Share premium	20,000	Purchase of Machinery	29,900
Debentures	1,000	Purchase of Furniture	1,100
Funds Flow	48,700	Payment of tax	8,000
Decrease in working capital	1,400	Payment of dividend	15,000
	1,14,100		1,14,100

(It is presumed that last years provisions were completely paid in the current year. Provision for taxation and proposed dividend have been treated as non-current liability).

Working Notes

(a) Machinery A/c	Rs.		Rs.
To opening balance	40,300	By depreciation	15,000
To purchases of machinery	29,900	By closing balance	55,200
(balancing figure)	70,200		70,200

(b) Furniture and Fittings			
To opening balance	3,200	By depreciation	800
To purchases	1,100		3,500
(balancing figures)			
	4,300	By closing balance	4,300

(c) Profit from Operation		
Net profit	9,000	
Add depreciation	15,800	
(15,000 + 800)		
Provision for tax	10,900	
Proposed dividend	12,000	
Appropriation to		
Reserve	5,000	
	43,700	43,700
		52,700
Less net profit balance		
on 1st January		4,000
		48,700

Illustration III

From the figures given below prepare a statement showing application and source of funds for the year 19×6.

Liabilities & Capital	31st Dec. 19×5	31st Dec. 19×6
Share capital equity	Rs. 4,00,000	Rs. 4,50,000
8% preference shares capital	2,200,000	1,00,000
Debentures	1,00,000	2,00,000
Reserves and surplus	1,10,000	2,70,000
Current Liabilities	90,000	1,80,000
	9,00,000	12,00,000

Assets:	31st Dec. 19×5	31st Dec. 19×6
Fixed assets (net)	Rs. 5,10,000	Rs. 6,20,000
Investments	40,000	1,00,000
Current assets	3,40,000	4,75,000
Discount on debenture	10,000	5,000
	9,00,000	12,00,000

You are informed that during the year; (a) A machine with a book value of Rs. 50,000 was sold for Rs. 30,000 (b) Preference share redemption was done at a premium of 10% on 31st December 19×6 (c) Dividend at 15% was paid on equity shares for 19×5 and (d) Depreciation charged during the year Rs. 70,000.

Solution III

Schedule of Changes in Working Capital

	Increase (Rs.)	Decrease (Rs.)
Current assets	1,35,000	
Current liabilities		90,000
Net increase in working capital		45,000
	1,35,000	1,35,000

Funds Flow Statement

Sources		Applications	
Equity share capital	50,000	Preference capital (including premium)	1,10,000
Debenture	1,00,000	Fixed asset acquired	2,30,000
Sales of fixed assets	30,000	Payment of equity dividend	60,000
Funds flow	3,41,000	Payment of preference dividend	16,000
		Investment acquired	60,000
		Net increase in working capital	45,000
	5,21,000		5,21,000

Working Notes

(1)

Fixed assets A/c

To balance	5,10,000	By depreciation	70,000
To purchases (balancing figure)	2,30,000	Sale of fixed asset	50,000
		By closing balance	6,20,000
	7,40,000		7,40,000

(2)

Scrapped assets A/c

To balance	50,000	By cash	30,000
		By loss on sale	20,000
	50,000		50,000

(3) Funds Flow Statement
Reserves and surplus

(balance on 31st Dec. 19×6)		Rs. 2,70,000
Add loss on sale of fixed asset	Rs. 20,000	
Discount on debenture	5,000	
Preference dividend declared	16,000	
Equity dividend declared	60,000	
Depreciation	70,000	
Premium on preference shares redeemed	10,000	
	1,81,000	1,81,000
		4,51,000
Less reserves and surplus (balance on 31st Dec. 19×5)		1,10,000
		3,41,000

Illustration IV

From the following balance sheet for the years 19×6 and 19×7 prepare a schedule of changes in working capital and a funds flows statement:

	19×6	19×7		19×6	19×7
	Rs.	Rs.		Rs.	Rs.
Share capital	1,00,000	1,00,000	Buildings	50,000	45,000
General reserve	20,000	25,000	Plant	27,800	29,000
Net Profit	19,000	15,000	Investment	15,000	18,100
Sundry creditors	8,000	5,400	Stock	35,000	40,000
Provision for taxation	22,000	31,500	Bills receivable	3,000	4,000
			debtors	21,0000	25,000
Provision for doubtful debts	2,000	2,700	Bank	19,200	18,500
	1,71,000	1,79,600		1,71,000	1,79,600

The following additional information is also available

(a) Depreciation: Building 4,000
Plant 3,500

(b) Provision for taxation of Rs. 25,000 was made during the year.

(c) Interim dividend of Rs. 10,000 was paid during the year.

Solution IV

Schedule of Changes in Working Capital

	Increase (Rs.)	Decrease (Rs.)
Stock	5,000	
Debtors	4,000	
Bank		700
Sundry creditors	2,600	
Provision for doubtful debts		700
Net increase in working capital (balancing figure)		11,200
	12,600	12,600

Sources and Applications of Funds

Sources	Rs.	Applications	Rs.
Funds from operations	43,500	Purchase of plant	4,700
Sale of building	1,000	Investment purchased	2,100
		Interim dividend paid	10,000
		Increase in working capital	11,200
		Tax paid	15,500
	44,500		44,500

Working Notes

(1) Provision for tax

To bank (being tax paid)	15,500	By balance (opening)	22,000
To balance (closing)	31,500	By profit & loss A/c	25,000
	47,000		47,000

(2) Fund from operation

Net profit			Rs. 15,000
Add transfer to general reserve		5,000	
Provision for tax		25,000	
Depreciation Building	4,000		
Plant	3,500	7,500	
Interim dividend paid		10,000	
		47,500	47,500
			62,500
Less net profit			19,000
Funds from operation			43,500

Questions

1. Distinguish between funds and working capital.
2. What are the main sources of funds?
3. What is the most important source of funds for a firm and how is it calculated?
4. A firm has depreciation of Rs. 15,000 and a net income of Rs. 33,500. What is its total funds from operation?
5. A firm has depreciation of Rs. 45,000 and a net loss of Rs. 27,700. What are the total funds from operations for the firm?
6. Explain the major sources and uses of working capital.
7. What are the uses of a statement of sources and applications of funds?
8. What is the difference between a funds flow statement and cash flow statement?

Problems:

1. A firm had a net income of Rs. 250,000 and paid dividends of Rs. 125,000. How much did retained earnings change?
2. A firm has the following amounts in the building account:

	19×2	19×1
Building	10,500	8,200
Less accumulated depreciation	(1,000)	(800)

   (a) How much new equipment did the firm buy as a minimum in 19×2.

   (b) How much depreciation did it charge in 19×2 if Rs. 100 was written off as accumulated depreciation?

3. A firm has net plant and equipment of Rs. 5,20,000 in

19×1 and Rs. 5,90,000 in 19×2. The depreciation was Rs. 50,000. What was the effect of flow of funds?

4. A firm's balance sheet shows the following:

	19×2	19×1
Building	800	550
Less depreciation	(200)	(100)

The net income for 19×2 is Rs. 70,000. It wrote of Rs. 90,000 of machinery with accumulated depreciation of Rs. 10,000. Calculate the firm's funds from operations?

5. **J.K. Company**
Comparative Balance Sheet
December 31

	19×6	**19×5**
Assets		
Cash	Rs. 40,000	Rs. 50,000
Accounts receivable (net)	1,00,000	70,000
Inventory	2,00,000	1,60,000
Equipment	5,00,000	4,00,000
Accumulated depreciation	(1,60,000)	(1,40,000)
Investments	1,50,000	40,000
Total assets	8,30,000	5,80,000
Liabilities and Stockholders' Equity		
Accounts payable	25,000	20,000
Accrued liabilities	5,000	10,000
Capital stock-m-common-m-Rs. 10 par	5,00,000	4,00,000
Capital in excess of par	2,00,000	1,00,000
Retained earnings	1,00,000	50,000
Total liabilities and stockholders' equity	8,30,000	5,80,000

Additional data:

1. Net income was Rs. 1,00,000 for the year.
2. Fully depreciated equipment costing Rs. 20,000 was sold for Rs. 5,000 and equipment costing Rs. 90,000 was purchased for cash.
3. Depreciation expense for the year was Rs. 30,000.
4. Investments were purchased Rs. 1,10,000.

5. An additional 10,000 shares of common stock were issued for cash at Rs. 20 per share.

6. Cash dividends of Rs. 50,000 were declared.

Required: Prepare a statement of sources and applications of funds for the year ended 31st Dec. 19×6.

6. The comparative Balance Sheet of Neha and Company for the two years 19×1 and 19×2 are as given below:

	19×1	19×2
Assets	Rs.	Rs.
Current Assets	40,000	62,500
Land	7,500	12,500
Building	90,000	1,11,250
Accumulated depreciation	(12,500)	(21,250)
Total Assets	1,25,000	1,65,000
Liabilities & Owner's Equity:		
Current Liabilities	22,500	15,000
Long-term debt	25,000	50,000
Equity Capital	30,000	42,500
Retained Earning	47,500	57,500
Total liabilities & owner's equity	1,25,000	1,65,000

The following adjustments are required:

a. Depreciation for the year was Rs. 8,700.

b. A dividend of Rs. 5,000 was paid.

Required: Prepare a funds flow statement for Neha and Company for the year 19×2.

7. The following are the summarized balance sheets of XYZ Ltd. on December, 19×6 and 31st December, 19×7.

Liabilities	Rs.	Rs.
Share Capital	10,00,000	16,00,000.00
Debentures	6,00,000	6,00,000
Profit and Loss Account	2,00,000	5,00,000
Creditors	2,00,000	1,80,000
Provision for:		
Bad and Doubtful Debts	12,000	6,000
Depreciation on Land and Building	40,000	44,000
Depreciation on Plant and Machinery	60,000	70,000
	21,12,000	30,00,000

Assets		
Plant & Machinery (at cost)	7,20,000	12,90,000
Land & Buildings (at cost)	6,00,000	8,00,000
Stocks	6,00,000	7,00,000
Bank	40,000	80,000
Preliminary Expenses	14,000	10,000
Debtors	1,38,000	1,20,000
	21,12,000	30,00,000

Additional Information:

(i) During the year, apart of the machinery, costing Rs. 50,000 (accumulated depreciation thereon Rs. 14,000) was sold for Rs. 12,000.

(ii) Dividend of Rs. 80,000 was paid during the year.

8. **From the following financial statements prepare a funds flow statement for 19×7 and also a schedule of changes in working capital.**

	19×6	19×7		19×6	19×7
Current Liabilities:	Rs.	Rs.	Current Assets	Rs.	Rs.
Provision for taxation	10,500		Cash	18,000	22,500
Sundry Creditor for goods	34,500	15,000	Book debts	40,000	29,000
Bills Payable	30,500	26,000	Inventories	90,000	1,10,000
Total current	65,000	51,500	Total current assets	1,48,000	1,61,500
Mortgage loan	28,000	38,000	Plant & Equipment	2,80,000	2,95,000
Share capital	2,00,000	2,25,000	Other assets	5,000	8,000
Reserves and surplus	1,40,000	1,50,000			
Total Liabilities	4,64,500	4,64,500	Total Assets	4,34,000	4,64,500

CONDENSED INCOME STATEMENT

	19×6	19×7
	Rs.	Rs.
Sales	4,30,000	4,95,000
Cost of goods sold*	3,65,000	3,80,000
	65,000	1,15,000
Selling and administration	90,000	85,000
Other expenses	9,000	6,500
Interest	2,000	3,000
Total expenses	1,01,000	94,500
(Including depreciation 19×6)	15,500	15,000
Profit (loss) before tax	(36,000)	20,500
Provision for taxation	-	10,500
Net Profit (loss)	(36,000)	10,000

9. **Balance Sheets and Income Statement of Ritu Limited as on December 31, 19×6 & 19×7**

Liabilities	19×6	19×7	Assets	19×6	19×7
	Rs.	Rs.		Rs.	Rs.
Account payable	15,000	25,000	Cash balance	5,000	2,000
Cash credit	13,000	10,000	Accounts receivable	10,000	8,000
Outstanding expenses	2,000	3,000			
Long-term loan	30,000	20,000	Loan and advances	5,000	
Share Capital	30,000	30,000	Inventories	20,000	25,000
Net Profit	10,000	12,000	Fixed assets (net)	60,000	65,000
	1,00,000	1,00,000		1,00,000	1,00,000

The following additional information is available:

a. Depreciation on fixed assets was Rs. 7,000.

b. Income tax of Rs. 8,000 was paid during the year.

c. Cash Dividend of Rs.10,000 were paid during the year.

d. A fixed asset costing Rs. 8,000 was sold for Rs. 5,000 on which depreciation of Rs. 4,000 had been accumulated during the year.

6

Statement of Cash Flows

In this Chapter, we discuss the content and development of the new statement of cash flows as recommended by the FASB. An example to illustrate the preparation of a statement of Cash Flow is also given.

Effective management of cash flow is the primary objective of all financial managers. Information about cash flows is important to achieve the objectives of every business organisation like survival, profitability, growth and the efficient use of corporate resources. Careful planning and prediction of cash resources ensures that the organization always has enough cash to meet its payment obligations on schedule.

Apart from the Income Statement and the Balance Sheet, a third statement commonly used in financial accounting is the Statement of Cash Flows. Until recently, a financial statement showing the sources and uses of working capital or some other type of liquid resources was prepared, which was termed as a 'funds flow statement'. However, the statement of changes in financial position or funds flow statement prepared by different companies varied greatly in content because of the different interpretations of the term 'funds'. This created problems for the investors, specially when the investor wanted to compare the funds flow statement of various companies. Hence, the FASB provided guidelines to all companies to prepare a new statement instead of the funds flow statement, known as the 'statement of cash flows[1] which will be guided by the generally accepted accounting principles. The FASB has also given guidance on how the new statement of cash flows should be prepared.

The statement of cash flow provides information about the firm's cash inflows and outflows as related to operating, investing or financing activities during the period. The three categories of cash flows as classified and explained by the FASB are explained briefly below:

I. Operating Flows

Operating flows include all cash inflows and outflows other than those associated with investing and financing activities. Some examples of cash flows from operating activities include:

Cash inflows	Cash outflows
Cash received from customers.	Payment of salaries and wages.
Interests received on investments[2].	Payment of interest and income taxes.
Dividends received on investments.	Cash payments for inventory.

II. Investing Activities

Cash flows relating to investing activities include:

Cash inflows	Cash outflows
Cash received from selling assets such as plant, equipment, etc.	Amount given as loans to borrowers.
Cash proceeds from repayment of loans.	Cash payments to acquire assets such as plant, equipment etc.
Cash received from sale of investment.	

III. Financing Activities

Cash inflows and cash outflows classified under the heading financing activities include the following:

Cash Inflows	**Cash outflows**
Cash received from long-term and short-term borrowing.	Payments of dividends to owners.
Cash received from issuing stock. This does not include interest payments which are classified earlier as operating activities.	Repayment of borrowing (i.e. repayment of loans)

To briefly summarize, the statement of cash flows should assist creditors, shareholders, investors, managers and others in assessing such factors as:

- Ability of the company to generate cash flows.
- Ability of the company to meet its obligations and to pay dividend.
- The company must have sufficient cash to carry out its expansion plans in the near future.
- Need for external financing to meet the planned requirement.
- Cash and non-cash aspects of the company's investment and financing decisions for the period.
- Reasons for differences in the beginning and ending balancing of cash at the end of the accounting period.

Preparing a Statement of Cash Flows

Two approaches have been permitted by the FASB for presenting the statement of cash flows. The first approach, called the direct method reports cash inflows and cash outflows separately. The statement of cash flows is prepared by examining the income statement and the information about changes in all the balance sheet accounts except cash, during the period. The second approach, called the **indirect method** reconciles the reported net income and the net cash flow from operations. This method does not report the inflows and outflows separately nor describe the major outflows. It only prepares a reconciliation statement which reconciles the net income and cash flow from operations.

Generally, organizations prefer the direct method for preparing a statement of cash flows. The FASB has also expressed its preference for the direct method. Organizations using the direct method must also provide a reconciliation of net income to net cash flow from operations. This is so because many external users of financial statements are interested in the reconciliation statement. Hence, a firm using the direct method is also required to provide such a reconciliation.

However, both the direct and the indirect method result in the same net cash flow from operating activities.

The following examples illustrate the preparation of a cash flow statement.

Illustration I

From the information given below, prepare a statement of cash flows for the Milling Trading Ltd. according to the Direct Method. The income statement for the current year and information about changes in the company's balance sheet accounts over the year are summarized below:

Milling Trading Ltd.
Income Statement
For the year ended 30th June 19x1

Sales		Rs. 90,000
Less Cost of goods sold		20,000
Gross profit on sale		70,000
Less Operating Expenses		
Depreciation	3,000	
Other operating expenses	14,000	17,000
Operating income		Rs. 53,000
Other Income and Expenses		
Gain on sale of investment	10,000	
Interest income	6,000	
Gain on sale of marketable securities	4,000	
Interest expense	–5,000	15,000
Income before taxes		68,000
Income taxes		28,000
Net income		Rs. 40,000

Information about changes in the company's balance sheet accounts during the year are summarized below:

1. Inventory decreased by Rs.10,000 and accounts payable decreased by Rs.15,000.
2. The liability for accrued interest payable decreased by Rs.8,000 during the year.
3. Accounts receivable decreased by Rs. 7,500.
4. Accrued interest receivable increased by Rs. 4,000 during the year.
5. The liability for accrued income taxes payable increased by Rs. 9,000 during the year.
6. Short-term prepayments of operating expenses decreased by Rs.6,000 and liabilities for operating expenses increased by Rs. 2,000.
7. The other debit and credit entries in other balance sheet accounts during the year are:-

	Dr.	Cr.
Marketable securities	8,000	14,000
Notes Receivable (cash loans made to others)	7,000	5,000
Plant assets	18,000	16,000
Notes payable (S-T borrowings)	12,000	15,000
Bonds payable		70,000
Capital stock		30,000
Additional paid in capital	40,000	
Retained earnings	33,000	40,000

8. The Rs.33,000 debit to retained earning represents dividends declared and paid during the year. The Rs.40,000 credit entry represents the net income shown in the Income Statement.
9. The Rs.16,000 credit to plant assets accounts represents the book value of all plant assets sold during the year.
10. All investing and financing activities were cash transactions.

11. Cash and cash equivalent at the beginning of the year were Rs. 2,13,000 and Rs. 3,65,000 at the end of the year.

Required

1. Prepare a statement of cash flows for the year 19x1 using the direct method.

Solution I:

Milling Trading Ltd.
Statement of Cash Flows
for the year ended 30th June 19x1

Cash flows from operating activities		
Cash received from customers (1)	97,500	
Interest received (2)	2,000	
Cash provided by operating activities		99,500
Cash paid to suppliers and employees (3)	(Rs.31,000)	
Interest paid (4)	(13,000)	
Income taxes paid (5)	(19,000)	
Cash disbursed for operating activities		(63,000)
Net cash flow from operating activities (99,500 - 63,000)		Rs.36,500
Cash flows from investing activities:		
Purchases of marketable securities	(8,000)	
Proceeds from sale of Marketable securities (6)	18,000	
Loans made to borrowers	(7,000)	
Collection on loans	5,000	
Proceeds from sales of plant assets (7)	(18,000)	
Net cash used by investing activities		6,000
Cash flows from financing activities:		
Proceeds from short-term borrowings	15,000	
Payment to settle short-term debts	(12,000)	
Payment from issuing bonds payable	70,000	
Proceeds from issuing capital stock (8)	70,000	
Dividends paid	(33,000)	
Net cash provided by financing activities		1,10,000
Net increase (decrease) in cash (36,500 + 6,000 + 1,10,000)		1,52,500
Cash and cash equivalent at the beginning of the year		2,13,0C0
Cash and cash equivalents at the end of the year		3,65,500

Working Notes

1.	Cash received from customers		
	Net sales		90,000
	Add decrease in documents		
	Receivable		7,500
			97,500
2.	Interest Received:		
	Interest Income		6,000
	Less Increase in accrued		4,000
	interest receivable		
	Interest received		2,000
3.	Cash paid to suppliers and employees:		
	Cash paid for purchase of mercandise:		
	Cost of goods sold		20,000
	Less decrease in inventory		10,000
	Net purchases		10,000
	Add decrease in accounts payable to		
	suppliers		15,000
	Cash paid for purchase of mercandize		25,000
	Cash paid for operating expenses:		
	Operating expenses		17,000
	Less depreciation	3,000	
	Decrease in pre-payment	6,000	
	Increse in accrued	2,000	
	Liabilities for		
	operating expenses		11,000
	Cash paid for operating expenses		6,000
	Cash paid to suppliers and employees		31,000
	(25,000 + 6,000)		
4.	Interest paid:		
	Interest expense		5,000
	Add decrease in accrued		
	interest payable		8,000
	Interest paid		13,000
5.	Income taxes paid:		
	Income taxes expense		28,000

	Less increase in accrued income tax payable	9,000
	Income taxes paid	19,000
6.	Proceeds from sales of marketable securities:	
	Cost of marketable securities sold (credit entries to the marketable securities account)	14,000
	Add gain on salesof marketable securities	4,000
	Proceeds from sales of marketable securities	18,000
7.	Proceeds from sale of plant assets:	
	Book value of plant assets sold	16,000
	Less loss on sales of plant assets	
	Proceeds from sales of plant assets	16,000
8.	Proceeds from issuing capital stock account	30,000
	Add amounts credited to Additional paid in capital account	40,000
	Proceeds from issuing capital stock	70,000

Illustration II

The comparative balance sheets and income statement for XYZ Corporation for the years 19x6 and 19x7 are presented below:

XYZ Corporation
Income Statement
For the Year Ended December 31, 19x7

Sales		16,50,000
Cost of Goods Sold		9,20,000
Gross Margin from Sales		7,30,000
Operating Expenses (including Depreciation Expense of Rs. 12,000 on Buildings and Rs. 23,100 on Equipment and Amortisation Expense of Rs. 4,800)		4,70,000
Operating Income		2,60,000
Other Income (Expense)		
Interest Expense	(55,000)	
Dividend Income	3,400	

XYZ Corporation
Comparative Balance Sheets
December 31, 19x6 and 19x5

	19x7	19x6	Change	Increase or Decrease
	Assets			
Cash	1,15,850	1,21,850	(6,000)	Decrease
Accounts receivable (net)	2,96,000	3,14,500	(18,500)	Decrease
Inventory	3,22,000	3,01,000	21,000	Increase
Prepaid Expenses	7,800	5,800	2,000	Increase
Long-Term Investments	36,000	86,000	(50,000)	Decrease
Land	1,50,000	1,25,000	25,000	Increase
Building	4,62,000	4,62,000	-	-
Accumulated Depreciation, Building	(91,000)	(79,000)	(12,000)	Increase
Equipment	1,59,730	1,67,230	(7,500)	Decrease
Accumulated Depreciation, Equipment	(43,400)	(45,600)	2,200	Decrease
Intangible Assets	19,200	24,000	(4,800)	Decrease
Total Assets	14,34,180	14,82,780	48,600	

Liabilities and Stockholders' Equity

Accounts Payable	1,33,750	2,33,750	(1,00,000)	Decrease
Notes Payable (current)	75,700	1,45,700	(70,000)	Decrease
Current Liabilities	5,000	-	5,000	Increase
Income Taxes Payable	20,000	-	20,000	Increase
Bonds Payable	2,10,000	3,10,000	(1,00,000)	Decrease
Mortgage Payable	3,30,000	3,50,000	(20,000)	Decrease
Common Stock-m-Rs. 10 par value	3,60,000	3,00,000	60,000	Increase
Paid-up Capital in Excess of Par Value	90,000	50,000	40,000	Increase
Retained Earnings	2,09,730	93,330	1,16,400	Increase
Total Liabilities and Stockholders' Equity	14,34,180	14,82,780	(48,600)	

Gain on Sale of Investments	12,500	
Loss on Disposal of Equipment	(2,300)	(41,400)
Income Before Taxes		2,18,600
Income Taxes		52,200
Net Income		1,66,400

The following additional information was taken from the company's records:

a. Long-term investments that cost Rs.70,000 were sold at a gain of Rs. 12,500; additional long-term investments were made in the amount of Rs. 20,000.

b. Five acres of land were purchased for Rs. 25,000.

c. Equipment that cost Rs. 37,500 with accumulated depreciation of Rs. 25,300 was sold at a loss of Rs. 2,300; new equipment costing Rs. 30,000 was purchased.

d. Notes payable in the amount of Rs. 1,00,000 were repaid; an additional Rs. 30,000 was borrowed by signing notes payable.

e. Bonds payable in the amount of Rs. 1,00,000 were converted into 6,000 shares of the common stock.

f. The Mortgage Payable account was reduced by Rs. 20,000 during the year.

g. Cash dividends declared and paid were Rs. 50,000.

Required:

1. Prepare a schedule of cash flows from operating activities using the (a) direct method and (b) indirect method.

2. Prepare a statement of cash flows using the indirect method.

Solution II.

1. (a) Schedule or cash flows from operating activities – direct method.

XYZ Corporation
Schedule of Cash Flows from Operating Activities
For the Year Ended December 31, 19x7

Cash Flows from Operating Activities		
Cash Receipts from		
Sales	16,68,500[1]	
Dividends Received	3,400	16,71,900
Cash Payments for		
Purchases	10,41,002[2]	
Operating Expenses	4,27,000[3]	
Interest Payments	55,000	
Income Taxes	32,200[4]	15,55,300
Net Cash Flows from Operating Activities		1,16,600

1. Rs. 1,650,000 + Rs. 18,500 = Rs. 1,668,500
2. Rs. 920,000 + Rs. 100,000 + Rs. 21,000 = Rs. 1,041,000.
3. Rs. 470,000 + Rs. 2,000 - Rs. 5,000 - (Rs. 12,000 + Rs. 23,1000 + Rs. 4,800) = Rs. 427,100.
4. Rs. 52,000 - Rs. 20,000 = Rs. 32,200.

1. (b) Prepare a schedule of cash flows from operating activities—indirect method.

XYZ Corporation
Schedule of Cash Flows Operating Activities
For the year ended December 31, 19x7

Cash Flows from Operating Activities		
Net Income		1,66,400
Adjustments to Reconcile Net Income to		
Net Cash Flows from Operating Activities		
Depreciation Expense, Buildings	12,000	
Depreciation Expense, Equipment	23,100	
Amortisation Expense, Intangible Assets	4,800	
Gain on Sale of Investments	(12,500)	
Loss on Disposal of Equipment	2,300	
Decrease in Accounts Receivable	18,500	
Increase in Inventoy	(21,000)	
Increase in Prepaid Expenses	(2,000)	

Decrease in Accounts Payable	(1,00,000)	
Increase in Accrued Liabilities	5,000	
Increase in Income Taxes Payable	20,000	(49,800)
Net Cash Flows from Operating Activities		1,16,600

2. Prepare a statement of cash flows—indirect method.

XYZ Company
Statement of Cash Flows
for the year ended December 31, 19x7

Cash Flows Operating Activities		
Net Income		1,66,400
Adjustments to Reconcile Net Income to		
Net Cash Flows from Operating Activities		
Depreciation Expense, Buildings	12,000	
Depreciation Expense, Equipment	23,100	
Amortisation Expense, Intangible Assets	4,800	
Gain on Sale of Investments	(12,500)	
Loss on Disposal of Equipment	2,300	
Decrease in Accounts Receivable	18,500	
Increase in Inventory	(21,000)	
Increase in Prepaid Expenses	(2,000)	
Decrease in Accounts Payable	(1,00,000)	
Increase in Accrued Liabilities	5,000	
Increase in Income Taxes Payable	20,000	(49,800)
Net Cash Flows from Operating Activities		1,16,600
Cash Flows from Investing Activities:		
Sale of Long-Term Investments	82,500[1]	
Purchase of Long-Term Investments	(20,000)	
Purchase of Land	(25,000)	
Sale of Equipment	9,900[2]	
Purchase of Equipment	(30,000)	
Net Cash Flows from Investing Activities		17,400
Cash Flows from Financing Activities		
Repayment of Notes Payable	(1,00,000)	
Issuance of Notes Payable	30,000	
Reduction in Mortgage	(20,000)	
Dividends Paid	(50,000)	

Net Cash Flows from Financing Activities	(1,40,000)
Net Increase (Decrease) in Cash	(6,000)
Cash at Beginning of Year	1,21,850
Cash at End of Year	1,15,850
Schedule of Non-cash Investing and Financing Transactions	
Conversion of Bonds Payable into Common Stock	1,00,000

Questions

1. Briefly state four uses of the statement of cash flows?
2. What is the most important source of cash for most successful companies?
3. Describe the three types of activities that are reported on the statement of cash flows? Give examples of each.
4. What does the term cash in the statement of cash flows mean?
5. What are the purposes of the Statement of Cash Flows?
6. Why do companies prepare a statement of cash flows when most of the information in it is available from a companies comparative balance sheets and the income statement.

Problems

1. Given below is the Income Statement for Arjun Ltd.

Income Statement
for the year ended June 30, 19x6

Sales		50,00,000
Cost of Goods sold:		
Beginning Inventory	12,50,000	
Purchases (net)	30,00,000	
Goods Available for Sale	42,50,000	
Ending Inventory	13,00,000	
Cost of Goods Sold		29,50,000
Gross Margin from Sales		20,50,000
Operating Expenses:		
Sales and Administrative Salaries Expenses	11,00,000	
Other Sales and Administrative Expenses	6,24,000	

Total Operating Expenses	17,24,000
Income Before Income Taxes	3,26,000
Income Taxes	70,000
Net Income	2,56,000

Required:

1. **Prepare a schedule of cash flows from operating activities using the direct method.**
2. **Preparing a schedule of cash flows from operating activities using the indirect method.**

2. Income Statement for a Company is as follows:

Income Statement
For the year ended December 31, 19x6

Sales		9,44,000
Cost of Goods Sold		5,73,400
Gross Margin from Sales		3,70,600
Operating Expenses (including Depreciation Expense of Rs.42,860)		1,74,800
Operating Income		1,95,800
Other Income Expenses		
Interest Expense	Rs. (16,000)	
Interest Income	6,200	
Loss on Sale of Investments	(10,000)	(19,800)
Income Before Income Taxes		1,76,000
Income Taxes		50,000
Net Income		1,26,000

Relevant accounts from the comparative balance sheets for December 31, 19x6 and 19x5 are as follows:

	19x6	19x5
Amounts Receivable (net)	37,000	47,000
Inventory	79,200	69,900
Prepaid Expenses	4,800	17,800
Accounts Payable	69,800	45,450
Accrued Liabilities	9,300	17,600
Income Taxes Payable	10,000	35,000

Required:

1. Prepare a schedule of cash flows from operating activities using the direct method.
2. Prepare a schedule of cash flows from operating activities using the indirect method.
3. Preparing the statement of cash flows using the direct method.

AV Ltd. have developed the following data from the accounting records of the company for the year ended 30th June, 19x6.

(i) Cash payments to acquire plant assets, Rs. 29,700.

(ii) Cost of goods sold, Rs. 1,91,300.

(iii) Proceeds from issuance of equity shares, Rs. 4,000.

(iv) Collection of interest, Rs. 2,200.

(v) Payment of cash dividends, Rs. 24,200.

(vi) Equipment acquired by issuing short-term note payable, Rs. 8,200.

(vii) Payment of salaries, Rs. 46,800.

(viii) Credit sale, Rs. 2,91,950.

(ix) Loan to another company, Rs. 6,250.

(x) Collection of accounts receivable, Rs. 2,81,300.

(xi) Payment to suppliers, Rs. 2,39,250.

(xii) Proceeds from sale of plant assets, Rs. 11,200, including Rs. 3,400 loss.

(xiii) Interest revenue, Rs. 1,900.

(xiv) Cash dividends received, Rs. 2,050.

(xv) Depreciation expense, Rs. 29,950.

(xvi) Cash sales, Rs. 85,950.

(xvii) Payment of Long-term debt, Rs. 25,000.

(xviii) Proceeds from Short-term debt, Rs. 9,800.

(xix) Salary expense, Rs. 47,650.

(xx) Interest expense and payments, Rs. 6,650.

(xxi) Loan collections, Rs. 6,400.

(xxii) Payment of Short-term note payable by issuing common share, Rs. 15,500.

(xxiii) Amortisation expense, Rs. 1,450.

(xxiv) Income Tax expense and payment, Rs. 18,950.

(xxv) Cash balance: June 30, 19x5—Rs. 19,650; June 30, 19x6

Required: Prepare AV Ltd.'s statement of cash flows for the year ended 30th June, 19x6.

4. Shown below is the income statement for Jyoti Corporation for the year:

Sales		7,00,000
Cost of goods sold		3,50,000
Gross Profit		3,50,000
Opening Expenses:		
Salaries expense	70,000	
Depreciation expense	15,000	
Rent expense	28,000	1,13,000
Net Income		2,37,000
Additional Information	**Jan. 1**	**Dec. 31**
Accounts receivable	50,000	45,000
Inventory	65,000	95,000
Prepaid Rent	8,000	6,000
Accounts payable	30,000'	20,000
Salaries payable	8,000	10,000

Calculate;

a. Amount of cash collected from customers for the year.

b. Cash paid to suppliers.

c. Net cash flow from operating activities.

d. Cash paid to employees.

e. Cash payments for inventory.

5. The information below was obtained from the accounting records of the Sunny Manufacturing Company for the year ended Dec. 31, 19x6.

Proceeds from issuing Equity Stock	60,000
Payment of cash dividends	40,000
Loans	40,000
Proceeds from issuing short-term debt	1,20,000
Payments of long-term debt	55,000
Loan collection	80,000
Purchase of stock on credit	3,60,000
Salary expense	1,70,000
Collection of interest receivable	6,000
Payment of salaries	1,56,000
Credit Sales	8,00,000
Collection from customers	7,00,000
Cash sales	1,60,000
Interest expense and payments	25,000
Proceeds from sale of plant assets including gain on sale	30,000
Payments to suppliers	6,50,000
Depreciation expense	40,000
Income Tax expense	40,000
Acquisition of machinery	1,30,000
Cost of goods sold	6,40,000
Cash Balance: Dec. 31, 19x6	2,00,000

Prepare Sunny's statement of cash flows for the year ended Dec. 31, 19x6. Use the direct method.

6. Given the following data determine the cash flow from operating activities for 19x7.

	19x7	19x6
Cash	15,000	20,000
Accounts Receivable	40,000	36,000
Inventories	38,000	50,000
Accounts payable	18,000	20,000
Accrued expense	9,000	4,000
Net Income	63,000	70,000
Depreciation	12,000	10,000

7

Financial Statement Analysis

Financial Statement Analysis consists of applying analytical tools and techniques to financial statements and other relevant data to obtain useful information. This information helps to identify significant relationships between data and trends in those data that assess the Company's strengths and weaknesses. In addition, the information can also be used to make predictions about the company. For example, the analyst may be interested in an internal financial analysis to assess the firm's liquidity, profitability or solvency over a period of time. Alternatively, external financial analysis may be performed if the objective is to determine the firm's creditworthiness or investment potential.

Because of the varying needs of decision makers, the many categories of users, the different levels of knowledge and the general nature of financial statements, several types of analysis can be performed, on a company's financial statements. This chapter discusses one such technique viz. ratio analysis. It is used as a primary tool for examining the financial performance of an organization.

Ratio Analysis

A ratio is a relationship between two numbers by dividing one number by another. Financial ratios help the analyst in making meaningful comparisons of a firm's financial data at different points of time and with other firms.

Financial statement like the Income Statement and the Balance Sheet are of limited value as sources of information because they simply summarize what has happened by using certain accounting conventions. A profit of Rs. 50,000 or a sales of Rs. 1,00,000 may convey very little about the performance of a company. But if these figures are expressed as ratios, in the form of a percentage or a rate, then they have more meaning. Also ratios have more meaning when compared with some benchmark. The benchmark could be trend of a ratio over time, or it could be an industry average for firms of the same size or company backgrfound and so on.

Hence some important aspects which should be kept in mind when analyzing ratios are:

1. Ratios taken alone mean very little. They should be compared with others ratios, norms, standards, etc.
2. The analyst should decide the ratios which are appropriate in a specific situation and what combination of ratios to use.
3. Ratios give clues about the strengths and weakness of a firm.

Objective of Ratio Analysis

1. Ratios help to make comparisons and evaluation of past performance and also to provide a basis for making decisions in the future.
2. The analysis of financial information helps the management seeks indicators of why goals were or were not achieved and thus help to identify trends that may be helpful in the planning process.
3. Ratio analysis is an important tool which helps the management diagnose a situation in advance. For example prediction of bankruptcy and failure by evaluating the solvency position of the organisation.

Kinds of Ratios

Stockholders and potential stockholders employ several

ratios to help them evaluate management performance in using the resources of an organisation. Financial ratios may be classified in terms of four basic categories, each representing an important aspect of the firm's financial condition:

1. Liquidity Ratios
2. Profitability Ratios
3. Leverage Ratios
4. Turnover or Efficiency Ratios.

Example

The following example will be used to calculate and illustrate the technique of ratio analysis.

Profit and Loss Account for Arjun Ltd. for the year ended 30th June 19x1

	Rs.		Rs.
Opening Stock	1,35,000	Sales	11,50,000
Purchases	8,25,000	Closing Stock	1,10,000
Gross Profit	3,00,000		
	12,60,000		12,60,000
General Expenses	35,000	Gross Profit	3,00,000
Administrative Expenses	45,000		
Selling Expenses	30,000		
Depreciation	40,000		
Interest	25,000		
Income Taxes	40,000		
Net profit after taxes	85,000		
	3,00,000		3,00,000
Preference Dividend	10,000		
Equity Dividend	45,500		

Balance Sheet as on 30th June 19x1 for Arjun Ltd.

Liabilities & Owner's equity		Assets	
Current Liabilities	Rs.	Current Assets	Rs.
Creditors	1,20,000	Cash	2,35,000
Accounts payable	65,000	Debtors	1,45,000

		Stock	1,10,000
Total current liability	1,85,000	Total current Assets	4,90,000
Long-term Liabilities	Rs.	Fixed Assets	Rs.
Debentures	3,15,000	Land	3,20,000
Owner's equity		Buildings	2,35,000
Equity Share Capital	4,50,000	Machinery	1,20,000
(45,000 shares)		Furniture	50,000
10% Preference share capital	1,00,000		
Reserve	1,65,000		
Total liabilities & owner's equity	12,15,000		12,15,000

I. Liquidity Ratios

A firm's ability to meet its immediate obligations can be measured through the use of liquidity ratios. Liquidity ratios indicate the immediate solvency of the company. The current ratio and the acid-test ratio are commonly used for measuring liquidity.

(a) Current ratio: This ratio relates current assets to current liabilities and is designed to assist the decision maker in determining a firm's ability to pay its current liabilities from current assets. The current assets are cash or assets expected to turn into cash within the current year while the current liabilities are those that must be paid within the current year.

The Current Ratio is calculated as:

Current Ratio = Current Assets / Current Liabilities

The current ratio for Arjun Ltd. in the given example can be calculated as shown below:

$$\text{Current Ratio} = \frac{4,90,000}{1,85,000} = 2.65:1$$

The current ratio for Arjun Ltd. for the year 19×1 is 2.65: 1.

In the other words, for every rupee of current liabilities there is Rs. 2.65 in current assets. So a ratio of 2.65 means that Arjun Ltd. has more than enough cash to meet its immediate obligations.

At one time, there was an old rule of thumb that the current ratio should be at least 2:1 to provide the proper margin of safety; however some industries may require more or less. Thus, in actual practice, the current ratio tends to vary by the type and nature of business. Everything is relative in the financial world and there are no absolute norms.

(b) Acid-test ratio (Quick ratio): This ratio is a more rigorous test of a firm's ability to pay its obligations. The quick ratio takes into account the fact that some accounts classified as current assets are less liquid than others. Current assets often include slow moving inventory items and other items which are not very liquid. For example, inventories may take several months to sell; also prepaid expenses only serve to offset otherwise necessary expenditure as time elapses. These are subtracted from current assets to arrive at quick assets which are divided by current liabilities to get the acid-test ratio. Thus, the quick ratio attempts to measure the immediate debt paying ability of the firm.

$$\text{Acid-test Ratio} = \frac{\text{Quick Assets}}{\text{Current Liabilities}}$$

For Arjun Ltd. the quick ratio is:

$$\frac{3,80,000}{1,85,000} = 2.05:1$$

This ratio is a more conservative measure as it relates the "pool" of cash and immediate cash inflows to immediate cash outflows. The old rule of thumb here was that a quick ratio of at least 1:1 would keep the creditors happy. A low ratio could indicate possible difficulties in the payment of bills. For Arjun Ltd. the quick ratio is 2.05 and it appears to be good.

Financial ratios are based on a given income statement and balance sheet. And in a dynamic world we have to supplement the financial statement given at a point of time with a trend analysis of changes that have occurred over time.

II. Profitability Ratios

Profitability is an important measure of a company's operating success. The profitability ratios measure the firm's ability to generate profits and are of central interest to security analysts, shareholders and investors. Profitability is an important measure of a company's operating success. There are two major categories of profitability ratios:

— Return on assets

— Return on owner's equity.

The different variations of the Profitability ratio are:

(a) Gross Profit Margin: This ratio is calculated by dividing gross profit by sales.

$$\text{Gross Profit Margin} = \frac{\text{Gross profit}}{\text{Sales}} \times 100$$

The Gross Profit Margin for Arjun Ltd.

$$= \frac{3,00,000}{11,50,000} \times 100 = 26.08\%$$

This ratio can be used as an indicator of the efficiency of the production department. For Arjun Ltd. the ratio is 26.08% and this should be interpreted in relation to the industry average, as profit margin varies widely by type of business.

(b) Net Profit Margin : This ratio is calculated as

$$\text{Net Profit Margin} = \frac{\text{Net profit}}{\text{Sales}} \times 100$$

$$= \frac{85,000}{11,50,000} \times 100 = 7.4\%$$

This ratio should also be compared with the past few years to analyze how the profitability of the company has changed over a period of time.

(c) Return on total assets: This ratio is a measure of the profitability of all financial resources invested in the firm's assets. It evaluates the use of total funds without any regard to the sources of funds. Return on total assets can be measured in two ways:

$$\frac{\text{Net profit}}{\text{Total Assets}} = \frac{85{,}000}{12{,}15{,}000} \times 100 = 6.99\%$$

Net prfofit before interest is used so that earnings will not be influenced by the manner in which the assets are financed.

$$\frac{\text{Net profit plus interest}}{\text{Total Assets}}$$

$$\frac{85{,}000 + 25{,}000}{12{,}15{,}000} = 9.05\%$$

The rationale for the second formula is that total assets include debt, and thus interest should be added to net profit. Hence, return on total assets is a measure of Management's efficiency in using all resources at its disposal.

(d) Return on net worth: The ratio of special interest to shareholders, is the return on net worth, which is net profit divided by shareholders' equity. Shareholders equity is

$$\text{Return on net worth} = \frac{\text{Net profit after taxes}}{\text{Shareholder's equity}}$$

$$= \frac{85{,}000}{7{,}15{,}000} = 11.89\%$$

equal to equity share capital plus preference share capital plus shareholders' reserve. For Arjun Ltd. this ratio is 11.89%. Even though there is no absolute norm, a 15 per cent return on net worth is generally considered to be quite satisfactory. Compared to this theoretical norm, Arjun Ltd. needs to improve its return on net worth in the coming years.

Top executives view this ratio with a great deal of interest and would choose the return on net worth to measure the overall performance of management. For shareholders, it is the measure of how well the company is using, either directly or indirectly the capital they have provided.

(e) Return on Capital Employed (ROCE)

$$\text{ROCE} = \frac{\text{Net profit after taxes}}{\text{Capital employed}}$$

$$= \frac{85,000}{10,30,000} \; 8.25\%$$

The capital employed has been worked out by deducting current liabilities from the total assets. The return on capital employed indicates how the management has used the funds supplied by creditors and owners. The higher the ratio, the more efficient the company in using funds entrusted to it. This ratio represents the interests of the owners and the long-term creditors. The return on capital employed for Arjun Ltd. is 8.25%

(f) Return on Shareholders' Equity (ROSE): This ratio shows how the management has been able to utilize the resources at its disposal. It is used to measure the profitability of the firm in relation to the amount invested by the shareholders.

$$\text{ROSE} = \frac{\text{Net profit after taxes}}{\text{Shareholder's Equity}}$$

$$= \frac{85,000}{4,50,000} = 18.88\%$$

For Arjun Ltd. ROSE is 18.88%.

(g) Times-Interest Earned Ratio. This ratio of times interest earned measures the ability of the company to meet its interest charges out of its annual operating earnings. The ratio indicates the number of times the firm is covering its interest and is calculated as under:

$$\frac{\text{Net profit before interest \& taxes}}{\text{Interest charges}}$$

For Arjun ltd., the ratio

$$= \frac{85,000 + 40,000 + 25,000}{25,000}$$

$$= \frac{1,50,000}{25,000} = 6 \text{ times}$$

Arjun Limited's income available to meet its interest responsibilities is about 6 times the amount of its interest expense. Usually if interest is covered several times, the long-term creditors consider this an acceptable margin of safety.

(h) Price Ratios: These ratios are primarily aimed at analyzing the overall earnings performance of the Company as an indication of the value of the share they own. Price ratios can be measured in two ways:

Earnings per share (EPS): This ratio attempts to measure the value of a share of stock by attributing to it a portion of the company's earnings.

$$\text{E.P.S.} = \frac{\text{Net profit after taxes} - \text{Preferred Dividend}}{\text{Number of Equity Shares outstanding}}$$

$$= \frac{85,000 - 10,000}{45,000} = 1.67$$

To interpret this ratio, a year-to-year comparison over the past few years can be very useful. The EPS for Arjun Ltd. is 1.67.

Price-Earnings Ratio (P/E): The second ratio, considered to be the most widely used, is the P / E ratio, which is the market value per share divided by the earnings per share. It is the most important measure used by investors to judge the worth of the company.

$$\text{P / E Ratio} = \frac{\text{Market price per share}}{\text{EPS}}$$

$$= \frac{30^*}{1.67} = 17.96 \text{ times}$$

For Arjun Ltd., assuming that the market price per share is Rs. 30, the P / E ratio is 17.96 times.

The P/ E ratio should be compared with the share market as a whole, of other companies in the same industry, and of the company in the last few years.

(i) Dividend Ratios: Finally, there are three ratios which are of interest to shareholders and investors interested in dividends paid by a company. The three ratios are as follows:

Dividend Per Share (DPS):

$$DPS = \frac{\text{Equity share dividend}}{\text{No. of Equity Shares}} = 45,500 = 1.01$$

Dividend Payout Ratio

$$\text{Dividend payout ratio} = \frac{DPS}{EPS}$$

$$= \frac{1.01}{1.67} = 60.47\%$$

Dividend Yield

$$\text{Dividend Yield} = \frac{DPS}{\text{Market price per share}}$$

$$= \frac{1.01}{30} = 3.37\%$$

The dividend payout ratio tells us what percentage of the firm's earnings are being paid to equity shareholders in the form of dividends. For Arjun Ltd., this is 60% which indicates that the company is paying 60% of its earnings to shareholders in the form of cash dividends, retaining 40% for company needs.

The Dividend Yield is of potential interest to shareholders,

---

* Assume that the market price per share for Arjun Ltd. is Rs. 30/-

who are considering purchasing the firm's stock. This ratio which is 3.37% for Arjun Ltd. gives the current return to the investor as a percentage of his investment. Shareholders will try and search for companies which match with their objectives. For example, a retired individual may be interested in current income while someone else may be more interested in long-term capital gains and have little interest in current income.

III. Leverage Ratios

Leverage ratios are also known as debt or solvency ratios and are designed to assist the decision maker in deciding whether a firm has little or too much debt. Debt represents borrowed funds and though is a cheaper source of finance, it is also a riskier one. This is so because a firm which has debt in its capital structure has to pay fixed obligation in terms of interest charges irrespective of profit earned.

(a) Debt Equity Ratio: The first of these ratios is the debt to equity, which is the total long-term debt divided by Shareholders' Equity.

$$D/E\,Ratio = \frac{Total\,Debt}{Shareholder's\,Equity}$$

$$= \frac{5,00,000}{7,15,000} = .69:1$$

For Arjun Ltd. the Debt-Equity ratio is 0.69: 1. This means that Arjun Ltd. has financed approximately 69% of its assets with borrowed funds, which appears to be on the higher side. In future, Arjun Ltd. may have difficulty trying to borrow additional funds.

Another variation of the Debt-Equity ratio is by using only Long-Term Debt to Shareholders' Equity.

$$D/E\,Ratio = \frac{Long-Term\,Debt}{Shareholder's\,Equity}$$

$$= \frac{3,15,000}{7,15,000} = .44:1$$

Lower the Debt-Equity ratio, the higher the degree of protection enjoyed by the creditors.

(b) Debt-Assets Ratio which is calculated by dividing total debt by total assets.

$$= \frac{\text{Total Debt}}{\text{Total Assets}} = \frac{5,00,000}{12,15,000} = .41:1$$

Arjun Ltd.'s debt-asset ratio is .41: 1. The leverage ratios are significant to lenders as well as investors and give important information about the prospects for future financing. Also, the degree of risk as a result of debt financing is provided by these ratios. If the debt has been increasing over a period of time in the capital structure of a company, this may indicate an increase in risk for the company's shareholders.

In general, debt should not exceed 50 per cent of the total sources of funds. For a risky business, it should be less than 50 per cent.

IV. Turnover Ratios (also known as Activity Ratios or Efficiency Ratios):

These ratios measure how efficiently the firm has utilized its resources. Efficiency ratios can be measured in terms of net fixed assets, total assets, accounts receivable and inventory.

(a) Fixed Assets Turnover Ratio: The fixed assets turnover ratio measures the efficiency with which a company uses its fixed assets to generate sales. It is calculated as under:

$$\text{Fixed Assets Turnover Ratio} = \frac{\text{Sales}}{\text{Fixed Assets}}$$

$$= \frac{11,50,000}{7,25,000} = 1.58 \text{ times}$$

The efficiency with which Arjun Ltd. utilizes its fixed assets is 1.58 times. This appears to be low as larger the fixed asset turnover ratio, the larger will be the income on each rupee invested in the assets of the business. However, for a proper comparison, this ratio should be compared with industry average.

(b) Total Assets Turnover: The total asset turnover shows the relationship between rupee volume of sales and total assets used in the business. It is calculated as under:

$$\text{Total Asset Turnover} = \frac{\text{Sales}}{\text{Total Assets}} = \frac{11{,}50{,}000}{12{,}15{,}000} = .94 \text{ times}$$

For Arjun Ltd., the total asset turnover ratio is .94 times i.e. each rupee of total assets produced Re. 0.94 of sales.

For proper comparison, this ratio should also be compared with the industry average.

(c) Accounts Receivable Turnover (also known as Debtors Turnover):

Credit plays an important role in today's environment. It is, hence, imperative for a company to manage its receivable in an effective manner. Two ratios which are normally analyzed to examine the firm's collection record are: Accounts Receivable Turnover and Average Collection period. Accounts receivabale turnover is the number of times per year that the average amount of receivables is collected. This ratio is calculated by dividing net credit sales by debtors.

Accounts Receivable Turnover

$$= \frac{\text{Net Credit Sales (or net sales)}}{\text{Debtors}}$$

$$= \frac{11{,}50{,}000}{1{,}45{,}000} = 7.93 \text{ times}$$

Higher the accounts receivable turnover, better it is for the company. For Arjun Ltd. this ratio is 7.93 times, indicating that the company collects its average receivable almost 8 times a year. In a world of inflation, a company can have substantial cash flow problems if its sales are tied up in receivables for long period of time.

(d) Average Collection Period: This ratio determines how rapidly the credit accounts of a firm are being collected. For Arjun Ltd., the average collection period.

$$= \frac{\text{No. of days in a year}}{\text{Debtors turnover}}$$

$$= \frac{365 \times 1,45,000}{11,50,000} = 46.02 \text{ days}$$

is 46 days. This indicates that an average of 46 days is required to collect the accounts receivable. This figure must be interpreted in relation to the normal collection period for the company, past performance and the general economic environment. If the average collection period is too high, this indicates that the customers are slow in paying the bills and some may not pay at all. Other things being same, lower the average collection period, more efficient is the firm in managing its accounts receivable.

(e) Inventory Turnover: While analyzing inventory turnover ratio, it must be remembered that having too much or too little in inventory stock is not desirable. Too much inventory ties up additional funds, needs space and may become obsolete. Insufficient inventory can result in lost sales and time consuming delays.

Inventory turnover shows how many times the average rupee invested in inventory were turned over during a period. It is computed as follows:

$$\text{Inventory turnover} = \frac{\text{Cost of goods sold}}{\text{Average Inventory (or closing stock)}}$$

Generally, a higher inventory turnover ratio is considered desirable and indicates that inventory is being handled more efficiently. But if a higher turnover is due to the company's keeping less stock, then this may result in the company incurring large ordering costs, lower sales due to inadequate inventory and so on.

Hence comparison must be made with firms in the same industry, past performance and industry averages.

Final consideration in Financial Statement Analysis

In considering financial statement analysis, managers, investors and creditors must recognize that they can learn much about a company's strengths, weaknesses, problems, liquidity, profitability and solvency if they can skill fully use the financial statements. They must know what information is desired and how the information has to be used.

Ratios are not ends in themselves but usually serve as a good starting point in evaluating an organization. In interpreting the findings of ratio analysis, the analyst must be sure that their comparisons are valid - especially when the comparison is of items for different period or different companies. Further, accounting practices must be followed consistently if valid inter-period comparisons have to be made. The analyst must also be concerned about the influence of different external factors, such as competitive conditions in the industry and general business conditions, and also about the impact of inflation on financial statements.

Illustrative Problems

I. From the following data of the balance sheet as on 31.3.XI, calculate the following ratios : Shareholder's funds to total assets; shareholder's funds to fixed assets; receivable turnover ratio, net profit to sales; net profit to total capital employed; net profit to net capital employed; net profit to shareholders' funds; net profit to share capital; captial gearing as expressed by debt equity ratio; book value per share. For the year under consideration, the total sales were Rs. 120,000. The net profit for the year was Rs. 20,000. The face value of each share is Rs. 10.

Balance sheet as on 31.3.XI

Liabilities	Rs.	Assets	Rs.
Share capital (30,000 shares)	30,000	Land	4,000

Retained earnings	10,000	Buildings	8,000
Long-term loan	16,000	Machinery	28,000
Accounts payable	6,000	Investment	6,000
Creditors	8,000	Inventory	6,000
		Receivable	6,000
		Cash	12,000
	Rs. 70,000		Rs. 70,000

Solution :

The various ratios are calculated as follows :

(*a*) Shareholders' funds to t otal assets

$$= \frac{40000}{70000} = 57.14\%$$

(*b*) Shareholders' funds to fixed assets

$$= \frac{40000}{40000} = 100\%$$

(*c*) Receivables turnover ratio

$$= \frac{120000}{6000} = 20 \text{ times}$$

(*d*) Net profit to sales

$$= \frac{20000}{120000} \times 100 = 16.67\%$$

(*e*) Net profit to total capital employed

$$= \frac{20000}{60000} \times 100 = 20\%$$

(*f*) Net profit to net capital employed

$$= \frac{20000}{56000} \times 100 = 35.7\%$$

(*g*) Net profit to shareholders' funds

$$= \frac{20000}{40000} \times 100 = 50\%$$

(*h*) Net profit to share capital

$$= \frac{20000}{30000} \times 100 = 66.67\%$$

(*i*) Debt to equity ratio

$$= \frac{16000}{40000} = 0.4:1$$

(*j*) Book value per share

= Shareholder's funds/Number of shares

$$= \frac{40000}{3000} = \text{Rs.}13.33$$

II. Prepare a balance sheet as at the end of the accounting year on the basis of the following information :

Current ratio 2.5

Quick ratio 1.5

Net working capital Rs. 60,000

Retained earning Rs. 40,000

Accounts payable Rs. 10,000

Accounts receivable Rs. 35,000

Fixed assets as percentage to the total assets 0.75

There is no long-term loan.

Solution :

(a) The current ratio and the net working capital, can help us calculate current liabilities and the current assests

$$\frac{\text{Current assets}}{\text{Current liabilities}} = 2.5$$

and, current assets - current liabilities = Rs. 60,000

Thus the value of current liabilities is Rs. 40,000 and current assets is Rs. 1,00,000. Since accounts payable is Rs. 10,000, the other current liabilities are Rs. 30,000.

The information related to quick ratio can be used to calculate the cash in hand.

$$\frac{\text{Accounts receivable} + \text{Cash}}{\text{Current liabilities}} = 1.5$$

Accounts receivable + Cash = 1.5 × Rs. 40,000

= Rs. 60,000

Rs. 35,000 + Cash = 60,000

Therefore, Cash = Rs. 25,000

Total current assets = Rs. 1,00,000

Cash = Rs. 25,000

Accounts receivable = Rs. 35,000

∴ Inventory = Rs. 40,000

We shall now use the information related to fixed assets as percentage of the total assets in order to calculate the value of fixed assets.

Fixed assets/Total assets = 0.75

Fixed assets = 0.75 × total assets

Fixed assets = 0.75 × (fixed assets + current assets)

Therefore, 0.25 fixed assets = 0.75 × Rs. 1,00,000

Hence, fixed assets = Rs. 3,00,000

The share capital figure can be found out as a balancing figure from the final balance sheet. The balance sheet as at the end of the year is as follows :

Liabilities	Rs.	Assets	Rs.
Share capital	320,000	Fixed assets	3,00,000
Retained earnings	40,000	Inventory	40,000
Not payable	10,000	Accounts receivable	35,000
Other current liabilities	30,000	Cash	25,000
	Rs. 4,00,000		Rs. 4,00,000

3. The balance sheet and supplementary data for the Sunny Corporation are shown below:

Sunny Corporation
Balance Sheet
December 31, 19x6

Assets		
Cash		Rs. 50,000
Marketable securities		30,000
Accounts receivable		70,000
Inventory		1,50,000
Building	Rs. 4,00,000	
Less Accumulated depreciation	1,00,000	3,00,000
Total assets		6,00,000
Liabilities and Stockholders' Equity		
Accounts Payable		30,000
Bank loans payable		20,000
Mortgage notes payable, due in 19x9		30,000
Bonds payable, 10% due December 31, 19x9		1,00,000
Common share, Rs. 100 par value		
Retained earnings		1,20,000
Total liabilities and stockholders' equity		6,00,000

Supplementary data:

1. 19x6 net income: Rs.60,000
2. 19x6 cost of goods sold: Rs. 5,40,000.
3. 19x6 sales: Rs. 9,00,000.
4. Inventory, December 31, 19x5: Rs. 1,00,000.
5. Interest expense: Rs. 20,000.
6. 19x6 net income before interest and taxes: Rs. 1,30,000.

Required: Compute the following ratios:

a. Current ratio.

b. Acid-test Ratio.

c. Accounts receivable turnover.

d. Inventory turnover.

e. Total assets turnover.

f. Equity ratio.

g. EPS of common shares

h. Times interest earned ratio.

Solution:

$$\text{a. Current ratio} = \frac{\text{Current Assets}}{\text{Current Liabilities}} = \frac{\text{Rs. }300,000}{\text{Rs. }50,000} = 60:1$$

$$\text{b. Acid – test Ratio} = \frac{\text{Quick Assets}}{\text{Current Liabilities}} = \frac{\text{Rs. }150,000}{\text{Rs. }50,000} = 3.01:1$$

$$\text{c. Accounts receivable turnover} = \frac{\text{Net sales}}{\text{Accounts receivable}} = \frac{\text{Rs. }90,000}{\text{Rs. }70,000}$$

$$= 12.85 \text{ times}$$

$$\text{d. Inventory turnover} = \frac{\text{Cost of goods sold}}{\text{Average inventory}} = \frac{\text{Rs. }5,40,000}{\text{Rs. }5,40,000}$$

$$= 1 \text{ times}$$

$$\text{e. Total assets turnover} = \frac{\text{Total Assets}}{\text{Equity Ratio}} = \frac{\text{Rs. }9,00,000}{\text{Rs. }60,0000} = 1.51 \text{ times}$$

$$\text{f. Equity ratio} = \frac{\text{Stockholder's Equity}}{\text{Total Assets}} = \frac{\text{Rs. }4,20,000}{\text{Rs. }600,000} = 70\%$$

$$\text{g. EPS} = \frac{\text{Net Income}}{\text{Number of equity shares}} = \frac{\text{Rs. }60,000}{3,00} = \text{Rs. }20/-$$

$$\text{h. Times interest earned} = \frac{\text{Net income before interest and taxes}}{\text{interest expenses}}$$

$$= \frac{\text{Rs. }1,30,000}{\text{Rs. }20,000} = 6.5 \text{ times}$$

4. Neha Electronics is considering an investment in one of the 2 companies — AV Ltd. & SK Ltd. The Balance Sheets and Income Statement of the 2 companies are given below:

Balance Sheets
(in thousands)

	AV Ltd.	SK Ltd.
Assets	**Rs.**	**Rs.**
Bank	2,000	4,500
Debtors	2,000	6,500
Stock	2,000	5,000
Plant and Equipment (net)	20,000	35,000
Other Assets	4,000	5,000
Total Assets	30,000	56,000
Liabilities and Shareholders' Equity		
Accounts Payable	2,500	3,000
Current Liabilities	1,500	4,000
Debentures	10,000	30,000
Common Share (Re. 1 par value)	1,000	3,000
Paid-in Capital in Excess of Par Value, Common	9,000	9,000
Reserves	6,000	7,000
Total Liabilities and Shareholders' Equity	30,000	56,000

Income Statements
(in thousands)

	AV Ltd.	SK Ltd.
	Rs.	Rs.
Sales	53,000	86,000
Less Cost of Goods Sold	37,000	61,000
Gross Margin from Sales	16,000	25,000
General Operating Expenses:		
Selling Expenses	7,000	10,000
Administrative Expenses	4,000	5,000
Interest Expense	1,200	3,000
Income Taxes Expense	1,800	3,400
Total Operating Expenses	14,000	21,400
Net Income	2,000	3,600

In addition to the information on the financial statements dividends paid were Rs. 500 for AV Ltd. and Rs. 600 for SK Ltd. The market prices of the stocks were Rs. 35 and Rs. 25 respectively.

Required: Conduct a comprehensive ratio analysis of the two companies and comment upon your results.

Solution :

1. Liquidity analysis AV Ltd. SK Ltd.

a. Current Ratio $\frac{\text{Rs. }6,000}{\text{Rs. }4,000} = 1.5$ $\frac{\text{Rs. }16,000}{\text{Rs. }7,000} = 2.3$

b. Quick ratio Rs. $\frac{4,000}{4,000} = 1.0$ $\frac{\text{Rs.}11,000}{\text{Rs.}7,000} = 1.6$

AV Ltd. **SK Ltd.**

2. Efficiency analysis

(a) Receivable turnover $= \frac{\text{Rs.}53,000}{\text{Rs.}2,000} = 26.5 \text{ times}$ $\frac{\text{Rs.}86,000}{\text{Rs.}6,500} = 13.2 \text{ times}$

(b) Average collection period $\frac{\text{Rs.}365}{26.5} = 13.8 \text{ days}$ $\frac{\text{Rs.}365}{13.2} = 27.7 \text{ days}$

(c) Inventory turnover $\frac{\text{Rs.}37,000}{\text{Rs.}2,000} = 18.5 \text{ times}$ $\frac{\text{Rs.}61,000}{\text{Rs.}5,000} = 12.2 \text{ times}$

3. Profiability analysis

(a) Gross profit margin $\frac{\text{Rs.}16,000}{\text{Rs.}53,000} = 30.2\%$ $\frac{\text{Rs.}25,000}{\text{Rs.}86,000} = 29.1\%$

(b) Net perfect margin $\frac{\text{Rs.}1,800}{\text{Rs.}53,000} = 3.4\%$ $\frac{\text{Rs.}3,400}{\text{Rs.}86,000} = 4.0\%$

(c) Total asset turnover $\frac{\text{Rs.}53,000}{\text{Rs.}30,000} = 1.8 \text{ times}$ $\frac{\text{Rs.}86,000}{\text{Rs.}56,000} = 1.5 \text{ times}$

(d) Fixed asset turnover $\frac{\text{Rs.}53,000}{\text{Rs.}24,000} = 2.2 \text{ times}$ $\frac{\text{Rs.}53,000}{\text{Rs.}40,000} = 1.3 \text{ times}$

(e) Return on asset $\frac{\text{Rs. }1,800}{\text{Rs. }30,000} = 6.0\%$ $\frac{\text{Rs.}3,400}{\text{Rs.}56,000} = 6.1\%$

(f) Return on equity $\frac{\text{Rs.}1,800}{\text{Rs.}16,000} = 11.3\%$ $\frac{\text{Rs.}3,400}{\text{Rs.}19,000} = 17.9\%$

(g) Earnings per share (EPS) $\frac{\text{Rs.}2,000}{\text{Rs.}1,000} = \text{Rs.}2.00$ $\frac{\text{Rs.}3,600}{\text{Rs.}3,000} = \text{Rs.}1.2$

(h) Dividend per share $\frac{\text{Rs.500}}{\text{Rs.1,000}} = .5$ $\qquad \frac{\text{Rs.600}}{\text{Rs.3,000}} = .2$

(i) Dividend payout ratio $\frac{\text{Rs.5}}{\text{Rs.2}} = 25\%$ $\qquad \frac{\text{Rs.2}}{\text{Rs.1.2}} = 16.7\%$

4. Loerage analysis

(a) Debt to equity ratio $\frac{\text{Rs.14,000}}{\text{Rs.1,600}} = .9$ $\qquad \frac{\text{Rs.37,000}}{\text{Rs.19,000}} = 1.9$

(b) Interst coverage ratio $\frac{\text{Rs.1,800} + 1,800 + 1,200}{\text{Rs.1,200}}$ $\qquad \frac{\text{Rs.3,400} + 3,400 + 3,00}{\text{Rs.3,000}}$

$= \frac{\text{Rs.48,000}}{\text{Rs.1,200}} = 4\text{ times}$ $\qquad \frac{\text{Rs.9,800}}{\text{Rs.3,000}} = 3.3\text{ times}$

5. Market analysis

(a) Price / earning ratio $\frac{\text{Rs.35}}{\text{Rs.2}} = 17.5\text{ times}$ $\qquad \frac{\text{Rs.25}}{\text{Rs.1.2}} = 20.8\text{ times}$

(b) Dividends yield $\frac{\text{Rs.5}}{\text{Rs.35}} = 1.4\%$ $\qquad \frac{\text{Rs.2}}{\text{Rs.25}} = .8\%$

		AV Ltd.	SK Ltd.	Company with Favourable Ratio*
1.	Liquidity analysis			
	a. current ratio	1.5	2.3	Sk Ltd.
	b. Quick ratio	1.0	1.6	Sk Ltd.
2.	Efficiency analysis			
	a. Receivable turnover	26.5 times	13.2 times	Av Ltd.
	b. Average days' sales uncollected	13.8 days	27.7 days	Av Ltd.
	c. Inventory turnover	18.5 times	12.2 times	Av Ltd.
3.	Profitability analysis			
	a. Gross perfect analysis	30.2%	29.1%	Av Ltd.
	b. Net profit margin	3.4%	4.0%	Sk Ltd.
	c Asset turnover	1.8 times	1.5 times	Av Ltd.
	d. Fixed asset turnover	2.2 times	1.3 times	Av Ltd.

	e.	Return on assets	6.0%	6.1%	Sk Ltd.
	f.	Return on equity	11.3%	17.9%	Sk Ltd.
	g.	Earnings per share	Rs. 2.00	Rs. 1.2	Non-comparable
	h.	Dividend per share	.5	.2	Av Ltd.
	i.	Dividend payout ratio	25%	16.7%	Av Ltd.
4.	Leverage analysis				
	a.	Debt to equity ratio	0.9	1.9	Sk Ltd.
	b.	Interest coverage ratio	4 times	3.3 times	Av Ltd.
5.	Market analysis				
	a.	Price/earning ratio	17.5 times	20.8 times	Sk Ltd.
	b.	Dividends yield	1.4%	8%	Av Ltd.

Analysis: The above indicates a comparative analysis of the company which has more favourable ratios. The liquidity ratios are more favourable for SK Ltd. while the efficiency ratios are more favourable for AV Ltd. The profitability analysis shows a mixed trend with net profit margin and return on equity being more favourable for SK Ltd. The EPS is higher for AV Ltd., but is strictly speaking non-comparable because of a substantial difference in the number of common shareholders of the two companies. In the classification of long-term solvency analysis, the debt-equity ratio is better for SK Ltd. while the interest coverage ratio is more favourable for AV Ltd. Finally the price/earning ratio is more favourable for SK Ltd. showing the performance of the firm as expected by investors. The investors judgment about the firm's performance is higher for SK Ltd. The dividend yield partially shows the shareholder return in relation to the market value of the share. This is higher for AV Ltd. Thus, in order to take a decision regarding investment in the two companies, more information if available, would help in taking the right decision keeping in view the long-term viability of the companies concerned. If earlier years' data is available, it would be very helpful in taking a sound decision. Prior years' information would also help in conducting a trend analysis.

5. The following ratios have been calculated for the Tyre industry for two companies :

Company ABC and Company XYZ Ratios for two years have been given. From the given information comment upon the financial position of the two Companies.

Current Ratio	19x1	19x2
1	2	3
ABC	1.70	1.70
XYZ	1.07	1.16
Quick Ratio		
ABC	1.30	1.30
XYZ	0.78	0.90
Debt-Equity Ratio		
ABC	1.80	2.30
XYZ	2.70	3.10
Coverage Ratio = Net Prof. before Int. & Taxes / Int. Charges		
ABC	2.60	2.80
XYZ	1.70	1.10
Stock Turnover Ratio		
ABC	7.40	7.60
XYZ	7.90	8.20
1	2	3
Debt Turnover Ratio = Sales/Debtor's Velocity Ratio		
ABC	5.45	3.70
XYZ	8.20	8.20
Av. Collector period = 365* Debtor/Sales		
ABC	67 days	100 days
XYZ	45 days	45 days
Total Asset Turnover Ratio = Sales / Total Assets		
ABC	1.20	0.90
XYZ	1.70	1.50
EPS		
ABC	7.30 (Rs.)	11.80 (Rs.)
XYZ	6.80 (Rs.)	8.40 (Rs.)
P/E		
ABC	7.90	33.90
XYZ	9.30	16.60

D.P.S.		
ABC	4.00	3.50
XYZ	2.75	2.75
Gross Profit/Sales		
ABC	11.10%	15.30%
XYZ	8.26%	6.30%
Net Profit / Total Assets		
ABC	6.60%	8.10%
XYZ	2.30%	2.30%
Operating Expense Ratio = (Cost of goods sold + O.E.)/Sales		
ABC	88.90%	84.70%
XYZ	91.40%	93.70%
Return on Capital Employed		
ABC	12.00	15.40
XYZ	18.40	17.30
ROSE = Net Profit / Shareholders Equity		
ABC	0.30	0.40
XYZ	0.12	0.10
Dividend Payout Ratio = DPS / EPS* 100		
ABC	55.00	29.60%
XYZ	40.00%	32.70%

ANALYSIS OF THE RESULTS

Current Ratio

Current ratio of 2:1 is considered ideal but in actual practice 1:1 ratio is found to be more acceptable than 2:1. A high ratio of more than 2:1, say 3:1 indicates undertrading and over capitalisation. Conversely, a low ratio indicates overtrading and under capitalisation.

Taking major players in the tyre industry into consideration the industry average works out to be 1:4:1. The current ratios for both companies, ABC & XYZ are generally acceptable but company XYZ's current ratio is on the lower side showing slightly significant overtrading or undercapitalisation.

However one cannot solely rely on the current ratio due to the following reasons:

— Manufacturers do window dressing of their balance sheets to show their current ratios in good light.

— All assets included in current assets are not equally readily realisable in cash to meet the demand of the current liabilities.

Quick Ratio: A Quick Ratio of 1:1 is generally considered ideal. From the quick ratios of company ABC and company XYZ it is obvious that ABC's short-term financial position is better than company XYZ's which implies that it will be in a better position to meet the creditors requirements in the short term.

Stock Turnover Ratio

Both the companies have nearly the same stock turnover ratio which appears satisfactory considering the general industry performance. It may be noted that a low turnover ratio indicates dull business or over investment in the industry.

Debtors Turnover Ratio

The industry average was 45 days in period 19x1 but it increased to 60 days in 19×2.

The calculations show that as the collection period for company ABC is more than the industry average. It implies that the company has:

— Overinvestment in receivables.

— Over extension of credit.

— Liberalisation of the credit terms.

— Lack of effective collection policy.

Company ABC's high debtors-turnover ratio might be due to its efforts in wooing dealers and customers with easy credit terms.

Debt Equity Ratio

A debt equity ratio of 1:1 is generally considered ideal and acceptable.

However, in the case of these two companies the debt-equity ratio is higher than the industry average. Specifically, the debt equity ratio for company XYZ is significantly higher. One important reason here could be the buying of any fixed asset or modernisation of its existing plans.

Normally, higher the interests of the proprietor as compared to that of the creditors lower will be the debt equity ratio and sounder would be the financial structure of the company.

Interest Coverage Ratio

Company ABC is in a much better position as compared to company XYZ. Its net profit situation is healthy so that it is able to meet its interest obligation better as compared to company XYZ.

Gross Profit Ratio

A Gross Profit Margin of 25-30% is generally accepted as good.

Profit margins of both the companies are extremely low. Considering the nature of the tyre industry, some possible reasons could be.

— There has been a recession in the tyre industry.

— Rapid addition of installed capacity.

— Comparatively low demand levels.

This has forced tyre manufacturers to go for price cutting thereby bringing the profit margins down.

Operating Expenses Ratio

Higher the operating ratio, the less favourable it is because it would leave a smaller margin to meet the interest, dividends etc. In general, operating expenses ratio is expected to be in the range of 75-85 per cent.

The operating ratios of both the companies though slightly on the higher side can be considered to be satisfactory.

Return on Assets

This is a good measure of profitability. The return on assets for both the companies is unsatisfactory but this has to be analysed in terms of the general recessionary conditions prevailing in the industry.

Return on Capital Employed

The return on capital Employed for both the companies is low. One possible reason could be that both companies have invested heavily in modernisation and diversification. Returns on investment will start improving after the mandatory gestation period.

Company XYZ has utilized the capital more efficiently than company ABC.

Return on Shareholder's Equity

This is a very crucial ratio as it gives the prospective investor an idea whether the investment would be worth making in terms of the returns involved. On this basis neither of the two companies performance is satisfactory. Company XYZ especially has a very low ROSE which is a definite disincentive for the investors.

EPS

Earnings per share of both the companies show an increasing trend; though in absolute terms, they are not very encouraging. This is understood given the difficult conditions existing in the tyre industry.

Net profits available to equity shareholders in relation to the amount of capital invested by them is higher in the case of company ABC. This higher return on equity capital might induce an investor to invest in company ABC rather than company XYZ other things remaining constant.

P/E Ratio

In 19x1 company XYZ had a higher P/E ratio as compared to company ABC whereas the situation got reversed in 19x2. This might probably be due to the investors expectations about the two companies.

Dividend Payout Ratio

There is a declining trend in this ratio for both the companies. Generally an investor would like to invest in a company with a high payout ratio. But this is not always necessary. The decline in the dividend payout ratio for both, the companies in 19×2 could be due to the fact that the companies were financing their expansion programmes out of the income earned. However investors who are interested in appreciation of the stock price may still like to invest in such companies inspite of them having a low dividend payout ratio.

Questions

1. Briefly describe the factors that might limit the comparability of one firm's current ratio with that of another firm in the same industry.
2. How do trend percentages differ from comparative financial statements?
3. How are financial ratios classified?
4. An increase in profit from one year to the other is always a good sign of financial strength. Elucidiate with examples.
5. What is the purpose of the statement of changes in financial position?
6. Is a high inventory turnover ratio always a good sign? Explain.
7. What is the purpose of the acid-test ratio? How is it related to the current ratio.
8. A firm has a profit margin of 15 per cent and an asset turnover of 5. What is its ROI?
9. Aa firm has a P/E ratio of 12/1. What rate of return do investors demand on this share?
10. How do solvency ratios differ from liquidity ratios?
11. A firm's accounts receivable has declined in the current year, compared to the previous year, although its sales remained constant in the two years. What does this mean for the average of the accounts receivable.

12. How does a firm calculate its P/E ratio. Of what use is this ratio to investors? Give examples to illustrate your answer.
13. What are the weaknesses of financial statement analysis?
14. Explain the difference between current assets and quick assets. Give examples to illustrate your answer.
15. Why does a firm calculate profitability ratios? Who has a primary interest in them?
16. Briefly explain the information obtained from the dividend notes. Also explain the three ratios used in this effort.
17. When is a higher inventory turnover ratio desirable?
18. What are the weaknesses of financial statement analysis as a source of information. Illustrate with examples.
19. Elucidiate some of important ratios which managers should calculate to assess whether the firm's financial position has improved or deteriorated during the past year.
20. Briefly enumerate the weaknesses of ratio analysis.

Problems

I. The following account balances are taken from the ledger of the Arnold Company:

	December 31, 19x6	December 31 19x5
	Rs.	Rs.
Allowance for doubtful accounts	40,000	30,000
Prepaid expenses	20,000	30,000
Accrued liabilities	1,40,000	1,20,000
Cash in Bank A	7,00,000	6,50,000
Bank overdraft in Bank B (credit balance)	-0-	25,000
Accounts payable	4,70,000	3,95,000
Merchandise inventory	8,95,000	9,50,000
Bonds payable, due in 19x8	4,20,000	3,90,000
Maraketable securities	1,00,000	90,000
Accounts receivable	5,00,000	4,85,000

Required:

a. Compute the amount of working capital for both the years.

b. Compute the current ratio for both the years.

c. Compute the acid-test ratio for both the years.

d. Comment briefly on the company's short-term financial position.

II. The following are the financial statements of Sunny Ltd.

Sunny Ltd.
Balance Sheet
December 31, 19×2

	Rs.
Assets	
Cash	40,000
Receivable	80,000
Inventory	1,20,000
Prepaid Expense	3,000
Machinery	1,60,000
Building	20,000
Total Assets	4,23,000
Liabilities and owner's equity	
Retained Earnings	92,000
Equity Capital	2,25,000
Liabilities	5,000
Accounts payable	26,000
Notes payable	50,000
Total Liabilities and Owner's Equity	4,23,000

Income Statement for the year Dec. 31, 19×2

	Rs.	Rs.
Sales		10,00,000
Less Cost of Sales:		
Opening Stock	1,00,000	
Purchase	7,90,000	
Cost of goods available for sale	8,90,000	
Less Closing Stock	1,20,000	7,70,000
Gross Margin		2,30,000
Operating Expenses:		
Selling	90,000	
Administrative	80,000	1,70,000
Net Income		60,000

Required: Calculate the following ratios:

1. Current Ratio
2. Quick Ratio
3. Receivables Turnover
4. Average Collection Period
5. Net Income to Sales
6. Net Income to Total Assets
7. Return on Investment
8. Inventory Turnover
9. Gross Profit Margin

III. The financial data for two companies, A Ltd. and M. Ltd. is given below:

Balance Sheet	**A Ltd.**	**M Ltd.**
Current Assets		
	Rs.	Rs.
Cash	12,500	19,500
Short-term investments	3,000	6,500
Accounts Receivable	94,500	82,000
Inventory	1,05,500	91,500
Prepaid expenses	9,500	7,500
Total Current Assets	2,25,000	2,07,000
Fixed Assets	2,62,000	2,62,000
Total Assets	4,87,000	4,69,000
Current Liabilities	1,83,000	1,69,000
Other Liabilities	1,50,000	1,76,500
Preferred Stock 5% Rs. 100 par		12,500
Equity Shares: Rs. 10 par (7,500 shares)	75,000	
Rs. 5 par (10,000 shares)		50,000
Reserves & surplus	78,500	73,500
Total liabilities and shareholder's equity	4,87,000	4,69,000
Market price per share of equity stock	Rs. 14	Rs. 24

Selected Income Statement Data for Current year		
Net sales (all on credit)	Rs. 301,500	Rs. 259,500
Cost of Goods sold	227,000	193,500
Closing stock	40,000	30,000
Gross margin	34,500	36,000
Interest expense	6,500	17,000
Net Income	28,000	19,000

The investment strategy that you have been advised to follow is to purchase the shares of companies that are in good shape financially and have low price/earning ratio. Assume that all other factors have been analised and what is required now is ratio analysis.

Required: Calculate the following ratios for both the companies for the current year and decide which company's stock are better for your investment strategy:

1. Current Ratio
2. Quick Ratio
3. Debtors Turnover
4. Inventory Turnover
5. Debt-Equity Ratio
6. Times-interest-earned ratio
7. Return on net sales
8. Return on total assets
9. Return on Shareholder's equity
10. Earnings per share of equity shares
11. Book value per share
12. Price/Earnings ratio

IV.

	19x3	19x2
	Rs.	Rs.
Net Sales	8,50,000	5,20,000
Income before interest & taxes	2,20,000	1,70,000

	Rs.	Rs.
Net Income	1,00,000	1,20,000
Interest expense	20,000	16,000
Shareholders equity Dec. 31 (on Dec. 31, 19x1, Rs. 4,00,000)	6,10,000	4,80,000
Common Share par value Rs. 50 Dec. 31	5,20,000	4,60,000

Additional shares of common stock were issued on Jan. 1, 19x3.

Required: Compute for both 19x3 and 19x2:

a. EPS of common shares.

b. Rate of return on shareholder's equity.

c. Net Income to net sales ratio.

d. Times interest earned ratio.

Compare the ratios for the 2 years and comment on your results.

V. The following Balance Sheet and supplementary data are for the SK Company for 19x6:

SK Company
Balance Sheet
December 31, 19x6

Assets		
Current Assets:	Rs.	Rs.
Cash	2,00,000	
Marketable Securities	1,45,000	
Accounts Receivable	1,80,000	
Inventory	1,65,000	6,90,000
Property, Plant and Equipment:		
Plant assets, cost	34,00,000	
Less: Accumulated depreciation	2,25,000	3,17,500
	Total assets	38,65,000

Liabilities and Stockholders' Equity	**Rs.**	**Rs.**
Current Liabilities:		
Accounts payable	1,80,000	
Bank loans payable	80,000	2,60,000
Long-term Liabilities:		
Notes payable, due in 19x7	80,000	
Bonds payable	4,20,000	5,00,000
Shareholder Equity		
Common shares, par value Rs. 50 per share	22,00,000	
Paid in capital in excess of par	8,000	
Retained earnings	8,25,000	31,05,000
Total Liabilities and stockholders' equity		38,65,000

Supplementary Data:

1. 19×6 net income, Rs. 3,00,000.
2. 19×6 Income before interest and taxes, Rs. 6,00,000
3. 19×6 cost of goods sold was Rs. 7,00,000.
4. 19×6 net sales amounted to Rs. 15,00,000.
5. Inventory on December 31, 1986 was Rs. 1,50,000.
6. Total interest expense for the year was Rs. 26,000.

Required: Calculate the following ratios:

a. Current ratio.

b. Percentage of net income to shareholders' equity.

c. Inventory turnover ratio.

d. Average collection period of account receivable (assume 365 days).

e. EPS

f. Times interest earned ratio.

g. Shareholders equity ratio.

h. Percentage of net income to total assets.

i. Turnover of total assets.

j. Acid-test ratio.

VI. The exhibit below shows five items from the financial statements for three companies for a recent year:

For Year	Company A	Company B	Company C
	Rs.	Rs.	Rs.
Operating Revenues	28,90,200	15,69,800	8,75,500
Income before interest and dividends*	4,35,300	1,10,300	25,500
Net Income to equity shareholders**	2,10,000	6,20,000	20,000
Total Assets	75,80,500	10,90,600	1,25,300
Common Shareholder's equity	30,00,000	5,00,000	80,000

* Net Income + interest charages x (1-tax rate)

** Net Income - Preferred Share Dividend.

a. Calculate the income to sales ratio for each company. Which company seems to be most successful, according to this ratio.

b. How many rupee of sales on an average does each of the companies make for each rupee worth of average assets held during the year.

c. Calculate the rate of return on assets for each company. Which company seems to be most successful according to this ratio.

d. Compute the rate of return on Shareholder's equity for each company. Which company is most successful according to this ratio.

VII. Selected information taken from the Balance Sheet of Neha Corporation for the year ended 19x6 is as shown below:

Liabilities	Rs.	Assets	Rs.
Share Capital	3,50000	Cash	50,000
Retained Earnings	60,000	Accounts Receivable	70,000
Long-term liabilities	2,00,000	Inventory	1,40,000
Accounts Payable	40,000	Prepaid Expenses	30,000
Creditors	50,000	Plant & Equipment	2,80,000
		Buildings	1,30,000
	7,00,000		7,00,000

The sales and gross profit of the company during the year were Rs. 13,00,000 and Rs. 5,00,000 respectively.

Compute the following:

a. Current Ratio.

b. Quick Ratio

c. Working Capital

d. Gross Profit Ratio

e. Accounts Receivable Turnover (all sales were on credit)

f. Inventory Turnover

g. Debt-Equity Ratio.

VIII. **Ratio analysis for two similar companies**

	X Company	Y Company
	Rs.	Rs.
Total Assets	9,00,000	5,00,000
Total Liabilities	3,00,000	2,00,000
Average Inventory	3,40,000	2,40,000
Average Receivable	3,00,000	2,00,000
Sales (all credit)	26,00,000	22,00,000
Gross Profit as a percentage of sales	50%	40%
Operating expenses as a percentage of sales	40%	30%
Net Income as a percentage of sales	5%	3%

Compute the following for each company:

a. Net Income

b. Net income as a percentage of shareholders equity.

c. Accounts Receivable Turnover.

d. Inventory Turnover.

IX. **Solvency ratios:** Financial data for a company are as follows:

	19x6	19x5
	Rs.	Rs.
Total assets	70,50,000	59,25,000
Current Liabilities	20,35,000	10,30,000
Long-term debit	8,45,000	9,10,000
Shareholders equity	44,80,000	41,35,000
Earnings before	8,80,000	4,60,000
Interest and taxes	8,80,000	4,60,000
Loan obligations	50,000	50,000

a. Calculate the solvency ratios for 19x6 and 19x5. The company's tax rate is 50%.

b. Evaluate the solvency ratios for the company and comment upon the solvency position of the company for the past two years.

X. **Activity analysis:** Evaluate the accounts receivable turn over, inventory turn over and total asset turnover of the company for the two years and 19x7 and comment.

	19x6	19x5
	Rs.	Rs.
Sales	25,00,000	20,50,000
Cost of goods sold	12,35,000	10,25,000
Accounts Receivable	3,00,000	1,80,000
Inventories	6,10,000	4,23,000
Total asset	11,20,000	8,35,000

Using the following information, complete the balance sheet below:

Long term debt to net worth	0.4 : 1
Asset turnover	3 times
Average collection period	18 years
Inventory turnover	9 times
Gross profit margin	8%
Quick ratio	1:1

Balance sheet as at

	Rs.		Rs.
Equity share capital	20,00,000	Plant and Equipment	-
Retained earnings	20,00,000	Inventory	-
Long-term debt		Receivable	-
Payable	20,00,000		

XII. Following are the ratios relating to trading activities of a firm:

Receivable turnover	4
Inventory turnover	1.5
Payable turnover	6
Gross profit to sales	25%

Gross profit for the latest accounting year amount to Rs. 8,00,000. Bills receivable amount to Rs. 30,000 and bills payable Rs. 15,000.

Calculate:

(i) Sales (ii) Sundry Debtors (trade debtors) (iii) Closing inventory and (iv) Sundry creditors (trade creditors).

XIII. From the following information, prepare a balance sheet:

Working capital	1,50,000
Reserve and surplus	2,00,000
Bank overdraft	1,20,000
Current ratio	1.80
Liquid ratio	1.10
Fixed assets to shareholders' funds	0.75
Long-term liabilities	Nil

XIV. **Case Study Alpha Chemical Industries**

Alpha Chemical Industries is an organisation into the manufacture and sale of medicines. Since this is a highly competitive industry. The company must maintain an aggressive marketing posture to survive.

The company has recently appointed a new President to look into the affairs of the company. The management of the Alpha Chemicals is concerned about the future of the company and has decided to use ratio analysis to identify potential trouble areas so that the performance of the organization could significantly increase in the coming years.

In addition to the Balance Sheet and the Income Statement for the two years 19x8 and 19x9 the industry averages have also been given.

Questions

1. Is Alpha Chemical Industries a strong firm in this industry.
2. Identify the strengths and weaknesses of the company based on ratio analysis.
3. Do the changes in the ratios from 19x8 to 19x9 give evidence that the firm is growing stronger or weaker. Mention the ratios.
4. Give suggestions to the company to improve their performance in the coming years.

Industry averages for Financial Ratios

Current Ratio	1.50
Quick Ratio	1.3
Gross Profit Ratio	23.0%
Net Profit Ratio	8.0%
Return on Capital employed	9.0%
Return on Shareholders' equity	13.1%
Earnings per share	6.0
Debt Equity ratio	0.96
Interest coverage ratio	2.5 times
Total Asset turnover	0.85 time
Fixed Assets turn over	2.85 times
Debtors turnover	5 times
Average collection period	74 days
Stock turnover ratio	4.3 times

Balance Sheet as at 30th June 19x9

	19x9 (Rs. in 000s)	19x9 (Rs. in 000s)	19x8 (Rs. in 000s)	19x8 (Rs. in 000s)
I. Source of Funds				
1. Shareholder's Funds				
(a) Share Capital	264,800		2,50,000	
(b) Reserve & Surplus	2,600,780		2,1,90,000	
		2.8.65.580		24.40.000
2. Load Funds				
(a) Secured		2,70,800		98,000
(b) Unsecured				500
TOTAL		31,36,380		23,38,500

II. Application of Funds				
1. Fixed Assets				
(a) Gross Block	810,600		660,800	
(b) Less : Decpreciation	210.700		175.400	
(c) Net Block	5,99,900		4,85,400	
(d) Capital WOrk in Progress at cost including advances	80.000		50.000	
		6,79,900		5,35,400
2. Investment		790,500		10,25,000
3. Curent Assets, Loans and Advances				
a) Current Assets	1,500,800		1,140,790	
b) Loans & Advances	316,300		134.000	
	18,17,100		1,274,790	
Less :				
Current Liabilities and Provisions	400,600		360,000	
Net Current Assets		14,16,500		9,14,790
Miscellaneous Expenditure				63,310
Accounting Policies		2,49,580		
Notes on Accounts				
TOTAL		31,36,380		25,38,500

Profit and Loss Accont for the year ending 30th June, 19x9

	19x9 (Rs. in 000s)	19x8 (Rs. in 000s)
INCOME		
Sale	22,00,000	20,00,000
Other Income	147,000	71,450
TOTAL	23,47,000	20,71,450
EXPENDITURE		
Material Consumed	924,900	790,000
Power & Fuel	44,000	33,000
Repairs & Maintenance	66,000	50,000
Salaries, Wages & Other Benefits	125,800	92,000
Adminstrative & Selling Expenses	590,700	602,000
Interest	58,000	30,000
Depreciation	38,400	33,600
TOTAL	18,47,800	16,30,600
Profit for the Year Before Tax	4,99,200	4,40,850
Less : Provision for Income Tax	—	10,000
Net Profit for the year After Tax	4,99,200	4,30,850

APPENDIX

The Balance Sheet and Income Statement of two companies as per scheduled format are given here. You are required to calculate and analyze the ratios of the two firms. Comment on your results.

Company A
Balance Sheet
As at 31st March 19x2

	As at 31-3-19x2	As at 31-3-19x1
		Rs. Millions
SOURCES OF FUNDS		
Shareholders' Funds		
Capital	537.24	494.10
Share Application Money Pending Allotment	1.08	4.34
Warrant Option Money	-	46.57
Reserves and Surplus	12,326.01	10,436.79
Capital and Reserves & Surplus Erstwhile Croslands Research Laboratories Ltd.	-	568.20
	12,864.33	11,550.00
Load Funds		
Secured	1,413.67	2,334.18
Unsecured	3,620.46	2,810.64
	5,034.13	5,144.82
Total	17,898.46	16,694.82
APPLICATION OF FUNDS		
Fixed Assets	6,631.56	5,469.02
Gross Block	1,604.85	1,242.07
Net Block	5,026.71	4,226.95
Capital Works-in-Progress	715.67	378.95
	5,742.38	4,605.90
	2,800.55	2,644.35
INVESTMENTS		
Current Assets, Loans and Advances		
Inventories	3,301.52	2,759.44

Sundry Debtors	3,414.41	2,953.59
Cash and Bank Balances	577.24	402.57
Other Current Assets	1,098.73	726.40
Loans and Advances	3,611.32	4,752.62
	12,003.22	11,594.62
Less:		
Current Liabilities and Provisions		
Liabilities	1,953.78	1,369.33
Provisions	978.86	890.46
	2,932.64	2,259.79
	9,070.58	9,334.83
NET CURRENT ASSETS		
Miscellaneous Expenditure		
(to the extent not written off or adjusted)		
Deferred Revenue Expenditure	284.95	109.74
Total	17,898.46	16,694.82

Company A

Profit and Loss Account for the year ended 31st March 19x2

Rs. Millions

	Year ended 31.3.19x2	**Year ended 31.3.19x1**
Income		
Operating income	13,805.18	11,562.76
Other income (Net)	135.41	88.35
	13,940.59	11,651.11
Expenditure		
Materials	6,025.58	5,233.39
Manufacturing	1,561.35	1,200.90
Personnel	1,116.12	909.84
Selling, General and Administration	2,834.82	2,167.41
	11,537.87	9,511.54
Profit Before Interest & Depreciation	2,402.72	2,139.57
Interest (Net)	15.10	(48.47)
Depreciation	376.11	318.68

Profit Before Tax	2,011.51	1,869.36
Provision for Tax	145.00	265.00
Profit After Tax	1,866.51	1,604.36
Balance as per last Balance Sheet	396.73	340.36
Prior period items		
Erstwhile Croslands Research Laboratories Ltd.	(124.42)	(6.17)
Pension Provision	(59.88)	-
Tax - Earlier Years	59.43	7.16
	2,138.37	1,945.71
Transfer from:		
Investment Allowance Reserve	5.49	-
Foreign Projects Reserve	0.49	0.41
Debenture Redemption Reserve	189.77	60.00
Balance available for appropriation	2,334.12	2,006.12
Appropriations		
Dividend	530.73	379j.05
Tax on Dividend	53.07	26.44
Transfer to Reserves		
Foreign Projects Reserve	12.27	4.90
Debenture Redemption Reserve	13.60	60.00
General Reserve	1,200	1,139.00
Surplus carried forward	525.45	396.73
	2,334.12	2,006.12

Company B
Balance Sheet as at 31st March 19x2

Rs. in 000's

		31-3-19x2		31-3-19x1
I. SOURCES OF FUNDS				
1. Shareholders' Funds				
(a) Share Capital	264873		264873	
(b) Reserves & Surplus	2742768	3007641	2673782	2938655
2. Loan Funds				
(a) Secured	518584		271818	
(b) Unsecured	107280	625864	-	271818
Total		3633505		3210473
II. APPLICATION OF FUNDS				
1. Fixed Assets				
(a) Gross Block	1091578		915676	

(b) Less: Depreciation	214570		213735	
(c) Net Block	877008		701941	
(d) Capital Work in Progress				
(at cost including advances)	127369	1004377	81035	782976
2. Investments		767866		797550
3. Current Assets, Loans and Advances				
(a) Interest Accrued on Investments	1212		20041	
(b) Inventories	615105		549914	
(c) Sundry Debtors	1046667		879794	
(d) Cash and Bank Balances	39384		53062	
(e) Loans & Advances	321185	2023553	306362	1809173
Less:				
Current Liabilities and Provisions				
(a) Liabilities	340081		316043	
(b) Provisions	96683	436764	85573	401616
Net Current Assets		1586789		1407557
Miscellaneous Expenditure		274473		222390
Accounting Policies				
Notes on Accounts				
Total		3633505		3210473
Income				
Sales		2499359		2203313
Other Income		23874		144723
Total		2523233		2348036
Expenditure				
Material Consumed		1011619		924909
Conversion Charges		10687		-
Excise Duty		235072		244461
Power & Fuel		63857		44307
Repairs & Maintenance		83608		65062
Salaries, Wages & Other Benefits		159748		125810
Administrative & Selling Expenses		465589		347290
Interest		84810		55958
Depreciation	83014		38459	
Less: Amount transfer from Amalgamation Reserve	25043	57971	-	38459
Total		2172961		1846256
Profit for the year Before Tax		350272		501780
Less: Provision for Income Tax		15000		-
Net Profit for the year After Tax		335272		501780

Add: Balance as per Last Balance Sheet	1840	1560
Add: Excess Provision for Proposed Dividend on Equtiy Shares of earlier Year	1669	-
Available for Appropriations	338781	503340
Appropriations		
Provision for Proposed Dividends on Equity Share	79461	79500
Provision for Corporate Dividend Tax	7946	-
Reserve for Contingencies	-	220000
Transferred to General Reserve	249000	202000
Balance Transferred to Balance Sheet	2374	1840
Total	338781	503340

Comparataive Ratio Analyses of Two Firms in the same industry

S.No.	Ratio Calculated	Co. A.	Co. B
1.	$\text{Current ratio} = \dfrac{\text{Current Assets}}{\text{Current Liabilities}}$	5.13	4.658
2.	$\text{Quick Ratio} = \dfrac{\text{Current Assets} - \text{Inventory}}{\text{Current Liabilities}}$	3.91	3.25
3.	$\text{Cash Ratio} = \dfrac{\text{Cash} = \text{Mktable Securities}}{\text{Current Liabilities}}$	1.23	1.848
4.	$\text{Interval Measure} = \dfrac{\text{Current Assets} - \text{Inventory}}{\text{Average Daily Oprating Expend.}}$	346.48 Days	251
5.	$\text{Net Working} = \text{Captial ratio} = \dfrac{\text{Net Working Capital}}{\text{Net Assets}}$	0.56	0.44
	Leverage Ratios		
6.	$\text{Debt Ratio} = \dfrac{\text{Total Debt}}{\text{Total Debt} + \text{Net Worth}}$	0.31	0.172
7.	$\text{Debt} - \text{Equity Ratio} = \dfrac{\text{Total Debt}}{\text{Net Worth}}$	0.44	0.208

		Co. A	Co. B
8.	Capital Employed to Net Worth $= \frac{\text{Capital Employed}}{\text{Net Worth}}$	1.44	1.208
9.	Interest Coverage Ratio $= \frac{\text{EBIT}}{\text{Interest}}$	44.11	5.13

Activity Ratios:

10.	Inventory Turnover $= \frac{\text{Cost of Goods Sold}}{\text{Average Inventory}}$	3.44	2.544
11.	Days of Inventory Holding = 360/Inventory Turnover	104.5	141.5
12.	Debtors Turnover = Sales / Debtors	3.92	2.38
13.	Collection Period = 360 / Debtors Turnover	90	150
14.	Net Asset Turnover = Sales / Net Assets	0.69	0.689
15.	Total Asset Turnover = Sales / Total Assets	0.71	0.612
16.	Fixed Asset Turnover = Sales / Net Fixed Assets	2.51	2.488
17.	Current Asset Turnover = Sales / Current Assets	0.99	1.228

Profitability Ratios:

18.	Gross Profit Margin $= \frac{\text{Sales} - \text{Cost of Goods Sold}}{\text{Sales}}$	17.7	18.77%
19.	Net Profit Margin = PAT/SALES	13.87%	13.4%
20.	Operating Expenses= Operating Expenses/Sales	82%	81.2%
21.	Earnings per Share=PAT/No. of Common Shjares	325%	126.6%
22.	Dividends per Share = Dividends/No. of Shares	78%	29.8%
23.	Return on Net Assets = EBIT/Net Assets	12.38%	11.9%

Analysis of the Ratios

In order to comment on the working of the two firms, let us consider the ratios one by one :

The **Current Ratio** of both the firms are very high, 5.13 and 4.66 respectively for Co. A and Co. B. This implies that both the industries employ a high amount of current assets, that is marketable securities, inventories and debtors, which can be converted into cash within a short period of time. The current ratio represents the margin of safety, that is, the ability of an organisation to withstand a crisis, and taking into account the ratios of both the firms, both have a relatively high margin of safety.

The **Quick Ratio** of both the firms are 3.91 and 3.25 respectively, thus signifying that the amount of assets that can be immediately converted into cash. Both the firms have a very high Quick Ratio, which can also be interpreted in terms of the satisfactory current financial condition of the company. As compared to the general quick ratio of 1:1, the quick ratio of both the firms is very high.

The **Cash Ratio** of the firms are 1.23 and 1.85 respectively. The cash ratio is a measure of instant liquidity, which is very high for the two firms.

The **Interval Measure** of the two firms is 346 and 251 days respectively. This implies that Company A has enough finance to sustain itself for 346 days while Company B has enough finance to sustain itself for 251 days, which is better than average.

The **Net Working Capital Ratio** of the two firms are 0.56 and 0.44 respectively. This shows that Co. A has a greater ability to meet its current liabilities than Co. B. As a measure of the firm's potential reservoir of funds, Co. A earns more points than Co. B.

Leverage Ratios

The **Debt Ratio** of the two firms are 0.31 and 0.17 respectively, which means that both the firms have a high Net Worth, that is, borrowed funds are much lesser than Equity. The Companies will stand to gain if their profit is more than the interest they have to pay on the borrowed funds.

The **Debt-Equity Ratio** of both the firms are 0.44 and 0.21 respectively. This implies that the firms employs lesser debt to finance its operations compared to the shareholder's equity.

The **Capital Employed** to **Net Worth** ratios are 1.44 and 1.21 respectively. This implies that the borrowed element for both the firms is much lesser than the Equity element.

The **Capital Employed** to **Net Worth** ratios are 1.44 and 1.21 respectively. This means that the borrowed element for both the firms is much lesser than the Equity element.

The **Interest Coverage Ratio** of the firms are 44.11 and 5.13 respectively. The ability to cover interest payment with earnings before payment of taxes is much higher for Co. A signifying that it is a safe firm to invest in. This is a very important ratio from the view point of the firm's creditors.

Analysis of Leverage Ratios for the two firms :

	Ratio	**Co. A**	**Co. B**
6.	Debt Ratio $= \dfrac{\text{Total Debt}}{\text{Total Debt + Net Worth}}$	0.31	0.172
7.	Debt – Equity Ratio $= \dfrac{\text{Total Debt}}{\text{Net Worth}}$	0.44	0.208
8.	Capital Employed $= \dfrac{\text{Capital Employed}}{\text{Net Worth}}$ to Net Worth	1.44	1.208
9.	Interest Coverage Ratio $= \dfrac{\text{EBIT}}{\text{Interest}}$	44.11	5.13

The Leverage Ratios are important for the creditors who are to give **Long term credit** to the company. Each company has to choose between Equity and Debt for financing itself. In case of Debt the company is under a legal obligation to pay it's creditors, but in case of Equity there is no such obligation. Moreover if rate of return for the company is greater than the interest it has to pay on borrowers then it makes more sense to have a high Debt component in the financing of the company. The Owner's Equity is considered as a margin of safety by the creditors; if Equity base is thin, the creditors risk will be high and it will become increasingly difficult for the firm to borrow additional funds. A high level of Debt also introduces inflexibility in the firm's operation due to increasing interference and pressures from the creditors.

However, for the two companies which are analysed the Equity component in funding is very high compared to the Debt component. These firms will be safe for long term creditors as the risk is low. From the **investors** point of view the companies will be a good opportunity to invest in case the company has been giving a rate of return higher than that which is to be paid on borrowed funds. Also as can be seen from the Interest Coverage ratios for the two companies Co. A has a significantly higher value as compared to Co. B. This is because Co. A not only has a much greater EBIT but also has to pay much lesser Interest Payments as compared to Co. B. Finally, from the Leverage Ratios it is clear that in times of low profits Co. B will be better for **investors** (because it has a lower Debt-Equity ratio) than Co. A.

14.	Net Asset Turnover= Sales / Net Assets	0.69	0.689
15.	Total Asset Turnover=Sales / Total Assets	0.71	0.612
16.	Fixed Asset Turnover= Sales / Net Fixed Assets	2.51	2.488
17.	Current Asset Turnover= Sales / Current Assets	0.99	1.228

From the above values of Inventory Turnover and Inventory holding days for the two firms we can say that Co. A has better management of it's inventory that Co. B. Also from the values of Debtors Turnover and Collection Period for the two firms we can see that Co. B has a very liberal and inefficient credit policy and is more likely to have larger bad debts as compared to Co. A. This knowledge is important for the **creditors** and **investors** of the company. A low Debtors turnover for Co. A indicates that its Debtors are prompt in the payment to the company and the chances of Bad Debt is lower and hence the profit of the company is more likely to be higher. This also indicates better management on the part of Co. A's management.

The Net Asset, Fixed Asset, Total Asset and Current Asset turnover ratios for the two firms are approximately the same and hence the only conclusion we can draw is that both firms can increase their sales by investing more money into Fixed Assets than by investing in Current Assets.

Profitability Ratios

The **Gross Profit Margin** for the two firms is 17.7% and 18.7% respectively. This indicates the ratio of Gross profit to sales for the two firms which is approximately same.

The **Net Profit Margin** for the two firms is 13.9% and 13.4% respecteively. One interesting point to be noted here is that although the Gross Profit of Co. B is greater the Net Profit of Co. B is a lesser proportion of its sales as compared to Co. A. This could be on account of the fact that depreciation, interest or taxes constitute a greater proportion of the sales for Co. B.

The **Operating Expenses Ratio** of the two firms is almost the same for the two firms at 82%.

The **Earnings Per Share** for the firms are 325% and 127% respectively. This means that Co. A has a much higher ratios of profit to its equity than Co. B. The return on Equity for Co. A will be much more than that for Co. B.

The **Dividends Per Share** for the two firms are 78% and 29% respectively. This clearly shows that the shareholders for Co. A are getting a much higher rate of return on their investments than those of Co. B.

Activity Ratios / Turnover Ratios

The **Inventory Turnover Ratios** for the two firms are 3.4 and 2.5 respectively. Assuming that the Inventory Turnover of Co. A to be industry average we can say that the Inventory Turnover of Co. B is low. Hence Co. B will take a longer time to sell it's inventory. Generally a high inventory turnover is an indicator of good inventory management whereas a low inventory turnover is an indicator of slow-moving or obsolete inventory.

The **Days of inventory holding** for the two companies are 104.5 and 141.5 days respectively. The days of inventory turnover for Co. B is on the higher side as compared to Co. A if Co. A is considered to be an indicator of industry average.

The **Debtors Turnover** for the two firms are 3.92 and 2.38 respectively. The higher debtors turnover indicates a more efficient management of credit.

The **Collection Period** for the two firms are 90 and 150 respectively. The collection period measures the quality of debtors since it indicates the speed of their collection. The shorter the Collection Period the better the quality if debtors of the firms. An excessively long Collection Period implies a very liberal and unefficient credit and collection performance. In such a case the chances of bad debt also increase. On the other hand too low a collection period indicates restrictive collection policy, and although Bad Debts may decrease the profitability of the firm is curtailed. It can be seen from the values that Co. A's debtors are much more prompt in their payments as compared to those of Co. B. Hence Co. A is likely to hve lower Bad Debts as compared to C. B.

The **Net asset turnover** for the two companies are 0.69 and 0.69 respectively. The **total asset turnover** for the two companies are 0.7 and 0.6 respecteively. **The fixed asset turnover** for the two firms are 2.5 and 2.49 respectively. All the above ratios are almost for the two firms and are indicative of the fact that both the companies are using their assets efficiently to maximise sales. The **Current Assets Turnover Ratio** for the two firms are 0.99 and 1.23 respectively. This means that for companies for every on rupee the company invests in current assets the sales increase by 1.0 to 1.2 times but for every rupee invested in Fixed Assets the sales increase by 2.5 rupees.

Analysis of the Turnover Ratios of the Two Firms:

Ratio	Co. A	Co. B
10. Inventory Turnover = $\frac{\text{Cost of Goods Sold}}{\text{Average Inventory}}$	3.44	2.544

11.	Days of Inventory = 360/Inventory Turnover Holding	104.5	141.5
12.	Debtors Turnover = Sales / Debtors	3.92	2.38
13.	Collection Period = 360 / Debtors Turnover	90	150

The **Return on Net Assets** for the two firms are 12.4% and 11.9% respectively. This means that Co. A has a greater rate of return on its Net Assets as compared to Co. B.

Analysis of the Profitability Ratios

Profitability Ratios:		**Co. A**	**Co. B**
18.	$\text{Gross Profit Margin} = \frac{\text{Sales} - \text{Cost of Goods Sold}}{\text{Sales}}$	17.7	18.77%
19.	Net Profit Margin = PAT/SALES	13.87%	13.4%
20.	Operating Expenses= Operating Expenses/Sales	82%	81.2%
21.	Earnings per Share=PAT/No. of Common Shjares	325%	126.6%
22.	Dividends per Share = Dividends/No. of Shares	78%	29.8%
23.	Return on Net Assets = EBIT/Net Assets	12.38%	11.9%

From the above ratios for Profitability it is evident that Co. A gives a greater earnings per rupee of equity invested than Co. B. This is mainly because of the greater amount of Net Profit of Co. A as compared to Co. B. Also the Dividend per rupee is much greater for Co. A than Co. B. Hence for **investors** Co. A is a better company to invest in as the returns they will earn are also much greater.

Final Analysis of the Two Firms

1. From the **Liquidity Ratios** it is evident that both companies are safe for the **creditor** for lending in short term as their **Liquidity** is well above the industry average.
2. From the **Leverage Ratios** for the two firms it can be seen that Co. A has a much higher **Interest Coverage Ratio** as compared to Co. B. Both firms have a high component

of Equity in their funding. Therefore Co. A is safer for **Creditors** as compared to Co. B.

3. From the **Turnover Ratios** it can be seen that both the companies have similar values of turnover. However in case of debtors turnover Co. A is much better off that Co. B. Also Co. A is much more efficient at Inventory turnover. Hence Co. A will be safer for **creditors, debtors** and **investors**.

4. From the **profitability** ratios it is evident that Co. A is a **better** firm for **investors** as it will yield a **higher rate of return** for the investors.

8

How to Read a Financial Statement

The Financial profile of a company is outlined in its profit and loss statement and balance sheet, and every manager should know how to read and interpret that profile.

For full details about a company, one has to refer to the company's published annual report. For purposes of illustration, we have selected a company XYZ whose consolidated Balance Sheet and Profit and Loss Statement are given for two years—year 1 and year 2.

Starting with the consolidated Balance Sheet (Table 1), we see several items grouped under the heading Current Assets. These are items that can be converted into cash within a year. The first item under this head is cash and bank balances. Most companies concentrate specifically on cash management, which means keeping actual cash to an absolute minimum and investing the remainder in short-term earning assets. The cash balance for the company XYZ for the year 2 is Rs. 184.03 lakhs which appears to be a little on the lower side, if compared in relation to the debts and other liabilities of the company.

The next item in the balance sheet is Rs. 1302.69 lakhs in sundry debtors. After cash this is the most liquid asset on the balance sheet as it can be converted into cash in a relatively short period. For company XYZ, the Accounts Receivable appears to be very high, in fact it has nearly doubled from year 1 to year 2.

Next on the balance sheet is Rs. 1483.99 lakhs for Inventories. In absolute terms, nothing much can be said about this figure. A comparison with sales, however, helps us in finding out if the figure of inventory is reasonable or not. For company XYZ, the figure of inventory appears to be quite reasonable.

Inventory, which appear in the Balance Sheet, could be valued at cost by the LIFO method or by the FIFO method.

In a period of Inflation and rising costs, the FIFO method tends to understate the true cost of inventory and overstate profits while the LIFO method matches current costs to current revenues, saves in terms of income taxes but understates the amount of inventory reported on the Balance Sheet. Companies differ in their operating structure and LIFO is not always appropriate.

The last item in current assets is Rs. 762.06 lakhs in loans and advances. Loans and advances are the amounts loaned to employees, advances given to suppliers and deposits made.

Fixed Assets: Under the Fixed Assets section we find a gross value of Rs. 1536.85 lakhs. This could be made up of various fixed assets like machinery, land, building, furniture, fixtures etc. Because all the fixed assets deteriorate over time and must be replaced one day, a depreciation reserve has been created. This reserve amounts to Rs. 618.12 lakhs and when this amount is subtracted from the Gross Value of Fixed Assets, the net Block becomes Rs. 918.74 lakhs. The other items under the category of fixed assets is investments worth Rs. 227.62 lakhs. Fixed assets are tangible assets of the company and their utility to the company will be realised over a long period of time.

The final asset listed in the Asset side of the Balance Sheet is capital, work-in-progress which is Rs. 52.19 lakhs.

Liabilities: The liability side of the Balance Sheet concerns with what the company owes to others. The Current Liabilities are those that will be due and must be paid with one year. Two items are listed under this head: Liabilities Rs. 1598.12 lakhs and provisions Rs. 223.71 lakhs. Thus the total amount under

Current Liabilities is Rs. 1821.83 lakhs. Compared to the current assets figure, the current liability appears to be satisfactory for the company under consideration.

Debt and Net Worth

The long-term debt of the company (i.e. debt maturing after a period of one year) is made up of two components: Secured Loans and Unsecured Loans. The secured loans denote borrowing of the firm against which specific securities have been provided. The unsecured loans denote borrowing of the firm against which no specific securities have been provided. There are no standard rules as to how much debt a company should have, but in general the debt ratio is an index to the relative conservation of management. In general, a debt to equity ratio of 50 per cent is considered safe and reasonable by most analysts. Beyond that, the company begins to move into the "increased-risk" or "high-leverage" category.

The debt-equity relationship is a sign of risk-reward relationship for a company. The more debt a company has in relation to its net worth, the riskier would the company become. Also, since debt is a relatively cheap source of capital, too little debt also implies the company is not using its capital in the best possible manner.

The last item in the liability side of the Balance Sheet is Shareholders' Funds. The shareholders' funds for the company XYZ for year (2) are Rs. 1579.35 lakhs. Shareholders equity reflects what the owners of the business have invested in the organization, both through the purchase of its shares or in the form of earnings that have been retained and not paid out in dividends. The share capital of the company is Rs. 315.55 lakhs. The Reserves and surplus are profits which have been retained in the firm. Surplus is the balance in the profit and loss account which has not been appropriated to any particular reserve account. The reserves and surplus of the company XYZ are Rs. 1263.80 lakhs.

In the case of this company, preferred shares have not been issued. Preferred shares, as the name suggests, take precedence over common shares in the payment of dividends and in liquidation of the company. Unlike interest on debt, dividends on preferred stock is not tax deductable. Yet, companies are many times forced to use it, for various reasons.

Shareholders' funds which is made up of snareholders' equity plus reserve and surplus is often called the net worth of a company.

After the thorough analysis of the Balance Sheet has been completed, the next statement to be examined is the 'Profit and Loss Statement'. (Table 2).

The total Income for the year (2) for company XYZ was Rs. 11510.21 lakhs. This is made up of Sales which is Rs. 11022.48 lakhs and other income which is Rs. 487.73 lakhs. This is the gross income of the company, from which all expenses must be paid, to find out the profit for the year.

The largest iiem under expenditure is manufacturing and other expenses which is Rs. 10671.25 lakhs. Next is Rs. 375.91 lakhs as Interest to be paid on various loans and advances. Finally, we have depreciation to the extent of Rs. 115.09 lakhs.

Total expenditure adds up to Rs. 11162.25 lakhs and when this is subtracted from Incomes, we get Rs. 347.96 lakhs as the profit before income taxes. From this figure we deduct Rs.65 lakhs as taxes for the year to arrive at the profit after taxes which is Rs. 282.96 lakhs.

Table 1
Balance Sheet of XYZ Company

Assets	Year 2 (Rupees in lakhs)	Year 1 (Rupees in lakhs)
Current Assets, Loans and Advances		
a. Inventories	1483.99	1444.37
b. Sundry Debtors	1302.69	683.05
c. Cash and Bank balances	184.03	280.82
d. Loans and Advances	762.06	837.84
Total current assets	3732.77	3246.08
Fixed Assets		
a. Gross Block	1536.86	1289.20
b. Less depreciation	618.12	507.39
c. Net block	918.74	781.81
d. Capital work in Progress	52.19	46.46
	970.93	828.27
Investments	227.62	95.58
Total Assets	4931.32	4169.93
Liabilities and Shareholders' Equity		
Shareholders Funds		
a. Capital	315.55	315.55
b. Reserves and Surplus	1263.80	1130.02
	1579.35	1445.57
Loan Funds		
a. Secured Loans	965.88	1074.07
b. Unsecured Loans	564.26	398.56
	1530.14	1472.63
Total Funds Employed	3109.49	2918.20
Current Liabilities		
a. Liabilities	1598.12	1028.91
b. Provisions	223.71	222.82
	1821.83	1257.73
Total Liabilities and Shareholders' Equity	4931.32	4169.93

Table 2
Profit and Loss Account of Company XYZ

Assets	Year 2 (Rupees in lakhs)	Year 1 (Rupees in lakhs)
Sales and Related Income	11022.48	3219.10
Other Income	487.73	338.90
Total Income	11510.21	3558.00
Expenditure		
Manufacturing and other Expenses	10671.25	7933.54
Depreciation	115.09	87.58
	10786.34	8021.12
Interest		
a. On Fixed loans	113.65	87.27
b. On other loans	262.26	128.55
Total Expenditure	11162.25	8236.94
Profit before taxes	347.96	321.06
Provision for taxes	65.00	50.00
Profit after taxes	282.96	271.06

9

Basic Cost Concepts for Planning and Control

Cost measurement and allocation are a significant aspect of financial and management accounting. Cost measurement and allocation techniques are used not only to assign incurred costs to products or services but also to plan future activities. In accounting, the term cost has a variety of meanings and a variety of cost concepts and measurement techniques are needed for internal planning and control.

The purpose of this chapter is to analyze the cost classifications and behaviour patterns that are widely used in management accounting. Such an analysis would help the management accountant specificallly when he is supplying information for planning and decision making purposes.

Types of Cost

Cost may be defined as the amount measured in terms of money, paid in consideration of goods and services received or to be received. Accountants and managers use many different cost concepts and these different costs are used for different purposes. It is the classification of cost which indicates to the managers how the term is being used and whether they can do anything about the cost or not.

Fixed Cost and Variable Cost

Costs are classified as fixed costs or variable costs depending on how the costs relate to changes in activity. Fixed costs are costs that remain constant in total within a relevant range of volume or activity. The concept of relevant range is important here. Relevant range is the range of activity in which a company expects to operate. Examples of fixed costs include depreciation, salary of a plant suprintendent, rent, advertising, insurance, etc. However, for pracical purposes, the notion of fixed cost may be slightly modified. Fixed cost can be expected to change over time due to certain variations, e.g., rent may increase or decrease or taxes may go up, due to factors independent of the firm's activity. Thus a cost is fixed only within a limited time period. Hence reference to a particular time period is essential to the concept of fixed cost because all costs tend to be variable in the long run. The diagram below illustrates the concept of fixed costs:

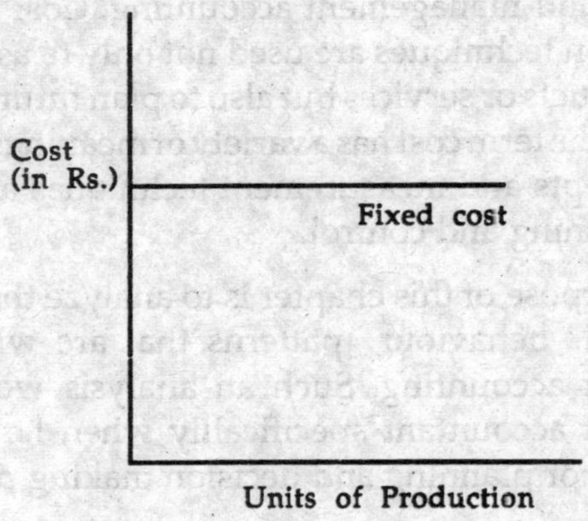

Total fixed costs are shown by a straight line drawn parallel to the horizontal axis because fixed costs do not respond to changes in volumes or activity.

Variable Costs

Total costs that change in direct proportion to changes in productive output or activity are Variable Costs. Typical variable costs include direct materials, direct labour, sales commissions and so on. Variable costs assume that there is a linear relationship between cost and volume of activity. The diagram below shows the relationship: Thus fixed costs are constant in total while Variable Costs are constant per unit.

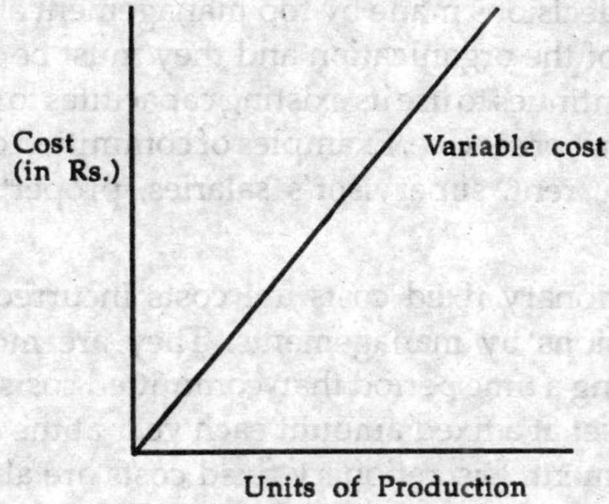

Semi-variable Costs

Some costs cannot be classified as either fixed or variable. These costs are known as semi-variable costs and they contain a fixed and a variable cost element. These costs may change, but not in direct proportion to changes in activity. Examples of semi-variable costs include repairs, monthly telephone charges, indirect materials, indirect labour, fuel and power. Telephone charges, for example, are made up of a service charge plus extra charges for extra telephones and long-distance calls. The service charges are fixed but the cost of additional telephones and long-distance charges are variable because they depend on monthly use. Maintenance is another good example of semi-variable costs. Some maintenance is required to prevent the deterioration of buildings and equipment while additional maintenance is required as the use of these asset increases. Thus semi-variable costs may be broken down into their respective fixed and variable cost parts for purposes of cost planning and control.

Committed versus Discretionery Fixed Costs

Fixed costs can be classified as "committed" or "discretionery" depending on their immediate impact on the organization. Committed fixed costs (also known as capacity costs) are costs that the company is required to incur, to maintain the current production capacity. These costs result from long-range decisions made by top management about the size and nature of the organization and they must be incurred if a company continues to use its existing capacitites to produce and sell its product or service. Examples of committed costs include depreciation, rent, supervisor's salaries, property taxes and depreciation.

Discretionary fixed costs are costs incurred because of policy decisions by managements. They are more likely to change during a time period than committed costs. These costs are usually set at a fixed amount each year at the discretion of the management. Discretionery fixed costs are also known as managed costs or programmed costs. Typical discretionery costs include advertising, research and development, employee training programmes and charitable contributions. Expenditures on discretionery fixed costs are usually regarded as investments in the future.

Product Costs and Period Costs

In manufacturing organization, a distinction is made between product costs and period costs. Product costs are costs assigned to products. These costs are identified as being either direct materials, direct labour or factory overheads and are traceable or assignable to products. They become an expense only when the products to which they are attached are sold. Product costs are related to manufacturing activities and include the following costs: raw materials used, depreciation on plant, expired insurance on plant, production supervisor's salaries, manufacturing supplies used, plant maintenance and so on.

Period costs are expired non-product costs and they are identified with measured time intervals and not with goods or services. They are any cost or an expense item of the income statement. Examples include selling and administrative costs, since selling and administrative expenses are used up in the same period in which they originate. Period costs are related to services consumed during the current period.

Direct and Indirect Cost

All costs incurred by a firm must be assigned to some cost objective. A cost objective could be a production department, a division of the firm or a unit of production. The key to the difference between the two terms direct cost and indirect cost is their traceability.

A manufacturing cost that is traceable to a specific product or an activity or a department is known as direct cost. Direct costs are fully traceable to a cost objective. For example, the salary of the manager of a particular department is easily traceable to that deparatment and hence is a direct cost for that department.

An indirect cost is a manufacturing cost that is not traceable to a specific product or cost objective and must be assigned using some allocation method. For example, the manufacturing overhead costs are not directly identifiable with any particular product or service and are hence indirect costs with respect to the product or service.

Managers are concerned with the portion of total cost that is direct and the portion that is indirect. If the majority of costs incured are direct and traceable, the manager is in a better position to understand and control these costs. But he will have no control over the portion of indirect cost his area must bear.

Controllable and Non-controllable Costs

All costs are controllable by someone in the organization, so the difference between controllable and non-controllable costs depends upon a point of reference. Time also plays a part in controllability.

A controllable cost is one that can be regulated in whole or in part from a particular manager's action and decisions. If the costs incurred by a particular cost centre cannot be controlled by the manager involved, then these costs are called uncontrollable costs.

Determining controllability is the key to a successful responsibility accounting system. If most of the costs incurred by a particular cost centre are controllable by the manager involved, he is in a good position to regulate his operations and show good profit performance.

However, identifying controllable costs at lower management levels is usually difficult because these managers rarely have the authority to acquire or supervise the use of sources. Thus, it is only at intermediate or at lower management levels, that cost can be said to be uncontrollable.

Direct cost and controllable cost are not necessarily the same. Similarly uncontrollable and fixed costs are also not always same. This is because cost behaviour characteristics are different from cost controllability. Also it is possible for a cost to be controllable in the long run but not in the short run. For example, insurance may have been paid in advance for the next 3-4 years or the manager may have committed the company to an advertising contract. The manager will have no control over the cost while the contract is in force. But when the contract expires, the manager is free to renegotiate the deal and hence has control over the cost in the long run.

Imputed Cost is the cost allocated for resources or use of a service which does not involve a cash outlay. They are hypothetical costs and are not recorded in the books of accounts.

Sunk Cost

Sunk costs are those costs that have already been incurred. Sunk costs cannot be changed by a decision and hence they are irrelevant in the decision-making process. The important point here is that if sunk costs are included in the decision-making process, it will make it difficult for management to focus on important decision variables.

Opportunity Cost

An opportunity cost is the cost that results from a foregone alternative. In choosing between alternatives, management desires to select the altrernative with the smallest total cost. By selecting one opportunity, management foregoes an alternative. The benefit from a rejected alternative is known as the opportunity cost of the alternative accepted. Also, since there are no cash receipts or cash expenditures incurred in connection with a foregone opportunity, opportunity costs are not entered in the accounting records. However, they are a significant part in the decision making process.

Imputed cost is used in a narrower context (as compared to the concept of opportunity cost) and generally relates to the interval events of the organization. Examples of imputed cost include interest on owners equity, rent of building owned by the firm etc. However in some cases, the concept of opportunity cost and imputed cost may be used interchangeably.

Thus, the various classification of costs and how they help the management to plan for future activities have been discussed in this chapter. A thorough knowledge of the cost behaviour and how costs will respond to changes in the volume of business activity, would specially help the managers assign incurred costs to products and services and help them in effective planning.

Questions

1. What can financial managers do to obtain greater control over costs?
2. Briefly distinguish between direct and indirect costs. Give examples to illustrate your answer.
3. "All costs are controllable at one level or the other". Discuss.
4. What can the management do to estimate the relevant range of activity?
5. Briefly discuss the following cost concepts with examples:
   a. Sunk Costs.
   b. Fixed versus Variable Cost.
   c. Discretionary Cost.

d. Period versus Product Cost.

e. Opportunity Cost.

f. Controllable and Non-controllable Costs.

g. How can management reduce indirect cost?

6. What should managers do to obtain greater control over cost? Elucidiate with examples.

7. 'Knowledge of cost behaviour is essential for effective planning'. Discuss with examples.

8. Briefly distinguish between Period Cost and Product Cost?

9. Distinguish between Opportunity Cost and Imputed Cost? Can the two terms be used interchangeably. Illustrate with examples.

10. "Sunk Costs are irrelevant costs". Discuss with examples.

10

Cost-Volume-Profit Analysis

To make profits is the first law of any business enterprise. If we eliminate the profit, the enterprise is also liable to be eliminated. Yet, very few managers know about the profit structure in their own company or the basic elements that determine the profit structure. Cost-Volume-Profit (CVP) analysis is an important tool that analyses the interplay of various factors that affect profits. CVP analysis shows the relationships among a business's costs, volume and profits. It is an important part of the budgeting activities of an organisation.

Cost-Volume-Profit (CVP) analysis is a tool used extensively in both the planning and control functions of an organisation. An organization may use CVP analysis as a planning tool when the management wants to find out the desired profit, when the sales volume is known. Alternatively, the management may begin with a target profit and then work out the level of sales needed to reach that profit level. As a control technique, CVP analysis is used to measure the performance of the different departments in a company. A basic application of CVP analysis is the break-even analysis. Break-even analysis stresses the relationship among the factors affecting profits. It is a simple and easy to understand method to show the effects of changes in volume on profits. Also the break-even analysis tries to determine the sales volume at which total revenue equals total costs so that profits are seen.

The present chapter discusses the various dimensions and application of CVP analysis from the view point of managers in taking suitable business decisions.

Break-Even Analysis

The break-even point is that volume of activity at which total revenue equals the sum of all variable and fixed costs. The activity can be expressed in unit or in rupee sales. The break-even is the point at which there is no profit or loss. The basic objective of break-even analysis is to find out the number of units of product that must be sold if a company is to operate without loss. In other words the no-profit-no-loss point is the break-even point.

Sales below the break-even point means a loss, while at sales above the break-even point, profits begin.

Break-Even Point

The break-even point can be determined by two methods:

1. The Algebraic method
2. The graphic method which comprises of (a) the break-even graph and (b) the profit-volume graph.

The following equations help us in finding the break-even point as per the algebraic method:

(i) S = VC + FC where S = Sales, VC= Variable Costs, FC= Fixed Cost

(ii) S - VC - FC = 0

Importance

The following are some of the more important applications of the break-even analysis:

1. What is the sales volume required to produce desired profits?
2. What is the minimum level of sales needed to avoid losses?

3. What will be the effect on profits of changes in fixed costs and variable costs?

4. How will the change in sales mix, in the context of multiproduct firm, affect profits?

5. What is the sales level required to earn a target profit?

6. Which product is most profitable?

7. What will be the effect of a simulations change in prices, costs and volume on profits?

Assumptions in CVP Analysis

1. All costs can be classified into two types: fixed costs and variable costs.

2. The total fixed cost remains constant with changes in sales volume.

3. The total variable cost per unit is constant but the total variable cost changes in direct proportion to sales volume.

4. Selling Price per unit remains constant i.e. it does not change with volume or because of other factors.

5. Sales mix does not change if there are multiple products or the firm manufactures only one product.

Contribution Margin

The contribution margin (C.M.) is the amount of revenue in excess of variable costs. To cover the company's fixed cost, this portion of the revenue is available. And after all fixed costs have been covered, this provides an operating profit. Hence contribution is a profit measure, although an incomplete one, since fixed costs are not covered. However, as we will discuss later, when contribution margin is expressed as a ratio or as a percentage of sales, it provides a sound alternative to the profit ratio.

The following example illustrates the calculation of the Break-even point:

Example

Assume that company X manufactures and sells a single product. The various per unit costs are:

Unit S.P.	=	Rs. 25
Unit V.C.	=	Rs. 15
Unit Contribution Margin	=	Rs. 10

Total fixed costs are Rs. 30,000 for the time period involved. Presently, the sales of the company are 1,00,000.

Solution

The different formula's for calculating the break-even point (B.E.) point are

$$\text{B.E. point (in sales units)} = \frac{\text{Fixed costs}}{\text{unit contribution margin}}$$

$$\text{B.E. point (in sales, Rs.)} = \frac{\text{Fixed costs}}{\text{C.M. expressed as a percentage of sales revenue}}$$

For the above question, the calculations are as under

$$\text{B.E. point (in sales, units)} = \frac{\text{Total fixed cost}}{\text{unit contribution margin}}$$

$$= \frac{30,000}{10} = 3,000 \text{ units}$$

Break-Even Point in Sales Percentage

Selling Price per unit	Rs. 25	100%
Variable cost per unit	Rs. 15	60%
Contribution Margin per unit	Rs. 10	40%

Break-even point in Sales (Rs.)

$$= \frac{\text{Fixed Cost}}{\text{C.M. expressed as a percentage of Sales Revenue}} = \text{Sales revenue required to break-even}$$

$$= \frac{30,000}{40\%} = \text{Rs.}75,000$$

The Break Even point in Sales (Rs.) can also be expressed as S.P. per unit x B.E. Point in units.

= 25 x 3,000 = Rs. 75,000

Each unit sold contributes Rs. 10 to cover fixed costs and profits. The Break-Even point for company X is 3,000 units. If the company realises a level of activity of more than 3,000 units, a profit will result, if less, a loss will be incurred. Profits will equal the number of units sold in excess of 3,000 units multiplied by the unit contribution margin. Thus at the 5,000 unit level, there is a profit of Rs. 20,000 (2,000 units above break even point x Rs. 10/-).

Sales (5,000 units @ Rs.25/-)	=	Rs. 1,25,000
Less Variable costs (5,000 units @ Rs. 15)	=	75,000
Contribution Margin	=	Rs. 50,000
Less Fixed Costs		30,000
Income before taxes		20,000

Profit Planning

The concept of break-even can be extended further to include profit planning. The objective of a business is not just to break-even but also to make a profit. To estimate the profitability of a business, it is possible to calculate the sales revenue required to produce the desired profit:

$$\frac{\text{Fixed Costs + Desired Profit}}{\text{Contribution Margin expressed as a percentage of sales revenue}} = \text{Sales revenue required to produce a desired profit}$$

Assume that the desired profit is Rs. 10,000. Using the data from the earlier examples, for company X, the sales revenue required to produce the desired profit can be calculated as follows:

$$= \frac{30{,}000 + 10{,}000}{0.4} = \text{Rs. } 1{,}00{,}000$$

The Break-Even Graph

Cost-Volume-Profit (or Break-Even) relationships can also be portrayed through the use of graphs. This method has the advantage of showing cost-volume-profit relationships over a range of sales. The graphic analysis permits managers to observe areas of profit or loss that would occur for a broad range of sales activity. The data from the earlier example are presented in a tabular form as below and are used to draw the break even chart:

Units of product sold	1,000	2,000	3,000	4,000	5,000	6,000
Total revenue	Rs. 25,000	50,000	75,000	1,00,000	1,25,000	1,50,000
Total Cost						
Variable	15,000	30,000	45,000	60,000	75,000	90,000
Fixed	30,000	30,000	30,000	30,000	30,000	30,000
Total Cost	Rs. 45,000	60,000	75,000	90,000	1,05,000	1,20,000
Profit (loss)	(Rs. 20,000)	(10,000)	(-0)	Rs. 10,000	20,000	30,000

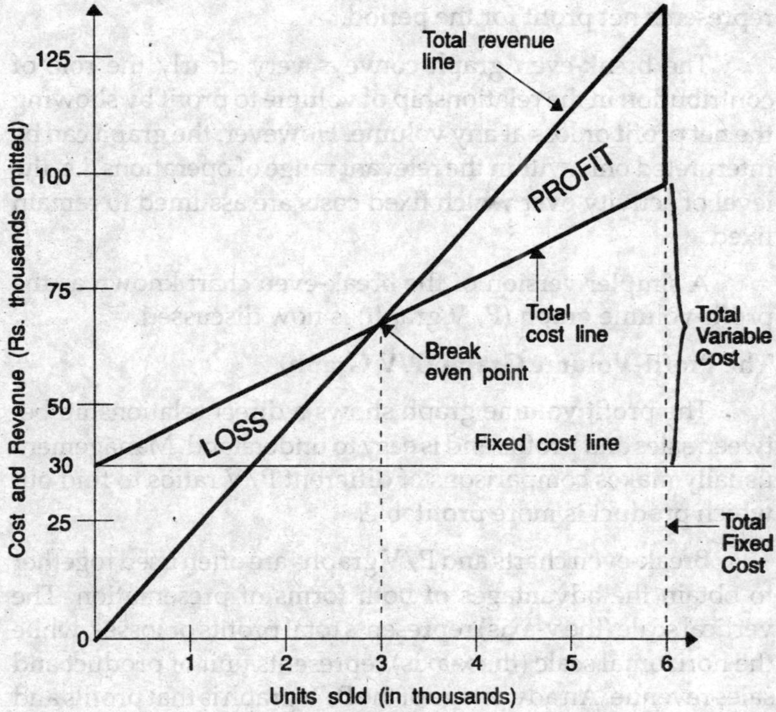

Fig. 1. *The Break even chart*

In plotting the graph it is assumed that the selling price remains at Rs. 25/- variable cost remains at Rs. 15/- per unit and fixed cost at Rs. 30,000 over the range of units sold.

The units sold areplotted on the horizontal scale while total revenue is shown on the vertical scale. The total revenue line is plotted, running from Rs. 0 at zero volume of sales to Rs. 1,50,000 representing sales of 6,000 units at Rs. 25/- per unit. The total cost line is the sum total of fixed cost (Rs. 3,000) and variable cost of Rs. 15/- per unit, plotted for various quantities of units to be sold. The intersection of the two lines indicates the break-even point. Below and to the left of the break-even point, the difference between the total cost line and the total revenue line reflects the net loss for the period. Conversely, the distance between these two lines to the right of the break-even point represents net profit for the period.

The break-even graph conveys very clearly the role of contribution in the relationship of volume to profit by showing the net profit or loss at any volume. However, the graph can be interpreted only within the relevant range of operations, i.e. the level of activity over which fixed costs are assumed to remain fixed.

A simpler version of the break-even chart known as the profit-volume graph (P/V graph) is now discussed.

The Profit-Volume Graph (P/V Graph)

The profit volume graph shows a direct relationship between sales and profits and is easy to understand. Management usually makes comparisons of different P/V ratios to find out which product is more profitable.

Break-even charts and P/V graphs are often used together to obtain the advantages of both forms of presentation. The vertical scale (the y-axis) represents total profits or losses, while the horizontal scale (the x-axis) represents unit of product and sales revenue. An advantage of the P/V graph is that profits and losses at any point can be read directly from the y-axis.

The data used earlier for preparing the Break-Even chart have been used to draw-up the P/V graph given above.

The intersection of the profit line with the horizontal line gives the break-even point. Points above the line measure profits while points below the line measure losses.

The P/V graph is a simple and convenient device of showing the extent to which profits are affected by changes in the factors that affect profit. For example, if unit selling prices, unit variable costs and total fixed costs remain constant, how many units are required to be sold so as to achieve a target profit, or percentage return on sales. Or, if variable costs per unit can be reduced, what additional profits can be expected at any given volume of sales.

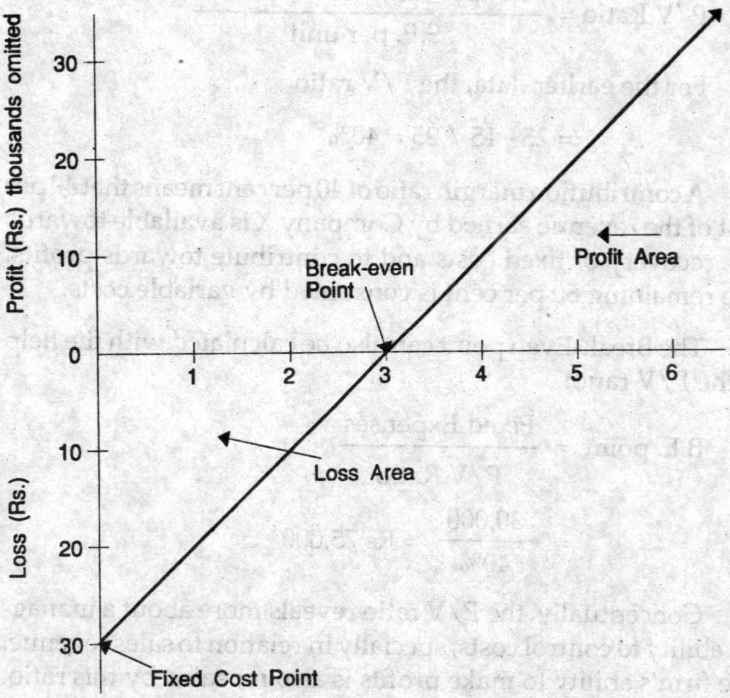

Fig. 2. *Gives the profit-volume graph.*

An advantage of the P/V graph is that profits and losses at any point can be read directly from the vertical scale. A major disadvantage is that the graph does not clearly reveal how costs vary with changes in activity. Hence, as mentioned earlier, both the P/V graph and Break-Even chart are used together by financial managers.

P/V Ratio

The Contribution Margin has earlier been defined as the amount of revenue in excess of variable costs. Contribution margin may be expressed on per unit basis (S.P. per unit minus variable cost per unit) or in total Rupees (Sales Revenue - Total variable costs), or as a percentage of sales. When the contribution margin is expressed as a percentage of sales, it is called the contribution margin ratio or profit-volume ration (P/V ratio). The P/V ratio is calculated as follows:

$$\text{P/V Ratio} = \frac{\text{S.P. per unit - V.C. per unit}}{\text{S.P. per unit}}$$

For the earlier data, the P/V ratio

$$= 25 - 15 / 25 = 40\%$$

A contribution margin ratio of 40 per cent means that 40 per cent of the revenue earned by Company X is available towards the recovery of fixed costs and to contribute towards profits. The remaining 60 per cent is consumed by variable costs.

The Break-Even point can also be calculated with the help of the P/V ratio:

$$\text{B.E. point} = \frac{\text{Fixed Expenses}}{\text{P/V Ratio}}$$

$$= \frac{30{,}000}{40\%} = \text{Rs.}75{,}000$$

Conceptually the P/V ratio reveals more about a managers ability to control costs, specially in relation to sales revenue. The firm's ability to make profits is also revealed by this ratio. With a high P/V ratio a firm makes greater profits when sales increase and more losses when sales decrease than a firm with a low P/V ratio.

Margin of Safety (M/S)

The difference between the actual sales volume and the break-even sales volume is called the margin of safety. It represents that proportion of the current sale which determines the profit of the firm.

The M/S ratio is calculated as :

$$\text{M/S ratio} = \frac{\text{Sales - Break Even Sales}}{\text{Sales}}$$

$$= \frac{1{,}00{,}000 - 75{,}000}{1{,}00{,}000} = 25\%$$

The Margin of Safety can be expressed as an absolute amount (Rs. 25,000) or as a percentage of sales (25%). The M/S ratio is an ideal index for ranking firms within an industry. Let us take the case of two firms showing exactly the same net income in their Income Statement but with a different M/S ratio. The firm with a high M/S ratio will withstand safely large decreases in sales volume while a firm with the low margin of safety will even with small decrease in sales volume start showing losses.

Assumptions and Limitations underlying CVP Analysis

The assumptions imposed by accountants in calculating the CVP ratios also serve as the possible limitations of the technique. Most CVP analyses are based on the concept of static cost.

1. All costs can be classified into two categories: fixed costs and variable costs. The assumption is not always true because certain costs like depreciation cannot be determined exactly. Different depreciation methods may yield different results. There is a third category of costs known as 'semi-variable' costs. These costs are also called mixed costs, because part of the cost is fixed and part is variable (for example, Telephone expenses).
2. Fixed costs will not change at all levels of sales within the assumed relevant range of activity.
3. Selling price per unit remains constant.
4. Variable costs vary in direct proportion to changes in activity i.e. as a percentage of sales revenue. They remain constant.
5. The sales mix is assumed to remain constant if more than one product is sold.
6. The projections are over a short period of time only.

The limitations and assumptions of CVP analysis mentioned above impair, but do not destroy the usefulness of the technique for managers as a useful profit planning tool.

Applications of CVP Analysis

CVP relationships provided information which is useful to managers in a wide variety of planning decisions. Managers use this analytical technique to accomplish far more than just the determination of a break-even point. The following problems are based on the information given earlier for company X:

1. A 10% reduction in selling price per unit.

Solution:

New S.P. per unit = Rs. 22.50.

New C.M. per unit = Rs. 22.50 - Rs. 15.00
Rs. 7.50

With Fixed Expenses remaining unchanged, the new B.E. point is

$$= \frac{30,000}{7.5} = 4,000 \text{ units}$$

The management may find the proposed change desirable, if in the long run, sales are expected to increase.

2. The management believes that with a 10% reduction in selling price per unit, demand is expected to increase by 25%. What effect would this change have on profits ? Is this a viable proposition ?

		Present Position
Sales		1,00,000 (4,000 @ 25)
Variable Expenses (4,000 @ 15)		60,000
Contribution Margin		40,000
Fixed Expenses		30,000
Net Profit		10,000
B.E. point	=	3,000 units
B.E.	=	Rs. 75,000
P/V ratio	=	40%
M/S ratio	=	25%

With a reduction in S.P. per unit and an increase in Sales by 25%, the relevant calculations are as shown below:

New S.P. per unit	=	Rs. 22.50
Sales	=	5,000 units
		Changed Situation
Sales (5,000 @ 22.50)		Rs. 1,12,500
Variable Expenses (5,000 @ 15/-)		75,000
Contribution Margin		37,500
Fixed Expenses		30,000
		7,500
B.E. point	=	4,000 units
B.E. sales revenue	=	90,000
P/V Ratio	=	33.3%
M/S Ratio	=	20%

The proposed change is not desirable as net profits have decreased by Rs. 2,500, B.E. point has increased to 4,000 units, and both the P/V ratio and M/S ratio have also decreased.

Hence these examples serve to demonstrate that cost-volume-profit analysis can be used to solve a variety of business problems. It is a powerful tool that is used in conjunction with variable costing in order to improve the decision making process.

Illustrative Problems

I. P/V ratio = 50%

Margin of Safety = 40%

Calculate the break-even point and the net profit if the sales volume is Rs. 50,00,000.

Solution:

Break-even Point

Sales	= 50,00,000
Margin of Safety (40%)	= 20,00,000
Break even point	30,00,000

Net profit

Profit = P/V ratio × M/S ratio × Sales

= 50% × 40% × 50,00,000

= Rs.10,00,000

II. The following information pertains to the half year ending 30th June 19x1:

Fixed Expenses	Rs. 30,000
Sales Value	Rs. 1,20,000
Profit	Rs. 30,000

The company has projected a loss of Rs. 6,000 for the second half of the same year ending 31st December 19×1.

Required:

a. The Break-even point, P/V ratio and Margin of Safety for six months ending 30th June 19x1.

B. If the selling price and fixed expenses remain unchanged in the second half of the year, what is the expected sales volume for the second half year.

c. The Break-even point and margin of safety for the whole year.

Solution:

$$\text{a. P/V ratio} = \frac{\text{Contribution} \times 100}{\text{Sales}}$$

$$= \frac{\text{Fixed expenses + Profit} \times 100}{\text{Sales}}$$

$$= \frac{60{,}000 \times 100}{1{,}20{,}000} = 50\%$$

$$\text{B.E. point} = \frac{\text{Fixed Expenses}}{\text{P/V ratio}} = \frac{30{,}000}{50\%} = \text{Rs. } 60{,}000$$

Margin of Safety = Sales - Break-even point

= 1,20,000 - 60,000 = Rs. 60,000

b. Contribution = Fixed Expenses - Loss

= 30,000 - 6,000 = Rs. 24,000

Contribution = Sales × P/V ratio

24,000 = S x 50%

or Sales = Rs. 48,000 for second half year.

c. For full year

Sales = 1,20,000 + 48,000 = Rs. 1,68,000

Fixed Expenses = 30,000 + 30,000 = Rs. 60,000

P/V ratio = 50% (due to no change in selling price).

Profit = 30,000 - 6,000 = Rs. 24,000

$$\text{Break-even point} = \frac{60{,}000}{50\%} = \text{Rs. } 1{,}20{,}000$$

Margin of Safety = 1,68,000 - 1,20,000

= Rs. 48,000

III. Cost-Volume-Profit Applications:

The income statement for the ABC company in contribution income statement format is given below:

ABC Company
Contribution Income Statement
For the Year Ended December 31, 19x6

Total Sales (66,000 units at Rs. 12.00 per unit)		Rs. 7,92,000
Less: Variable Production Costs		
(66,000 units at Rs. 4.40 per unit)	Rs. 2,90,400	
Variable Selling Costs		
(66,000 units at Rs. 2.80 per unit)	1,84,800	
Total Variable Costs		4,75,200

Contribution Margin		Rs. 3,16,800
Less: Fixed Production Costs	1,30,500	
Fixed Selling and Administrative Costs	48,200	
Total Fixed Costs		1,78,700
Income Before Taxes		1,38,100

The company's accountant has asked several members to describe their expectations of the business environment for the coming year. Each member was asked to write up his personal outlook, including changes in selling prices, product demand, variable production costs, variable selling costs, fixed production costs, and fixed selling and administrative costs.

(i) *Changes in Production Costs only.* The manager of production believes that variable production costs will increase by 10 per cent and that fixed production costs will rise by 5 per cent. With no other anticipated changes, what is the projected profit for the coming year?

Total sales (66,000 units at Rs. 12.00 per unit)		Rs. 7,92,000
Less: Variable production costs (66,000 units at Rs. 4.84)	Rs. 3,19,440	
Variable selling costs (66,000 units at Rs. 2.80 per unit)	1,84,800	
Total variable costs		5,04,240
Contribution margin		2,87,760
Less: Fixed production costs (Rs. 1,30,500 × 1.05)		1,37,025
Fixed selling and administrative costs		48,200
Total fixed costs		1,85,225
Projected Income before taxes		1,02,535

Thus, if the variable and fixed production costs do change and no adjustments to selling price or volume are made, the Company's profit will decrease by Rs. 35,565. Because both variable and fixed production costs are projected to increase, management may want to increase the selling price to offset the rise in costs. Increasing the number of units produced and sold also would help offset the higher fixed costs. Because the production has commented on only production costs, the controller should try to augment the forecast by having other managers develop projections in their areas of expertise.

(ii) *Changes in all cost areas* All costs will change, according to the manager of data processing. He believes that all variable costs will go up by 10 per cent, and that all fixed costs will rise by 5 per cent. He does not anticipate any other changes.

Total sales (66,000 units at Rs. 12.00 per unit)		Rs. 7,92,000
Less: Variable production costs		
(66,000 units at Rs. 4.84 per unit)	Rs. 3,19,440	
Variable selling costs		
(66,000 units at Rs. 3.08 per unit)	2,03,280	
Total variable costs		5,22,720
Contribution margin		2,69,280
Less: Fixed production costs (Rs.1,30,500 × 1.05)		1,37,025
Fixed selling and administrative costs		
(Rs. 48,200 × 1.05)		50,610
Total fixed costs		1,87,635
Projected income before taxes		81,645

Like the manager of production, the manager of data processing has concentrated only on projected costs. In this scenario, all costs are expected to increase. Profit decrease to Rs. 81,645.

(iii) *Changes in Demand and in all costs areas*. The manager of finance anticipates volume changes as well as changes in all cost areas. He believes that unit demand in 19×7 will increase by 8 per cent, all variable costs will go up by 20 per cent, and all fixed costs will decrease by 10 per cent.

Solution

Total sales (71,280 units at Rs. 12.00 per unit)		Rs. 8,55,360
Less: Variable production costs		
(71,280 units at Rs. 5.28 per unit)	Rs. 3,76,358	
Variable selling costs		
(71,280 units of Rs. 3.36 per unit)	2,39,501	
Total variable costs		6,15,859

Contribution margin		Rs. 2,39,501
Less: Fixed production costs (Rs. 1,30,500 × .9)	Rss. 1,17,450	
Fixed Selling and administrative costs (48,200 × .9)	43,380	
Total fixed costs		1,60,830
Projected income before taxes		78,671

The profit here further gets reduced. The manager of finance believes not only that all variable costs are going to increase but that volume also will increase.

Changes in Selling Price, Product Demand, and Selling Costs. According to the manager of sales, the company should increase the selling price by 10 per cent, which will cause demand to fall by 8 per cent. In addition, variable selling costs will go down by 5 per cent, and fixed selling and administrative costs will go up by 10 per cent.

Solution

Total sales (66,720 units at Rs. 13.20 per unit)		Rs. 8,01,504
Less: Variable production costs (66,720 units at Rs. 4.40 per units)	Rs. 2,67,168	
Variable selling costs (60,720 units at Rs. 2.66 per unit)	1,61,515	
Total variable costs		4,28,683
Contribution margin		372,821
Less: Fixed production costs	1,30,500	
Fixed selling and administrative costs	53,020	
Total fixed costs		1,83,520
Projected income before taxes		1,89,301

The manager of sales has the most optimistic outlook. Overall, in this scenario, profits increase by Rs. 51,201 (189,301-1,38,100).

Exhibit-1 is a comparative summary of the four executives' predictions.

IV. The following is the data for a company for the year 19x6:

Exhibit I: Comparative CVP Analysis
ABC Corporation
Summary of Projected Income Before Taxes
For the Year Ended December 31, 19x6

	VP Production	VP Data Processing	VP Finance	VP Sales
Total Sales	7,92,000	7,92,000	8,55,360	8,01,504
Less: Variable production costs	3,19,440	3,19,440	3,76,358	2,67,168
Variable selling costs	1,84,800	2,03,280	2,39,501	1,61,515
Total Variable Costs	5,04,240	5,22,720	6,15,859	4,28,683
Contribution margin	2,87,760	2,69,280	2,39,501	3,72,821
Less: Fixed production costs	1,37,025	1,37,025	1,17,450	1,30,500
Fixed selling and administrative costs	48,200	50,610	43,380	53,020
Total fixed costs	1,85,235	1,87,635	1,60,830	1,83,520
Projected income before taxes	1,02,535	81,645	78,671	1,89,301

Variable costs per unit:

	Rs.
Direct Materials	2,000
Direct labour	800
Factory overhead	1,400
Total fixed costs:	
Factory overhead	1,95,000
Other fixed costs	1,23,000
Selling price per unit	9,500

Required:

a. Compute the break-even point in units.

b. If the company sold 70 units in 19x6, how much profit did the firm realise.

c. How many units should the company sell to generate a profit of Rs. 84,800.

d. Calculate net income if the company increases the number of units sold by 20 per cent and reduces the selling price by Rs. 500 per unit.

Solution

1. Break-even units = $\frac{3,18,000}{5,300}$ = 60 units

2. Net income from sale of 70 units:

   = Rs. 5,300 per unit × 10 = 53,000

   The entire contribution margin of each unit sold in excess of break even represents profit.

3. Target sales units = $\frac{3,18,000 + 84,800}{5,300}$ = 76 units

4. Net income under specified conditions:

Total sales (84 units at Rs. 9,000 per unit)	Rs. 7,56,000
Less variable cost (84 units × 4,200)	3,52,800
Contribution margin	4,03,200
Less fixed cost	3,18,000
Projected income before taxes	85,200

V. The operating data of the MS Company for July are as follows:

	Fixed	Variable	Total
Sales			Rs. 20,00,000
Operating Costs:			
Cost of Goods Sold	Rs. 5,00,000	Rs. 6,10,000	11,00,000
Administrative Costs	1,15,000	30,000	1,45,000
Selling Costs	1,85,000	42,000	2,27,000
Total Costs	8,00,000	6,82,000	14,82,000
Profit			5,18,000

There were 1,00,000 units sold during July.

a. What is the break-even point in terms of units of product?

b. If sales can be increased to 2,00,000 units, determine the amount of profits.

c. For a revenue of Rs. 18,00,000, estimate the amount of profits.

Solution:

a. $$\text{Selling Price} = \frac{20,00,000}{1,00,000} = \text{Rs. } 20/\text{- per unit}$$

$$\text{Variable Cost} = \frac{6,82,000}{1,00,000} = 6.82 \text{ per unit}$$

Contribution Margin = Rs. 20 - 6.82 = 13.81 per unit.

Contribution margin percentage

$$= \frac{13.18}{\text{Rs.}20} = 66\%$$

$$\text{Break-even point} = \frac{\text{Fixed cost}}{\text{C.M. percent}} = \frac{8,00,000}{13.18}$$

$$= 60,698 \text{ units}$$

b. Profit = (13.18 × 2,00,000 - 8,00,000) = Rs. 18,36,000.

c. Profit = (.66 × 18,00,000-8,00,000) = Rs. 3,88,000.

VI. Given the following information for SM Company for October:

	Rs.
Sales	1,80,000
Fixed Manufacturing Costs	22,000
Fixed Marketing and Administrative Costs	14,000
Unit Price	9
Unit Variable Manufacturing Cost	6

Find:

a. Break-even quantity.

b. Quantity that would produce an operating profit of Rs. 33,000.

c. Break-even sales quantity if unit variable costs are reduced by 20 per cent per product unit, assuming no changes in total fixed costs.

d. Sales rupees required to generate an operating profit of Rs. 15,000.

e. Number of units sold in October.

Solution:

a. Break-even quality = $\frac{36,000}{9-6}$ = 12,000 units

b. $\frac{36,000 + 33,000}{9-6} = \frac{69,000}{3}$

= 23,000 units are required too produce an operating profit of Rs. 33,000

c. $\frac{36,000}{9-4.8} = \frac{36,000}{4.2}$ = 8571 units

d. $\frac{36,000 + 1500}{9-4.2} = \frac{51,000}{4.2}$ = 12,143 units

e. Units sold in October $\frac{1,80,000}{9}$ = 20,000 units

VII.

(i) Identify each of the following on the graph below:

a. The total cost line.

b. The total revenue line.

c. The total variable costs.

d. Variable cost per unit.

e. The total fixed costs.

f. The break-even point.

g. The profit area.

h. The loss area.

Solution

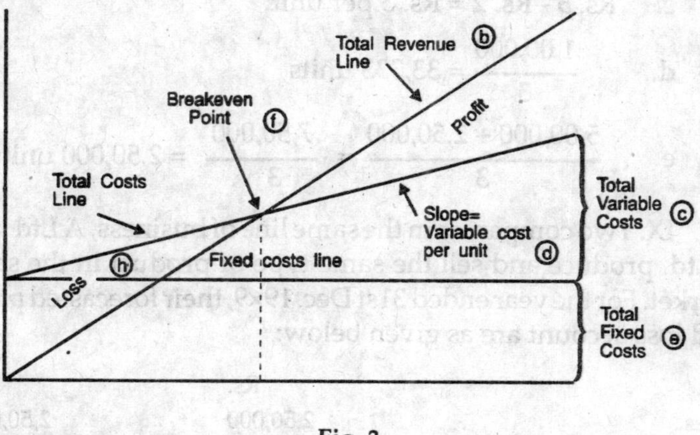

Fig. 3.

VIII. Anu Ltd. produces a product with the following costs and revenues for the year:

	Rs.
Total Revenues	5,00,000
Total Fixed costs	1,00,000
Total variable costs	2,00,000

Units produced & sold 1,00,000 units

a. What is the selling price per unit?

b. What is the variable cost per unit?

c. What is the contribution margin per unit?

d. What is the break-even point?

e. How many units should be produced by the company to produce a profit of Rs. 2,50,000 for the year?

Solution:

a. $\frac{5,00,000}{1,00,000 \text{ (units)}}$ = Rs. 5 per unit

b. $\frac{2,00,000}{1,00,000 \text{ (units)}}$ = Rs. 2 per unit

c. Rs. 5 - Rs. 2 = Rs. 3 per unit.

d. $\frac{1,00,000}{3} = 33,333$ units

e. $\frac{5,00,000 + 2,50,000}{3} = \frac{7,50,000}{3} = 2,50,000$ units

IX. Two companies in the same line of business, A Ltd. and B Ltd. produce and sell the same type of product in the same market. For the year ended 31st Dec. 19×9, their forecasted profit and loss account are as given below:

		Rs.		Rs.
Sales		2,50,000		2,50,000
Less:				
Variable costs of sales	Rs. 2,00,000		1,50,000	
Fixed costs	25,000	2,25,000	75,000	2,25,000
Forecasted net profit before tax		25,000		25,000

You are required to compute:

i. P/V ratio

ii. Break-even sales volume.

You are also required to state which company is likely to earn greater profits in conditions of:

(a) low demand and

(b) high demand.

Solution

		A Ltd.	B Ltd
		Rs.	Rs.
	Sales	2,50,000	2,50,000
	VC	2,00,000	1,50,000
	FC	25,000	75,000
	Profits	25,000	25,000
1.	P/V ratio	(1 - 2,00,000/25000) = 0.2	(1- 1,50,000/2,50,000) = 0.4
2.	B.E. Sales (FC/PV ratio) =	1,25,000	1,87,500

3. Company A Ltd. is likely to earn better profits for sales less than 2,50,000 and company B Ltd. for sales greater than 2,50,000.

X The sales turnover and profit during two periods were as follows:

Period I	Sales 20 lakh	Profit 2 lakh
Period II	Sales 40 lakh	Profit 4 lakh

Calculate

1. P/V ratio
2. Sales required to earn a profit of Rs. 4 lakh.
3. Profit when sales are Rs. 12 lakh. Assume that selling price and fixed costs are constant.

Solution

	Pd1	Pd2	Increase in pd 2 over pd 1
Sales	20 lakh	30 lakh	10 lakh
Profit	2 lakh	4 lakh	2 lakh
Increase in costs			8 lakh

As fixed costs are constant, the increase in costs reflects the increase in variable costs in tune with increase in sales volume. As such variable costs are 80% of sales as shown below:

$$\frac{8,00,000}{10,00,000} = 80\%$$

$\therefore$ P/V ratio = 100% - 80% = 20%

2. Fixed Expenses $= \frac{\text{Contribution - net profit}}{20\% \text{ of } 30,00,000 - 4,00,000} = 2,00,000$

$$\text{Required sales} = \frac{\text{FC + D Profit}}{\text{P/V ratio}}$$

$$= \frac{2,00,000 + 4,00,000}{20\%}$$

$$= \frac{6,00,000}{20\%} = \text{Rs. } 30,00,000$$

3. Sales x P/V ratio - Fixed cost

12,00,000 x 20% - 2,00,000

2,40,000 - 2,00,000 = Rs.40,000

XI. From the following information determine the amount by which the volume of sales must be increased for the company to break-even

	Rs.
Net sales	= 4,00,000
FC	= 2,00,000
Variable cost	= 2,00,000

Would your answer be different if the variable costs were Rs. 2,40,000?

Solution

$$\text{P/V ratio} = \frac{2,00,000}{4,00,000} = 50\%$$

$$\text{Break-even point} = \frac{2,00,000}{50\%} = \text{Rs. } 4,00,000$$

Hence sales should remain the same as the company is operating at the Break-even point.

(ii) $$\text{P/V ratio} = \frac{1,60,000}{4,00,000} = 40\%$$

$$\text{B.E. point} = \frac{2,00,000}{40\%} = 5,00,000$$

Sales should increase by 1,00,000 for the company to break-even as the present level of sales is Rs. 4,00,000 while the Break-even level is Rs. 5,00,000.

XII. The following information is given to you:

	Rs.	Rs.
Sales 4,000 units @ Rs. 20/- each		80,000
Materials consumed	30,000	
Variable OH	10,000	
Labour Charges	15,000	
Fixed overhead	13,000	68,000
Net profit		12,000

Calculate

(i) Break even point

(ii) Sales needed to earn a profit of 5% on sales

(iii) Extra units which should be sold to obtain the present profit if it is proposed to reduce the selling price by 10%.

Solution

(i) $$\text{V.C. per unit} = \frac{45{,}000}{4{,}000 \text{ units}} = 13.75 \text{ per units}$$

$$\text{B.E. point} = \frac{\text{F.C.}}{\text{C.M. per unit}} = \frac{13{,}000}{6.25}$$

$$= 2080 \text{ units}$$

(ii) Assume units to be sold as 'X'

Then Total Sales = V.C. + F.C. + Profit

$$20X = 13{,}75X + 13{,}000 + 5X$$

or $$1.25X = 13{,}000$$

or $$X = 10{,}400 \text{ units}$$

(If sales are 20X, then profit is 5 X as profit is given as 5% on sales)

Hence Sales in Rs.

$$= 10{,}400 \times 20 = \text{Rs. } 2{,}08{,}000$$

(iii) If S.P. is reduced by 10%

	Rs.
Present S.P.	20
Less of 10%	2
New S.P.	18.00
Less V.C. P. unit	13.75
C.M. per unit	4.25

$$\text{Units to be sold} = \frac{\text{FC + DP}}{\text{C.M. p.u.}}$$

$$= \frac{13{,}000 + 12{,}000}{4.25}$$

$$= 5882 \text{ units (approx.)}$$

∴ Extra units to be sold will be 1882 (5882 - 4,000)

XIII. A company showed a profit of Rs. 1,80,000 on a sales of Rs. 30,00,000. Variable expenses were Rs. 21,00,000.

Calculate :

1. B.E. Sales
2. B.E. Sales if V.C. increases by 10%
3. Break-Even Sales to maintain the profit as at present if S.P. is reduced by 10%.

Solution

$$\text{Sales} = \text{V.C.} + \text{FC} + \text{Profit}$$

$$30{,}000 = 21{,}00{,}000 + \text{FC} + 1{,}80{,}000$$

$$\therefore \quad \text{F.C.} = 7{,}20{,}000$$

1. $$\text{B.E. Sales} = \frac{7{,}20{,}000}{30\%} = \text{Rs. } 24{,}00{,}000$$

$$\text{P/V ratio} = \frac{9{,}00{,}000}{30{,}00{,}000} = 30\%$$

2. $$\text{Revised BEP} = \frac{7{,}20{,}000}{23\%} = \text{Rs. } 31{,}30{,}400$$

$$\text{P/V ratio} = \frac{6{,}90{,}000}{30{,}00{,}000} = 23\%$$

3. $$\text{P/V ratio} = \frac{6{,}00{,}000}{27{,}00{,}000} = 22.22\%$$

$$\text{Revised B.E. sales} = \frac{9{,}00{,}000}{22.22\%} = 40504 \text{ units (approx.)}$$

Questions

1. Identify specify types of variable and fixed costs, and compute the changes in these costs caused by changes in operating activity.
2. Define fixed cost, variablecost, semi-variable cost and give examples of each one of them.

3. Briefly analyse the cost behaviour patterns in a service-oriented business.

4. Why is an understanding of cost behaviour useful to managers? Give examples to illustrate your answer.

5. "Fixed costs remain constant in total but decrease per unit as productive output increases", explain this statement.

6. Define Cost-Volume-Profit analysis.

7. Briefly explain the significance of CVP analysis to management.

8. What assumptions are made in CVP analysis?

9. What is contribution margin and why is it important to management?

10. "An increase in fixed cost will always increase the break-even point". Elucidiate with examples.

11. Review the meaning of the following terms discussed in this chapter:

    a. Cost-Volume-Profit Analysis

    b. Break-even Point

    c. Margin of Safety

    d. Relevant Range

    e. Profit-Volume Analysis.

12. Is a company really breaking-even if it produces and sells at the break-even point? What costs might not be covered?

13. Define the term "Contribution Margin". What are some of its important assumptions?

14. What effect could the following changes, occurring independently have on (1) the break-even point, (2) the expected profit, and (3) the contribution margin:

a. a decrease in advertising.

b. an increase in variable cost.

c. an increase in fixed costs.

d. an increase in production volume.

e. an increase in the selling price of the product.

Problems

I. A company has the following revenue and cost data:

Total fixed costs	Rs. 50,000
Selling Price	Rs. 60 per unit
Contribution Margin ratio 40%	

Calculate:

a. The break-even point in rupees?

b. The variable cost per unit.

c. The sales revenue the company must generate to make a profit of Rs. 72,000.

d. The new break-even point if fixed costs are reduced by Rs. 5,250.

II. Cadbury Corporation sells three products, its fixed costs are Rs. 50,000. The revenue and cost data for the three products are as follows:

Products

	A	B	C
Sales	Rs.25,000	Rs. 37,500	Rs. 50,000
Variable costs	Rs. 15,000	Rs. 25,000	Rs. 27,500

a. Calculate the break-even point.

b. What would be break-even point be if the sales mix

next year is expected to be in the ratio of 2:2:1 with total sales being the same as this year.

III. a. Prepare a break-even chart with the help of the following data:

Fixed cost	= Rs. 1,20,000
Variable costs	= Rs. 3 per unit
Selling price	= Rs. 7 per unit
Output	= 50,000 units.

b. Determine the profit for each of the following situation:

(i) with the above data.

(ii) with a 10% increase in output & sales.

(iii) with a 10% increase in fixed costs.

(iv) with a 10% increase in variable costs.

(v) with a 10% increase in selling price.

IV. Music City, is a major producer of music organs. Product X has a large potential market. The summary data from 19x6 operations for product X are given below:

Variable costs per unit:

	Rs.
Direct materials	2,400
Direct Labour	800
Factory overhead	700
Selling expenses	600
Total fixed costs:	
Factory overhead	2,00,000
Advertising	50,000
Administrative expense	70,000
Selling price per unit	10,000

Required:

1. Compute the 19x6 break-even point in units.
2. Music City sold seventy-five product X models in 19x6. How much profit did the firm realise?
3. Management is pondering alternative courses of action for 19x7 (Treat each alternative independently).
   a. Calculate the number of units that must be sold to generate Rs. 1,00,000 profit. Assume that costs and selling price remain constant.
   b. Calculate net income if the company increases the number of units sold by 20 per cent and cuts the selling price by Rs. 500 per unit.
   c. Determine the number of units that must be sold to break-even if advertising is increased by Rs. 30,000.

V. XYZ Company anticipates fixed manufacturing, costs to be Rs. 1,26,500 and fixed general and administrative expenses to be Rs. 82,030 for the year. Variable manufacturing and selling costs per set will be Rs. 4.65 and Rs. 2.75 respectively. Each set will sell for Rs. 13.40.

1. Compute the break-even point in sales units.
2. Compute the break-even point in sales rupees.
3. If the selling price were increased to Rs. 14.50 per unit and fixed general and administrative expenses were cut by Rs. 30,000 what would the new break-even point be in units?
4. Prepare a graph to illustrate the break-even point found in 2.

VI. HM Company has a plant capacity of 1,00,000 units per year, but the 19x6 budget indicates that only 60,000 units will be produced and sold. The entire 19x6 budget is as follows:

	Rs.	Rs.
Sales revenues (60,000 units at Rs. 4)		2,40,000
Less: Cost of goods produced		
(based on production of 60,000 units)		
Materials (variable)	50,000	
Labour (variable)	40,000	
Variable manufacturing cost	45,000	
Fixed manufacturing costs	75,000	
Total cost of goods produced		2,10,000
Gross margin		30,000
Less: Selling and administrative costs		
Selling (10 per cent of sales)	24,000	
Administrative (fixed)	30,000	
Total selling and administrative costs		54,000
Net income (loss) from operations		24,000

1. Given the budgeted selling price and cost data, how many units would HM have to produce and selling to break-even?
2. Market research indicates that if HM were to drop its selling price to Rs. 3.50 per unit, it could sell 1,00,000 units in 19x6. At the new selling price, what is the company's new profit (loss) figure?
3. Would you recommend the new selling price in 2? Explain your answer.

VII. Neha Ltd. produces and distributes housing equipment. The present annual sales volume is 5,00,000 units, and the current selling price is Rs. 10.00 per unit. Variable costs amount to Rs. 6.00 per unit. Fixed costs are Rs. 1,00,000 per year.

1. (a) What is the present annual profit?

   (b) What is the present break-even point in units?

   (c) What is the present break-even point in rupees?
2. Compute the profit for each of the following changes (consider each situation independently):

a. A per unit increase of Rs. 2.00 in variable cost.

b. A 10 per cent decrease in fixed costs and a 10 per cent increase in sales volume.

c. A 10 per cent increase in fixed costs, a 20 per cent decrease in selling price, a 10 per cent decrease in variable costs per unit, and a 20 per cent increase in units sold.

3. Compute the new break-even point in units for each of the following changes:

(a) A 10 per cent decrease in fixed costs.

(b) A 10 per cent increase in selling price and Rs. 30,000 increase in fixed costs.

VIII. The income statement for Kumar and Co. is shown below:

Kumar & Co.
Income Statement for the Year Ended 19x1

	Rs.	Rs.
Sales		30,00,000
Cost of goods sold		19,00,000
Gross Margin		11,00,000
Sales Commission	4,40,000	
Annual salaries	2,50,000	
Other fixed costs	2,00,000	8,90,000
Net Income		2,10,000

Required:

a. What is the break-even point in sales volume for the company?

b. On what volume of sales was profit earned?

c. What break-even sales volume is needed to increase profits by 50 per cent?

IX. Mayfair Industries manufactures and distributes skates. Last year the company earned a profit of Rs. 30,000 on a sales volume of 80,000 units. The break-even sales volume was 50,000 units and the contribution margin ratio was 40 per cent.

Required:

a. Determine the contribution per unit sold.

b. What was the per unit selling price of the skates?

c. What was the variable cost of a skate.?

d. What was the total fixed costs?

e. Prepare an income statement for the year.

X. The operating results for the companies are given below:

	Company 1	Company 2
	Rs.	Rs.
Sales (20,000 units)	2,00,000	2,00,000
Variable costs	50,000	1,00,000
Contribution Margin	1,50,000	1,00,000
Fixed Costs	1,00,000	50,000
Net Income	50,000	50,000

Required:

a. Prepare a break-even chart for company 1 and company 2, indicating the break-even point, the contribution margin, and the areas of earnings and losses.

b. Compute the break-even point for both the companies.

c. If sales decline by 25 per cent for both the companies, prepare revised income statements for the 2 companies. Comment on your results.

XI. JP Company markets three lines of products. The accounting records of the three products yield the following information:

	Product ABC	Product XYZ	Product LMN
	Rs.	Rs.	Rs.
Sales	6,40,000	3,00,000	5,40,000
Variable expenses	1,28,000	1,50,000	2,16,000
Contribution Margin	5,12,000	1,50,000	3,24,000
Fixed expenses	3,76,000	2,40,000	2,52,000
Income (Loss) from operations	1,36,000	90,000	72,000

Average sale price is:

Rs. 4 for product ABC

Rs. 6 for product XYZ

and Rs. 10 for product LMN

Required:

1. Which product line is most profitable, which is least profitable.
2. Calculate the break-even sales in units for the company as a whole.
3. Prepare a contribution margin income statement for each product line, at the break-even point.
4. Assuming product XYZ is dropped altogether, that prepare a contribution margin income statement.
5. Is it economically viable to drop product XYZ? Explain.

XII. The ABC's Company income statement for the year ended 30th June is given below:

ABC Company

Income Statement for the year ended 30-6-19x8

	Rs.
Sales (1,00,000 units @ Rs. 50/-)	50,00,000
Variable costs	20,00,000
Fixed costs	10,00,000
Total costs	30,00,000
Pretax profit	20,00,000
Income Tax (50% rate)	10,00,000
	10,00,000

Required:

1. What is the break-even point in sales and units?
2. Suppose that a plant expansion will add $ 50,000 to fixed costs and increase capacity 50 per cent. How many units would have to be sold after the addition to break-even?
3. What would sales have to be after the plant expansion for the company to maintain its present pretax profit position?
4. Suppose that the plant operates at full capacity after the expansion. What profit will be earned?

XIII. ABC and XYZ are the owners of the Modern Processing Company and the Oldway Manufacturing Company, respectively. These companies manufacture and sell the same product, and competition between the two owners has always been friendly. Cost and profit data have been freely exchanged. Uniform selling prices have been set by market conditions.

ABC and XYZ differ markedly in their management thinking. Operations at Modern are highly mechanized and the direct labour force is paid on a fixed-salary basis. Oldway uses manual hourly paid labour for the most part and pays incentive bonuses. Modern's salesmen are paid a fixed salary, whereas Oldway's salesmen are paid small salaries plus commissions. XYZ takes pride in his ability to adapt his costs to fluctuations in sales volume and has frequently chided on Modern's "inflexible overhead".

During 19-2, both firms reported the same profit on sales of Rs. 1,00,000. However, when comparing results at the end of 19-3, Company XYZ was surprised by the following results:

	MODERN		OLD WAY	
	19.2	19.3	19.2	19.3
	Rs.	Rs.	Rs.	Rs.
Sales revenue	1,00,000	1,20,000	1,00,000	1,50,000
Cost and Expenses	90,000	94,000	90,000	1,30,000
Net Income	10,000	26,000	10,000	20,000
Percent on sales	10%	212/3%	10%	131/3%

On the assumption that operating inefficiencies must have registered XYZ and his accountant made a thorough investigation of costs but could not uncover any evidence of costs that were out of line. At a loss to explain the lower increase in profits on a much higher increase in sales volume, they have asked you to prepare an explanation.

You find that fixed costs and expenses recorded over the two-year period were as follows:

	Rs.
Modern	70,000 each year
Oldway	10,000 each year

Required:

1. Prepare an explanation for Company XYZ showing why Oldway's profits for 19.3 were lower than those reported by Modern despite the fact that Oldway's sales had been higher. Show relevant calculations to clerify the issue.
2. Indicate the volume of sales Oldway would have to have had in 19.3 to achieve the profit of Rs. 26,000 realized ny Modern in 19-3.
3. Comment on the relative future positions of the two companies when there are reductions in sales volume.

XIV. Consider two businesses with the following unit prices and fixed and variable costs:

Business A:

Selling price per unit	Rs. 100
Variable cost per unit	Rs. 20
Fixed cost of operations per year	Rs. 10,000

Business B:

Selling price per unit	Rs. 100
Variable cost per unit	Rs. 60
Fixed cost of operations per year	Rs. 5,000

Required:

1. Calculate the break-even point of each business in units.
2. Compute the profits of each business if sales in units are 10 per cent above the break-even point.
3. Which business would fare better if sales dropped to 5,000 units? Why?
4. Which business would fare better if the market collapsed and the price per unit fell to 50%? Why?

XV. **Business Decision Problem**: The XYZ Ltd. is operating at nearly 100 per cent of capacity. The company expects the demand for its product to increase by 20 per cent in 19x2. To meet the demand, the company is considering two alternatives. The first alternative will increase variable costs to 5 per cent of the selling price of the company's product, but will leave fixed costs unchanged. The second alternative will increase fixed cost by 10 per cent but have no effect on variable costs.

The condensed income statement for 19x1 is shown below:

	Rs.	Rs.
Sales		30,00,000
Costs:		
Variable	13,00,000	
Fixed	6,00,000	19,00,000
Net income before taxes		11,000

Required:

1. Calculate the break-even point for 19x2 under each of the two alternatives.
2. Determine projected net income before taxes for 19x2 under each of the alternatives.
3. Which alternative would you prefer and why?

11

Short-term Decisions

Short-run decisions concentrate on the maximum utilization of existing resources while long-term decisions are usually concerned with acquiring large capital investments. In the short-run, fixed costs remain unchanged so that the marginal cost, revenue and contribution of each alternative is relevant. In making business decisions, managers bring together all the relevant information, identify alternative courses of action and then decide on the course of action to be taken. Accountants normally consider a short-term decision as that which involves a period of one year or less. The basic distinction between short-term and long-term decisions is that the latter usually requires large capital investments and are not easily reversible, while maximising profitability is the best course of action in a short-run decision.

Very frequently, managers have to make decisions and choose from among various alternatives. This could involve dropping a particular product or adding a new line of product or making parts that earlier had been purchased or raising the price of the product and so on. Both qualitative and quantitative data are important in deciding among various alternative courses of action. Usually, quantitative data is utilized is making-decisions. However, many times a decision might be taken based on certain overriding qualitative factors that are economically not very sound.

To illustrate, a company will not replace an old machine with a fully automated new machine if the management's policy is to avoid laying off employees.

The present chapter analyzes three short-term decision-making situations with the help of examples.

The Concept of Relevant Information

In making business decisions, managers must identify the financial information relevant to a particular decision, i.e., information related to costs and revenue. Managers making business decisions always have to choose among alternative courses of action. In a choice among alternative courses of action, the only information that is relevant is the information which varies among the various actions being considered. Factors and information which remain the same among alternatives courses are not taken into account in making the business decisions.

For identifying and evaluating relevant financial information incremental analysis as a technique is generally preferred by accountants. Incremental cost refers to the increase in total cost due to the production of one additional unit. In quite a few situations, variable cost and incremental cost may be the same, but sometimes they are not. If the production of one additional unit of output extends activity beyond the relevant range, it causes both unit variable cost and fixed cost to increase.

To illustrate the concept of relevant information and incremental analysis, consider the following illustration:

A textile mill is expected to close for several months because of an expected labour strike. During the period of the strike, the textile mill is expected to incur costs of Rs. 40,000 per month. (These costs include depreciation charges, salaries to non-striking employees and interest expense). A chemical company is in need of some temporary storage space and has offered to rent the textile mill for one month at a rent of Rs. 30,000 per month. The management of the textile mill have estimated that they will have to incur approximately Rs. 8000 for cleaning up the space after the chemical company vacates the textile mill. Should the management accept or reject the offer based on the above information ?

Solution:

The operating income of the textile mill if it is rented for a month will be:

	Rs.	Rs.
Revenue		30,000
Cost		
Monthly expenses	40,000	
Clean up expenses	8,000	48,000
Operating income (loss)		(18,000)

However, Rs. 40,000 in expenses the textile mill will continue to incur whether or not the mill is rented to the chemical company. Hence, all the information given in this statement are not relevant to the decision at hand.

The incremental costs and revenue are the relevant factors that must be examined under the alternative courses of action. An incremental analysis for the textile mill will be as follows:

	Reject offer Rs.	Accept offer Rs.	Incremental analysis Rs.
Revenue	0	30,000	30,000
Costs			
Monthly costs	(40,000)	(40,000)	
Clean up costs	0	(8,000)	(8,000)
Operating income (loss)	(40,000)	(18,000)	22,000

The incremental analysis shows that accepting the chemical company's offer results in Rs. 30,000 of incremental revenue, but only Rs. 8,000 in incremental costs. Hence, the textile mill will stand to gain by reducing its operating loss for the month by Rs. 22,000 by accepting the chemical company's offer.

Hence, incremental analysis is an important tool for evaluating the effects of short-term changes in revenues and costs. We will now consider some of the typical short-term decisions. The situations discussed now are decisions involving make or buy, accepting a special order and dropping a product line.

I. Make or Buy Decisions

Management must often decide whether to make a particular product or whether to buy the product from outisde. The economics of the make or buy decision is usually based on an analysis of the cost implications. Make or buy decisions are quite easily resolved when the decision is based on the best utilization of the available resources so to achieve organizational goals.

Example

A firm is considering whether to make or buy a particular component. The manufacturing cost associated with the product is as follows:

	Rs.
Direct materials	15,000
Direct Labour	11,500
Variable Overheads	9,500
Fixed Overheads	14,000
Total Cost of Manufacturing	50,000
5,000 units per month	

Average manufacturing cost per unit (Rs. 50,000/5,000 units) ... Rs. 5/-

The cost to make the component must now be compared with the costs that would be incurred if the unit was purchased. The following table shows the relevant calculations:

	Decision	
	Make	**Buy**
	Rs.	Rs.
Direct Materials	15,000	-
Direct Labour	11,500	-
Variable overhead	9,500	-
Fixed overhead	14,000	12,000
Purchase price of part, Rs.9/- per unit (5,000 x Rs. 9)		45,000
Total cost to acquire	50,000	57,000
Saving if part is made	7,000	

The above table shows that if the firm buys the component it will still incur fixed overhead costs of Rs. 12,000. The cost of buying the part from outside sources is Rs. 9/- per unit. Hence making the component will cost Rs. 50,000 per month while buying the component will cost Rs. 57,000. The firm saves Rs. 7,000 by making the component.

II. Accepting a Special Order

In evaluating the merits of a special order decision, managers must consider not only their cost structures but also the potential effect of the special order on sales at regular prices. Special orders, either short-term or long-term require careful study.

Several factors should be considered in deciding whether to accept a special order or not. Also, many special-order decisions can have long-term consequences. Of major importance is the effect of accepting the special order upon the companies' regular sales volume and sales prices. A company cannot continue indefinitely without covering all its costs.

Other factors which need to be considered are:

(a) Is accepting the special order the best way of utilizing spare capacity ?

(b) Will acceptance of the special order at lower price lead other customers to demand lower prices also ?

(c) Effect of accepting the special order on fixed costs.

Example

A firm produces a product X that it sells for Rs. 40/-. The current production is at 50,000 units per month which represents 80% of capacity. Currently the fixed costs are Rs. 80,000 per month. The firm has an opportunity to utilize its spare capacity if it accepts an offer from a departmental store. The departmental store is willing to purchase 1250 units of product X at a price of Rs. 30/- per unit. Acceptance of the special order will increase fixed costs by Rs.10,000. The variable costs of product X are Rs.15/- per unit. Should the firm accept the special offer?

Solution

The present position is as follows:

		Rs.
Sales	50,000 @ 40/-	2,00,000
Less Variable cost	50,000 @ 15	75,000
Contribution		1,25,000
Less Fixed cost		80,000
Net profit		45,000

The cost-structure for the special order is as under:

Sales (1250 × 30)	37,500
Less Variable cost (1250 × 15)	18,750
Contribution	18,750
Less fixed cost	10,000
Net profit	8,750

In this example, accepting the special order increases net income by Rs. 8,750. Hence the firm should accept the special offer as it improves the profit picture.

Thus, based on purely quantitative data, the offer should be accepted. However, in some situations, certain qualitative factors also need to be considered, before a final decision is taken. Operating at capacity may help the firm avoid lay offs and other related problems. Also the firm must find out if accepting the special order is the most profitable way of using spare capacity.

III. Dropping a Product line

Frequently managers have to decide whether to discontinue/replace an unprofitable product line, so that the overall profitability of the company can be improved. This is specially applicable in case of a company which has a range of products, one of which is supposed to be unprofitable.

Illustration

Anu Ltd. manufactures three products, the income statement for which are given below. Management is considering whether or not to discontinue product Y as it is showing a loss. Based on the above data should product Y be dropped? What other factors would you take into account before making a final decision.

	Product X	Product Y	Product Z	Total
	Rs.	Rs.	Rs.	Rs.
Sales	60,000	50,000	80,000	1,90,000
Less variable cost	25,000	30,000	35,000	90,000
Contribution Margin	35,000	20,000	45,000	1,00,000
Fixed Costs				
Joint	8,000	9,000	10,000	27,000
Separate	15,000	15,000	18,000	48,000
Total	23,000	24,000	28,000	75,000
Net income	12,000	(4,000)	17,000	25,000

Solution:

If productY is dropped, the joint costs remain the same and have to be absorbed by the remaining products. (Rs. 3,000 by product X and Rs. 6,000 by product Y). The revised income statements will appear as shown below:

	Product X	Product Y	Total
	Rs.	Rs.	Rs.
Sales	60,000	80,000	1,40,000
Less variable cost	25,000	35,000	60,000
	35,000	45,000	80,000
Fixed Costs			
Joint	11,000	16,000	27,000
Separate	15,000	18,000	33,000
Total	26,000	34,000	60,000
Net income	9,000	11,000	20,000

Thus, dropping product Y with a loss of Rs. 4,000 reduces total profits by Rs. 5,000. Anu Ltd. would loose Rs. 20,000 contribution margin while saving only Rs. 15,000 in separate fixed costs. The common costs allocated to the other products will not change. Hence, dropping product Y reduces total profit by Rs. 5,000 (Rs. 20,000 lost contribution margin – Rs. 15,000 in fixed cost savings).

Other factors which need be considered are:

(a) Will dropping product Y result in the complete elimination of joint costs to product Y. If this is so, eliminating product Y may be a worthwhile decision?

(b) Will dropping product Y cause sales to increase for the company's other two products? If yes, then discontinuing product Y may be the correct decision. Thus the effects of expected changes in the sales of other products should also be examined.

(c) What alternative use can the company make of the production and the other facilities now used in manufacturing product Y?

(d) Various other factors should also be considered in a decision of whether to discontinue a product line. For example, the company may want to avoid laying-off employees or want to maintain a reputation for offering its customers a "full-line of products".

Illustrative Problems

Decision to eliminate unprofitable segments.

The Management of Ronny Ltd. wants to determine if Division A should be eliminated. Exhibit I below provides the Income statement for the company.

Exhibit I
Divisional Profit Statement

Income Statement	Division B	Division A	Total Company
Sales	Rs. 1,25,000	Rs. 10,000	Rs. 1,35,000
Less variable Cost	42,500	6,500	49,000
Contribution Margin	82,500	3,500	86,000
Less Traceable Fixed Cost	45,500	10,500	56,000
Divisional Income	37,000	(7,000)	30,000
Less Unallocated			
Fixed Cost			15,000
Income before Taxes			15,000

Exhibited II
Company profitability

Incremental Decision Analysis	Keep Division A	If it elects to Eliminate Division A	Cost to eliminate Division A	
	Rs.	Rs.	Rs.	
Sales	1,35,000	1,25,000	(15,000)	Sales decrease
Less Variable Cost	49,000	42,500	6,500	Cost reduction
Contribution Margin	86,000	82,500	(3,500)	C.M. decrease
Less Total Fixed Costs	71,000	60,500	10,500	Cost reduction
Income before Taxes	15,000	22,000	7,000	Profit increase

Exhibit II show that the profits of Ronny Ltd. increase by Rs. 7,000 if Division A is eliminated.

Exhibit III gives the incremental revenue and cost analysis for the Company.

Exhibit III
Incremental Revenue and Cost Analyis

Advantage of eliminating division A	**Amount**
Increase in Sales	
Decrease in costs (6,500 + 10,500)	Rs. 17,000
Total Advantage	17,000
Disadvantage of eliminating Division A	
Decrease in Sales	10,000
Increase in Costs	
Total Disadvantage	10,000

Incremental profit from eliminating division A is greater than the disadvantage of eliminating division A.

Hence, whether to discontinue a segment or not, contribution margin format helps in identifying traceable and avoidable fixed costs relevant to the decision whereas incremental revenue & cost analysis is helps in comparing the operating results with and without the segment.

Make or Buy

Alvin Enterprises is currently operating at 70 per cent capacity and producing 10,000 units a year. The Manager of Alvin Enterprises is considering various possibilities to increase its sales. At present Alvin Enterprises purchases its product from a supplier at a unit price of Rs. 30/-. Estimates show that Alvin Enterprises can manufacture the product at Rs. 11/- per unit direct material cost and Rs. 8/- direct labour cost. Variable factory overheads are Rs. 64,000 and fixed factory overheads are Rs. 90,000.

(a) Should the company Make or Buy?

(b) If the company could rent out the currently unused part of the factory for Rs. 1,500 a month would this affect your decision in part (a)?

Solution :

	Make	*Buy*	*Difference*
	Rs.	Rs.	Rs.
(a) Raw Materials	1,10,000	-	-
Direct Labour	80,000	-	-
Variable Overhead	64,000	-	-
Total Variable Cost	2,54,000	3,00,000	46,000

Alvin Enterprises can save Rs. 46,000 by making its own component.

(b) The opportunately cost of utilizing the factory space will be Rs. 18,000 per year. This will not alter the decision in (a) above but the net benefits will be reduced to Rs. 28,000.

Questions

1. Briefly explain the meaning of short-term as it relates to short-term decisions?

2. Briefly explain the meaning of the following concepts:

a. Make-or-buy decision.

b. Relevant cost.

c. Dropping a product line.

3. How do you determine which data are relevant to a make-or-buy decision?

4. For 'pricing a special order' when should fixed overhead costs be included/excluded from the analysis. Under what circumstances are fixed costs relevant to the pricing decision?

5. What is meant by relevant decision information? What are the important factors that should be taken into account in this decision?

6. What are the factors that must be considered in a decision to drop a product line?

7. What does the term short-term mean as it relates to short-term decision?

8. Explain the meaning of the term 'segment' analysis. Can all business firms use this concept successfully in their organisations? Elucidiate with example.

9. 'If it costs a firm Rs. 50/- to make a component that an outside agency can make for Rs. 40/- the firm should buy the component and save Rs. 10/- per unit Comment.

Problems

1. The ABC Electronics Company manufactures and sells three products. The income statement for the company is given below:

	Product A	Product B	Product C	Total
	Rs.	Rs.	Rs.	Rs.
Sales	10,000,000	6,00,000	4,00,000	20,00,000
Variable Cost	4,00,000	2,70,000	2,40,000	9,10,000
Contribution Margin	6,00,000	3,30,000	60,000	10,90,000
Fixed Cost	2,40,000	1,44,000	96,000	4,80,000

Joint Separable	1,00,000	80,000	70,000	2,50,000
	3,40,000	2,24,000	1,66,000	7,30,000
Net Income (loss)	2,60,000	1,06,000	(6,000)	3,60,000

Required:

1. Should the company drop product C? Explain.
2. Prepare a revised income statement assuming that product C was dropped?
3. Suppose that the sales of the ABC Electronics Company increase by 25% if product C is dropped? Will this change your answer? Explain.

2. Make or Buy:

The following are the estimated costs to produce a unit of item M for the next budget period:

	Unit Cost Rs.	Total Cost Rs.
Direct Materials	6.00	30,000
Direct Labour	18.00	90,000
Variable overhead	8.00	40,000
Joint fixed overhead	6.00	30,000
Separable fixed overhead	4.00	20,000
	42.00	2,10,000

Novex Ltd., a competitor has offered to make item M for Rs. 40 per unit, with no sacrifice in quality.

Required: Should the offer of Novex Ltd. be accepted? Explain.

3. Elimination of Unprofitable Segment

Frooti Company has three divisions: M.N.O. The divisional income summaried for 19 × 6 revealed the following:

Frooti company

	M	*N*	*O*	*Total*
	Rs.	Rs.	Rs.	Rs.
Sales	1,90,000	4,30,000	7,40,000	13,60,000
Variable Cost	50,000	3,20,000	4,80,000	8,50,000
Contribution Margin	1,40,000	1,10,000	2,60,000	5,10,000
Less Traceable Fixed Costs	1,00,000	1,50,000	1,50,000	4,00,000
Divisional Income	40,000	(40,000)	1,10,000	
Less Unallocated Fixed Costs	1,10,000			
Net income before Taxes	35,000			75,000

A detailed analysis of the traceable fixed costs revealed the following information:

	M	N	O
	Rs.	Rs.	Rs.
Avoidable Fixed cost	70,000	1,35,000	1,10,000
Unavoidable Fixed cost	30,000	15,000	40,000
Total	1,00,000	1,50,000	1,50,000

Is it profitable for the Company to eliminate one or more of its segments based on the 19x6 income statement. Prepare revised income statement if any division/s are eliminated.

4. The income statement for a Company producing 3 products is as shown below:

	Products		
	A	B	C
	Rs.	Rs.	Rs.
Sales	65,800	1,00,000	85,500
Less Variable cost	25,000	55,000	35,000
Total Contribution Margin	40,800	45,000	50,500
Less Allocated fixed cost	20,500	47,000	32,800
profit (Loss)	20,300	(2,000)	17,700

Should the Company drop product B. Prepare a revised income statement if product B was dropped.

5. Make or Buy

A Company produces an item 'X' for a radio assembly operation, the costs for which are given below:-

	Unit Cost	Total Cost
	Rs.	Rs.
Raw Material	45.50	400
Direct Labour	24.00	2,100
Variable overhead	15.00	8.00
Joint fixed cost	50.50	1,000
Separable fixed cost	15.00	200
Total Cost	150	4,500

Another company has offered to make the item X at a rate of Rs. 147/-. Should the Company accept the offer or not.

12

The Budgeting Process

All Organizations are involved in the budget-making process and budgetting is a part of the overall profit-planning and control process. Essentially the rules of good budgeting are based on common sense and sound business judgement.

By preparing a budget management is forced to look ahead. A budget specifies the events that must take place if the objectives of the organization are to be achieved.

The present chapter explains the three inter-related terms-Budget, Budgeting and Budgetary Control and then goes on to explain the basic principles used in budget preparation. The various types of budgets and the inter-relationship between them are also discussed. The chapter then highlights two special aspects of budgeting used frequently by managers to achieve the objective of an organization viz. Zero Base Budgeting and Performance Budgeting.

The budget is a formal quantitative expression of the goals of management. The act of preparing a budget is called budgeting. And the use of a budget to assist management in the controlling process is called budgetary control. However, in the budgetting process, the three terms sometimes tend to be used interchangeably. Thus through the process of budgeting, management specifies the events that must take place to ensure that target profit and other objectives will be achieved.

A budget is usually drawn up for an annual period. The

first step in the preparation of a budget is to look at actual expenditure and revenues for the previous year. With a good accounting system, expenditure for the prior year will be broken down and reported in considerable detail. Since many expenditures tend to vary with sales or volume of production, the estimate of these elements may be the most sensitive part of the entire budget. And a good manager will base his entire budget on the advise he gets from his sales and marketing people. Also a budget should contain enough information presented in an orderly manner so that its purpose is communicated to the user. Too much information or too little information clouds the accuracy of the budget.

Basic Principles of an Effective Budget

Preparation of an organization's budget forces management to look ahead and to analyze the various interrelationship in a business. It requires the entire management team work together to carry out the plans. The comparison of the actual performance with the budgeted one summarises the investigation of differences which serve as a feedback for future planning and control.

1. Preparation of a budget forces top management to set long-range goals. Also, it is necessary to name managers responsible for achieving the long-term goals. Once established, these goals serve as a benchmark against which managerial performance can be evaluated.

2. Success or failure of a budget is mainly determined by how well the human aspects of the process are handled. The budget can force the coordination of activity. Top management must communicate the importance of the budget time table to all so that coordination from all sections is forthcoming.

3. Budgets are important guides to the actions of management. However, they should always be treated as guides, not as absolute truths since budgets are finalized weeks or months in advance, unexpected changes may take place. A manager should not ignore these changes and

a procedure for taking care of these changes should be worked out as part of budget implementation.

4. Economic use of money, is facilitated through the process of budgeting. Budgets are prepared almost a year in advance and a time table with deadlines is also set for all levels and parts of the years' operating plans. All people in the organization become conscious of the need to conserve business resources resulting in efficient use of resources.

5. Budgetary control and planning operate together as key feature to a good management system. If investigation reveals that the plan is unsatisfactory, the plan is corrected. If investigation reveals that the plan is satisfactory but that performance can be improved, steps are taken to bring future performance in line with the plan. This system of feedback for future planning and control can lead to a better organization since theoretically in the budget, everything that needs to be done, is being done.

What does a Budget Look Like?

A budget is a financial plan of action. It does not have a standard form unlike a formal income statement or the balance sheet. A budget should not contain either too much information or two little information. Too much information clouds the meaning and accuracy of the data while too little information may result in overspending. Hence a budget should contain enough, if information presented in an orderly manner is to be properly communicated to the user. The information should be as accurate and meaningful as possible to the user of the budget.

The Budget Period

Budgets are normally drawn up for a year, with the year being divided into quarters or months. In some cases budgets are drawn up on the basis of an operating cycle—complete tracing of an activity from the time it is started until it is ended. The budget usually corresponds with the fiscal year so that meaningful comparisons of actual results with the budget can be made.

A budget that extends far into the future is liable to be less accurate. Also, if the budget is restricted to a quarter or a month, it tends to encourage a short-term perspective. Hence budgets are normally prepared for the year by quarters; with division into months as the immediate time approaches. Also, provision is made for reviewing and correcting the budgets frequently to incorporate the changes which may have taken place after the preparation of the budget.

Limitation of Budgeting

1. Budgeting is not an end in itself. Budgets are merely tools to make management more effective though they cannot take the place of management.
2. The success or failure of budgeting is largely determined by how well the human aspects of the process are handled. Managers at all levels must be educated in this area of activity and must feel that they are important links in the effective budgeting system.
3. In the development of budgets, one is dealing with projections and estimates and hence deviations can be expected. So it is important that the budget be checked and corrected whenever necessary.
4. Budgets must be adapted to new and changing conditions.

In the real world, it is extremely difficult to anticipate at budget time, all the things that may happen in the forthcoming year. Changes in the economic or industry conditions can pose serious problems for managers trying to make predictions about their own companies. Also, many future events almost defy accurate prediction, and unforeseen circumstances often develop, which makes it quite useless to compare actual results with the budgeted one.

Hence, management must recognise that the budget is not

unalterable, but it may require modifications, if conditions change.

Preparation of the Budgets or Types of Budgets

The nature of the business and its activities will determine the types of budgets that can be prepared. Each separate budget is prepared which gives the projected costs and revenues for that part of the company. All these separate budgets are then inter-related to form a single budget known as "The Master Budget Plan" which gives the forecasted financial statements for the entire company.

The Sales Budget: The starting point for the preparation of all other budgets is the sales budget. Sales predictions are made which are based as an analysis of past sales and an estimate of future economic prospects. Sales from past years are usually broken down by product line, regions, and sales-people. Management tries to accurately forecast future market conditions.

After the forecast is complete, the management tries to develop strategies and policies to obtain its desired market share. Also, planned sales may be overstated or understated, and so it is necessary to revise the sales budget frequently - probably after every month because of changing conditions in the economy and the company itself since sales tend to serve as a limiting factor for the preparation of all other budgets. This budget is probably the most important to the Master Budget.

The Sales Budget for the XYZ Company for the year 199x is presented in the Exhibit below:

XYZ Company Sales
Budget for the year ended 30th June 199x

	Total	First Quarter	Second Quarter	Third Quarter	Fourth Quarter
Product-I	2,00,000	50,000	80,000	40,000	30,000
Product-II	3,00,000	80,000	1,00,000	60,000	60,000

The Production Budget

In preparing a production budget, an important consideration to be kept in mind is the firm's inventory policy. The sales budget is the foundation for the production budget with adjustments for beginning inventory and inventory desired at the end of the budget period.

Production budgets, like the sales budgets, are developed on a unit basis. A production budget depends on 3 factors: (1) Sales forecast in unit as indicated in the sales budget, (2) Finished goods inventory level that management wants at the end of the period, and (3) Anticipated inventory at the start of the budget period.

The production budget also depends on a company's inventory policy. Inventories may be build up or liquidated depending upon the outlook adopted by management. Also the cost of carrying larger inventories should be compared with the cost of being out-of-stock when the firm cannot deliver. The production budget for the XYZ Company is shown here:

XYZ Company:
Production Budget for the year ended 30th June 199x

	Total	First Quarter	Second Quarter	Third Quarter	Fourth Quarter
Desired ending inventory	60,000	10,000	18,000	25,000	7,000
Cost of goods	30,000	7,000	6,000	9,000	8,000
Total needed	90,000	17,000	24,000	34,000	15,000
Opening inventory	25,000	6,000	5,000	6,000	8,000
Purchases	65,000	11,000	19,000	28,000	7,000

The Manufacturing Cost Budget

The Direct Materials Budget, the Direct Labour Budget, and the Manufacturing Overhead Budget make up the Manufacturing Cost Budget. Each of the three budgets is explained in brief below:

Direct Materials Budget

The materials required for the production schedule are estimated. Purchases are then made of the materials required depending upon the production cycle. Also, if the materials can be stored, with moderate cost, they can be purchased in large quantities when the prices are reasonable. Normally organisations try to keep reasonable levels of materials to match production requirements.

The Direct Labour Budget

In the preparation of the direct labour budget, production requirements are translated into labour requirements. The labour hours required to manufacture the product are estimated from the production budget. The standards hours are calculated from past records or past performance and are then adjusted for set-up time, idle time and other changes that may have taken place.

The labour hours are then multiplied by the various hourly labour rate to arrive at the total estimated labour cost.

The Manufacturing Overhead Budget

The Manufacturing overhead budget is made up of three important parts: (i) Indirect Materials, (ii) Indirect Labour; and (iii) Indirect Expenses like power, depreciation, repairs and maintenance, taxes, insurance, etc.

This budget provides management with ways and means of controlling overhead cost. For example, a small saving in one department, when multiplied for all other departments, may result in a substantial amount of savings for the entire organisation. The direct material and direct labour costs are normally fixed in advance and management has not much say in controlling these costs.

The Selling Expenses Budget

The selling expense budget is the responsibility of the sales department and includes selling expenses like sales salaries, sales commissions, advertising, sales office rent, shipping expenses, sale supplies etc. The selling expenses may be both fixed and variable.

The General and Administrative Expenses Budget

The general and administrative expenses are classified into fixed and variable costs so that this budget can be used as a means of controlling these costs. Most elements of this budget are fixed costs.

The Capital Budget

This budget tries to determine the capital investment requirements of the business, e.g., acquisition of machinery building, etc. The plans of the business to modernize or go in for additions of long-term investment will influence the cash budget in the current year. Therefore, capital expenditure decisions must be anticipated in advance and integrated into the master budget.

Cash Budget

The cash budget shows the budgeted cash receipts and cash disbursements for a future period of time. The cash inflows and cash outflows are brought together in a cash budget to show expected cash flows of the company. This summary of estimated cash flows, helps the company to plan future cash availability.

Financial plans are drawn up to anticipate periods of high and low cash availability. Large cash balances imply that the business has not been able to earn the best possible rate of return. Low cash reserves means that the business will be unable to meet its dues. In general, the company should have adequate cash balance to meet its forecasted cash requirements plus some additional reserve to meet unforeseen contingencies.

Forecasted Income Statement

The data from the different budgets prepared earlier is put together to prepare the forecasted income statement to show whether the profits as reflected in the budgets can be realized or not. The cost of goods sold is prepared from the information in the direct material, directlabour, and factory overhead budgets. The sale budget gives the figure of estimated revenue. The

Budget director can now add information from the selling expense and general and administrative expense budget, to prepare the forecasted income statement.

Forecasted Statement of Financial Position (Balance Sheet)

The forecasted statement of financial position depends upon the various individual budgets which have been prepared. The forecasted income statement and the cash inflow or outflow position must be known clearly before the forecasted statement of financial position can be prepared. Also, all the other transactions during the year as shown in the period budgets, must be classified and accordingly accounted for in the preparation of the statement of financial position.

A comparison of the estimated balance sheet with the actual statements can be used asa point of reference for the preparation of future budgets.

Budget Implementation

The implementation of budget is the responsibility of the budget director. The success of the entire exercise of budgeting depends on two important factors. **First** proper and clear communication to all key people involved in implementation of the budget. They should clearly know what is expected of them and how to achieve the goals. **Second** the co-operation and encouragement by the top management in achieving the targets as identified in the budgets. The top management should be willing to reward people who meet budget goals. Ideally top management and the lower level of management should work together to prepare and implement the budget successfully.

Budgeted statement of cash receipts and cash disbursements for the XYZ Company forthe year ended 30th June 19x1.

	Total	First Quarter	Second Quarter	Third Quarter	Fourth Quarter
Opening cash balance	85,000	20,000	15,000	30,000	20,000
Cash Receipts	60,000	15,000	6,000	26,000	13,000
Total cash available	1,45,000	35,000	21,000	56,000	33,000

Cash Disbursement					
Inventory	25,000	5,000	6,000	9,000	5,000
Asset Purchase	60,000	30,000	15,000	5,000	10,000
Operating Expenses	15,000	5,000	5,000	2,500	2,500
Total Disbursements	1,00,000	40,000	26,000	16,500	17,500
Minimum cash balance required	20,000	5,000	5,000	5,000	5,000
Total cash needed	1,20,000	45,000	31,000	21,500	22,500
Excess of cash available over cash disbursement	25,000	(10,000)	(10,000)	34,500	10,500

Budgeted Balance Sheet, 30th June 19x1

Current Assets	**Rs.**
Cash	25,000
Accounts Receivable	10,000
Inventory	20,000
Fixed Assets	
Land	30,000
	85,000

Liabilities and Owner's Equity

Current Liabilities	
Accounts payable	20,000
Accrued Expenses	5,000
Owner's Equity	40,000
Reserves and Surplus	20,000
	85,000

Special Aspects of Budgeting

1. Zero Base Budgeting

Zero-base Budgeting is the newest approach to budgetary planning and control. It was successfully developed and implemented in the seventies by Peter A. Phyrr. The approach became further popular when President Jimmy Carter, in 1979, required its use for the federal government.

There are at least two approaches to budgeting. The traditional method takes the current level of operations as the starting point for developing the future year's budget. In the traditional approach, it is assumed that all previous activities are essential for achieving the on-going objectives. However, the important limitations of the traditional approach are:

(a) Budgets tend to get larger and larger over the years as inefficiencies of earlier years are carried forward.

(b) New projects receive a raw deal being more susceptible to be dropped out in case of budget cuts.

(c) Alternative ways of achieving the same objectives are not identified. Things are taken for granted.

(d) Key problems and decision areas are not highlighted.

Thus, the traditional approach of using the existing budget as the starting point for developing the next budget needs reappraisal.

The second approach to budgeting is the Zero Base Budgeting approach. This approach is defined by Peter A. Phyrr[1] as:

"An operating, planning and budgeting process which requires each manager to justify his entire budget request in detail from scratch (hence Zero base) and shift the burden of proof to each manager to justify why he should spend any money at all".

This approach requires all activities be identified as 'decision package'.

The Zero Base Budgeting technique starts from the scratch each year and puts much less emphasis on what was budgeted in the past. The approach involves the evaluation and review of all activities and programmes on the basis of a cost-benefit analysis.

Key Elements of Zero-Base Budgeting

1. Identification of the objectives and developing an operating plan and budget for the coming year.

---

1. Peter A. Pyhrr: "Zero Base Budgeting", Wiley, New York, 1970.

2. Identifying alternative and efficient ways of achieving the current activity.

3. Evaluate budget reductions and expansions in a systematic manner to allow for a re-allocation of the resources, as per the priorities of the organization.

4. Diagnosing the unnecessary activities that budgeting often perpetuates.

Procedure of Zero-base budgeting

The basic steps involved in Zero-base budgeting are:-

I. Identification of decision units. The decision units are somewhat like cost-centres.

II. Analysis of each decision package in a decision unit. Once the decision units have been identified, managers try and analyze the decision packages in each decision unit. Each decision unit has several decision packages. For each decision package, managers evaluate the incremental benefits that they get from the incremental cost. The decision packages also try and find out alternative ways of accomplishing the same activity.

III. Ranking the decision packages so as to allocate the resources in the best possible manner. Ranking also helps the top management to determine the benefits of each decision package to the organization which will be evaluated by systematic analysis and ranked in order of importance.

Ranking establishes priorities amongst the functions as described in the decision package.

Generally, the manager at the level of divisional manager ranks the package. This allows them to trade of the expenditure amongst cost planning, maintenance, sales and administration.

Top management prepares a consolidated ranking to identify best allocation of resources. Management can now decide a cut off level on any or all rankings. It may decide to fund only the first fifteen packages a out of a total of twenty-five. This might mean funding for some new high priority programmes at the cost of other ongoing low priority ones.

IV. **Preparation of Budgets**: The final step is the preparation of budgets on the basis of decision packages and the availability of funds.

Advantages of Zero Base Budgeting

1. It ensures that all activities and programmes and their alternatives have been evaluated by the manager. This helps to allocate resources according to priority of the programmes as only the best programme is considered.
2. Zero Base Budgeting starts from the scratch each year and hence it can eliminate the unnecessary activities/ expenses that traditional budgeting often results in. This improves resource allocation and profitability of the organization.
3. The Zero Base approach requires integrated linkages to long-range plans and strategies. By constant reiteration of the process, both plan and budget are brought into consonance. Also, the plan is more responsive to market needs and more sensitive to profits.
4. The Zero Base budgeting techniques facilitate rational analysis and decision-making. Decision packages are ranked in order of importance.

Performance Budgeting

Performance budgeting involves the development of refined management tools (such as work measurement performance) so as to achieve the specific goals of the business over a period of time. The emphasis in performance budgeting is on the improvement of internal management, keeping in view the volume of work and its cost, that has to be accomplished during a financial year.

Performance budgeting is a convenient tool in the hands of management to achieve the objectives of an organization. In the short-run, it lays immediate stress on achieving the objectives as specified in the budget. In the long-run, it serves both as a tool for reviewing the efficiency of existing operations and their results and as a system of feeding the data for planning future services. It helps in making the organization sensitive and adaptive to the dynamic needs of the organization.

The first step in the technique of performance budgeting is the establishment, improvement and extenstion towards the programmes which help in achieving the specific and overall goals of the organization. The resources to be used should be clearly specified so that the financial responsibility at every level within the organization can be clearly specified.

The second step towards performance budgeting is to develop a yardstick for work measurement and also for determining performance standards. The most suitable method for a given performance should be devised and the aim should be to move towards higher levels of perfection. Suitable standards should be determined and variances between the actual and the budgeted may suggest the need for remedial action, thereby increasing the value of budget control.

The final step in performance budgeting is preparing the record keeping along functional lines. These records would indicate the variance between budgeted and actual costs. This helps the management in taking suitable action to correct the variances.

Thus, performance budgeting helps to organize the work in a systematic and scientific manner. It helps to provide information for the effective and efficient working of the organization towards the achievement of the business objectives of an organization.

Questions

1. Why is the concept of budgetary control important?
2. Why is the preparation of a cash budget important to a company?

3. Review the meaning of the following concepts discussed in this chapter:
   (a) Budgets as planning tools.
   (b) Budgets as control tools.
   (c) Cash Budget.
   (d) Master Budget.
4. Why is the sales forecast so important in developing the master budget?
5. Can budgeting and budgetary control lead to better management of an organisation? Explain.
6. "Budgeting leads to unnecessary spending". Do you agree? Elucidiate with examples.
7. What is Zero-base budgeting and what are its advantages?
8. What is performance budgeting? When can it be used.
9. Briefly explain the basic information needed to prepare a proper budgetary report.
10. "The ideal starting point for developing next years budget is our current budget". Do you agree? Explain with example.

13

Standard Costing and Variance Analysis

Control through standards and standards costs is considered by management to be a creative programme aimed at determining whether the resources of the organization are being used optimally or not. Standard costing is a system of accounting which makes use of predetermined standard costs for direct material, direct labour and factory overhead. Standard costs are usually determined during the budgetary control process because they are useful in preparing the flexible budgets and in evaluating performance. They help in setting realistic prices and in identifying the production costs that need to be controlled. A comparison of the actual costs with the standard costs gives us the variance. Correctly analyzed, variances show how adverse tendencies can be corrected. The present chapter discusses the technique of Standard Costing and Variance Analysis, which is aimed at profit improvement mainly by reducing materials, labour and overhead costs.

Definition of Standard Cost and Standard Costing

A standard cost is a scientifically predetermined cost that is usually expressed on a per unit basis. The Institute of Cost and Management Accountants (U.K.) defines standard costs as "a predetermined cost which is calculated from management's standards of efficient operation and the relevant necessary expenditure. It may be used as a basis for price fixing and for cost control through variance analysis".

The determination of standard cost is based on technical estimates for materials, labour and overhead for a selected period of time and for a prescribed set of working conditions.

The Institute of Cost and Management Accountants (UK) defines standard costing as "the preparation and use of standard cost, their comparison with actual cost and the analysis of variances to their causes and points of incidence."

Nature and Purpose of Standard Costs

The main purpose of standard costs is to provide management with information on the day-to-day control of operations. Standard costs are predetermined costs to provide a basis for more effective control over costs. The standard costs provide an indication of the criterion by which something can be analyzed. Actual costs are costs which have been incurred by the business. The difference between actual costs and standard costs is known as variance. The variances are identified and analyzed carefully, and are reported to managers for taking suitable corrective action. Thus, a standard cost accounting system can help a company to save money by setting realistic prices and reducing inefficiency.

Objectives of Using Standard Costs

The various objectives of using a standard costing system in an organization are:-

1. To control costs mainly by setting standards for each type of cost incurred - material, labour and overhead. It also helps in analyzing variances and hence judging the effectiveness of managers in controlling the costs for which they are held responsible.

2. To help in setting Budgets.

3. To provide useful and detailed information for managerial planning and decision-making.

4. Helps in assessing the performance and efficiency of the staff and management.

5. Standard costing is a control technique which follows the feedback control cycle. The feedback system may help in eliminating unwanted costs in the future and hence a possible reduction in the costs incurred can be achieved.

Advantage of Standard Costs

The following are some of the more important advantages of standard cost:

1. Standard costs serve as a yardstick against which actual costs can be compared. The difference between standard cost and actual cost is called variance. For proper control and performance measurement in the organisation variances should be measured and analyzed. This also ensures that regular checks are made upon the expenditure incurred.

2. If immediate attention is taken of the variances, control over costs in greatly facilitated. A proper standard costing system specifically helps in cost control and cost reduction.

3. Standard costs help in motivating the employees as the system can be used to provide an incentive scheme to the employees where the variance is minimum.

4. Production and pricing policies are formulated with certainty. This helps to keep the costs in-check.

5. If the standards are constantly being studied and revised they serve as a reliable basis for evaluating performance and controlling costs.

Type of Standards

Two important aspects which should be taken into account in selecting standards are (1) Is it possible to achieve the standards? i.e. are the standards attainable and (2) Frequency with which the standards are revised.

Four different concepts of standards are discussed below:

1. **Ideal Standards:** Also called perfect standards, they are established on a maximum efficiency level with no unplanned work stoppages. Ideal standards are tight standards which in practice may never be obtained as they do not provide for waste and inefficiency in any form. They represent the level of attainment that could be reached if all the conditions were perfect all of the time. Ideal standards are effective only when the individuals are aware and are rewarded for achieving a certain percentage (e.g. 90 per cent) of the standard.

2. **Basic Standards:** Basic standards are long-term standards and they remain the same after being computed for the first time. They are projections that are seldom revised or updated to reflect changes in products, prices and methods. Basic standards provide the base for comparing actual costs over time with a constant standard and are used primarily to measure trends in operating performance.

3. **Normal Standards:** These are average standards and are based on the performance achieved by a company during the last 3-4 years. These standards are set on a normal capacity which tends to average out the Company's peak and slack periods. Since these standards are easily attainable and do not reflect the goals to be attained, they are generally not used by organizations.

4. **Currently Attainable Standards:** A currently attainable standard is one that represents optimum attainable performance. It can be achieved with reasonable effort, i.e., if the firm operates with a "high" degree of efficiency and effectiveness. These standards make proper allowances for normal recurring interferences such as machine breakdown, delays, rest periods, unavoidable waste etc. It is assumed that these are unavoidable interferences and are a fact of life. However, allow-

ances are not made for any avoidable interferences with output.

The currently attainable standard is the most popular standard and they are acceptable to employees as they provide a definite goal and challenge to them.

Variance Analysis

Standard costs (SC) are an indication of what costs should be for a unit of production. The difference between actual cost (AC) and standard cost (SC) is called a variance. Variances can be analyzed to determine why they exist and this analysis can provide a basis for taking corrective action. If the actual cost is greater than the standard cost, the variance is unfavourable, if actual is less than the standard, the variance is favourable.

AC > SC = Unfavourable Variance

AC < SC = Favourable Variance

A system of variance analysis helps in identifying the difference in terms of costs between actual performance and desired performance and hence helps to pinpont efficient and inefficient operating areas. It helps in assigning responsibility to individuals and also helps to motivate individuals to achieve the performance targets.

The technique of variance analysis also helps to isolate the causes of differences between actual costs and standard costs. For proper control both favourable and unfavourable variance should be analyzed. The causes for the occurrence of variances alongwith the individuals responsible for variance can also be identified and analyzed. Hence the system of variance analysis helps management to find answers to the following two questions:

1. Are the variance due to loose or tight standards?
2. Have the standards been set scientifically?

The technique of variance analysis also helps management to rely on the principle of management by exception. Management is usually not concerned with analyzing all the performance reports. Rather, the management may decide that performance within ± 3 per cent of budget or standards is acceptable when examining performance reports. The management only examines more cost areas where differences exceed these limit.

Variances can be divided into three main broad categories:

I. Material Variances.

II. Labour Variances.

III. Overhead Variances.

I. Material Variances

Material variances include two factors: (1) the quantity of materials that should have been used to produce one unit of output and (2) the prices that should have been paid in acquiring this quantity of materials. The total material cost variance may result from difference between standard and actual quantities of materials used or between standard and actual prices paid for materials, or from a combination of these two factors.

Material Cost Variance : Material Cost Variance (MCV) is calculated as the difference between the standard cost of direct materials and the actual cost of direct materials for actual output.

MCV = (SQ for Actual Output x SP -AQ x AP)

where SQ = Standard quantity

AQ = Actual quantity

SP = Standard price

AP = Actual price

Material cost variance can be divided into Direct Material Price Variance and Direct Material Quantity Variance. The Material Price Variance is the difference between the standard price and the actual price multiplied by the actual quantity purchased. The Material Quantity Variance is the difference between the standard quantity used and the actual quantity multiplied by the standard price.

1. Material price variance (MPV) = Actual Quantity (Standard price- Actual price)
   = AQ (SP - AP)

2. Material quantity variance (MQV) = Standard Price (Standard quantity - Actual quantity)
   = SP (SQ - AQ)

Example

From the material related information giver below calculate the various material variances for the XYZ Company for the month of October:

	Standard					
	Quantity (kilos)	Unit Price	Total	Quantity (kilos)	Actual Unit Price	Total
Material X	5	3,00	15.00	4	3.00	12.00
Material Y	3	2.00	6.00	4	1.00	4.00

Solution MCV = MPV + MQV

MPV = Actual Quantity (Standard Price - Actual Price)

X = 4 (3 - 3) = zero

Y = 4 (2 - 1) = 4 (Favourable)

Total = 4 (Favourable)

MQV = Standard Price (Standard quantity - Actual quantity)

X = 3 (5 - 4) = 3 (Favourable)

Y = 2 (3 - 4) = 2 (Unfavourable)

Total = 1 Favourable

$$\text{DMCV} = \left(\text{Standard Price} \times \begin{matrix}\text{Standard}\\ \text{Quantity for}\\ \text{Actual output}\end{matrix}\right) - \left(\text{Actual Price} \quad \text{Actual Quantity}\right)$$

X = (3 x 5) - (3 x 4) = 15 - 12 = 3 (Favourable)
Y = (2 x 3) - (1 x 4) = 6 - 4 = 2 (Favourable)
5 (Favourable)

Thus MCV = MPV + MQV

5 (F) = 4 (F) + 1 (F)

5 (F) = 5 (F)

Material quantity or usage variance can be futher subdivided into two more variances, viz.,

1. Material Mix Variance

2. Material Yield Variance.

1. Material Mix Variance is that portion of the material quantity variance which arises due to the difference between the standard mix and the actual mix of different materials used in production. Material mix variance can be calculated as

Material mix variance

$$= \text{Total actual quantity} \left(\text{Standard price of standard mix} - \text{Standard price of actual mix} \right)$$

Alternatively, material mix variance can also be calculated as:

Material mix variance

$$= \text{Standard price} \left(\text{Revised standard quantity} - \text{Actual quantity} \right)$$

where,

Revised standard quantity (RSQ)

$$= \frac{\text{Standard qty. of each material}}{\text{Total standard quantity}} \times \text{Total actual quantity}$$

2. Material Yield Variance : Material yield variance arises due to the difference bewteen the standard yield (output) specified and the actual yield obtained. If the actual yield is greater than the standard yield, the variance is favourable and vice versa.

Material yield variance can be expressed as:

Material yield variance =

$$\begin{matrix}\text{Standard} \\ \text{rate per} \\ \text{unit of yield}\end{matrix} \left(\begin{matrix}\text{Actual} \\ \text{yield}\end{matrix} - \begin{matrix}\text{Standard} \\ \text{yield}\end{matrix} \right)$$

In the above example the Material Price Variance was favourable because the actual price of the materials purchased was less than the standard price. The quantity variance was also favourable since the actual quantity used was less than the standard prescribed. The responsibility for price variances generally lie with the purchasing department while the production department is responsible for quantity variances.

Labour Variances

The total labour cost variance is the difference between the actual labour costs incurred and the standard labour cost for the actual units produced. If the standard labour cost of actual output exceeds the actual labour cost, the variance is favourable and vice versa

Labour cost variance = [Standard hours for actual output × Standard rate – Actual hours × Actual rate]

Labour cost variance can be divided into labour rate variance and labour efficiency variance. Labour rate variance is the difference between the standard laboru rate and actual labour rate multiplied by the actual labour hours worked. The labour efficiency variance is the difference between standard hours worked specified for actual output and the actual labour hours worked. It is calculated by multiplying the difference between standard and actual hours by the standard rate per hour.

1. Labour Rate = Actual Time (Standard rate - Actual rate) Variance
2. Labour Efficiency = Standard rate (Standard time variance - Actual time)

Labour Rate Variance

This variance arises when labour is paid at a rate different from the standard wage rate. A rate variance usually occurs when a person is paid at a rate higher or lower than expected. The causes for labour rate variance are :-

- Payment at a rate higher or lower than the standard rate
- Change in the grades of employees
- Inclusion of new workmen
- Change in the method of compensation etc.

Labour Efficiency Variance

The time taken to do a job indicates the efficiency of workers. Hence the variance arises due to the difference between actual time worked and hours which should have been worked. This variance can usually be traced to departmental supervisions. An example would be when a highly paid worker performs a lower level task. The causes for labour efficiency variance are:

- Change in the skill-grade of the workers
- Extent of supervision
- Change in the method of production
- Change in tools
- Quality of materials
- Working conditions, etc.

Like Material Quantity Variance, Labour Efficiency Variance can also be divided into two types.

(1) **Labour Mix Variance:** That portion of direct labour efficiency variance which is due to the difference be-

tween standard and actual gang composition of the workers. It is calculated as:

$$\text{Standard rate} \times \left(\begin{matrix}\text{Revised} \\ \text{Standard} \\ \text{Time}\end{matrix} - \begin{matrix}\text{Actual} \\ \text{Time}\end{matrix} \right)$$

$$\text{Revised standard time} = \frac{\text{Total time of actual workers}}{\text{Total time of standard worker}} \times \text{Standard time}$$

(2) **Labour Yield Variance:** That portion of direct labour efficiency variance which is due to the difference between the standard yield specified and the actual yield obtained. It is calculated as:

$$\begin{matrix}\text{Standard} \\ \text{cost per unit}\end{matrix} = \begin{matrix}\text{Standard output} \\ \text{for actual unit} \\ \text{units}\end{matrix} \times \begin{matrix}\text{Actual} \\ \text{output}\end{matrix}$$

Example

The various Labour variances from the following labour related information for the XYZ Company for the month of October can be calculated as below :

Actual data

Hours worked = 6,000

Labour rate = Rs. 25/- per hour

Standard data

Hours worked = 4,000

Labour rate = Rs. 40/- per hour

Solution

Labour cost = (Standard hours for Actual output × Standard rate) – Actual hours × Actual rate)

Variance = (4,000 × Rs. 40) – (6,000 × Rs. 35)

= 1,60,000 – 1,50,000 = Rs. 10,000 (Favourable)

Labour rate = Actual Time (Standard rate – Actual rate)

Variance		6,000 (Rs. 40 – Rs. 25) = Rs. 90,000 (Favourable)
Labour Efficiency	=	Standard rate (Standard time – Actual time)
Variance		Rs. 40 (4,000 - 6,000) = Rs. 80,000 (A)
LCV	=	LRV + LEV or 10,000 (F)
	=	90,000 (F) + 80,000 (A) = 10,000 (F)

Overhead Variances

Controlling overhead costs is more difficult and complex than controlling direct materials and direct labour costs because it is difficult to assign the responsibility for overhead costs.

The total overhead cost variance can be sub-divided into a budget or spending variance* and an efficiency variance. The budget or spending variance is the difference between the budget and the actual cost for the actual hours of operation. This variance can be compared to the price and quantity variance developed for direct material and direct labour.

The efficiency variance measures efficiency in the use of the factor, e.g., machine hours employed in costing overheads to the products.

The formula for calculating the various overhead variances are as follows:

(a) Standard Rate per unit $= \dfrac{\text{Budgeted overheads}}{\text{Budgeted output}}$

(b) Standard Rate per hour $= \dfrac{\text{Budgeted overheads}}{\text{Budgeted hours}}$

(c) Standard hours for actual output $= \dfrac{\text{Budgeted output}}{\text{Budgeted hours}} \times \text{Actual Output}$

(d) Standard output for actual time $= \dfrac{\text{Budgeted output}}{\text{Budgeted hours}} \times \text{Actual output}$

* The budget or spending variance measure (1) the differences between the standard prices and actual prices of manufacturing overhead materials and services and (2) the difference between the standard and actual quantities used. Example

(e)	Recovered or Absorbed Overheads	= Standard rate × Actual Output
(f)	Budgeted Overheads	= Standard rate per unit × Budgeted output or Standard rate per hour × Budgeted hours
(g)	Standard Overheads	= Standard rate per unit × Standard output for actual time or Standard rate per hours × Actual output
(h)	Actual Overheads	= Actual rate per unit × Actual output or Actual rate per unit × Actual hours

The various overhead variances can now be put as follows:

Total overhead cost variance = Recovered overheads - Actual overheads

The total overhead cost variance may be segregated into.

(i) Variable overhead cost variance =
Recovered variable overheads – Actual variable overheads

(ii) Fixed overhead cost variance =
Recovered fixed overheads – Actual fixed overheads

Fixed overheads cost variance can be segregated into:

(i) Expenditure Variance =
Budgeted overheads – Actual overheads

(ii) Volume Variance = Recovered overheads – Budgeted overheads

Volume variance may be segregated into:

(i) Efficiency variance = Recovered overheads – Standard overheads

(ii) Capacity variance =Standard overheads – Budgeted overheads

The reasons for the overhead variance are:-

Fixed Overhead Expenditure Variance	Spending more money than budgeted
Fixed Overhead Volume Variance	Change in demand; Interruption of stoppage of work due to defective planning, shortage of material, absence of or faulty instructions, etc.
Fixed overhead	Actual efficiency in operations

Efficiency Variance	not as expected
Capacity Variance	Change in utilization of capacity from Lack of demand Lack of power Lack of raw materials etc.

For the XYZ Company for the month of October, calculate the various overhead variances from the information given below:

Normal overhead rate	=	Rs. 2/-
Actual hours operated	=	20,000
Allowed hours for actual Production	=	22,000
Allowed overheads for budgeted hours	=	Rs. 60,000
Actual overheads	=	Rs .62,000

Solution

Budgeted overhead = Rs. 60,000

Recovered overhead = Standard rate per hour x Standard hours for actual output.

= 2 x 22,000 = Rs. 44,000

Standard overhead = Standard rate per hour x Actual hours

= 2 x 20,000 = Rs. 40,000

Overhead cost = Recovered overhead - Actual overhead

Variance = 44,000 - 62,000

= 18,000 (Unfavourable)

The total overhead cost variance can be analyzed into a budget or spending variance and a volume variance.

Overhead Spending variance

= Budgeted overheads - Actual overheads

= 60,000 - 62,000

= 2,000 (Unfavourable)

Overhead Volume variance

= Recovered overheads - Budgeted overheads

= 44,000 - 60,000

= 16,000 (Unfavourable)

Exhibit I shows the total variances that have been discussed.

Interpreting through Variance Analysis

As noted earlier, a variance exists when standard costs differ from actual costs. The difference between standard cost and actual cost is called a cost variance. Cost variance for material labour and overhead result from a variety of different causes. Hence, in evaluating the efficiency of a manufacturing organization, these variances should be measured and analyzed. Every manager should try and answer two important questions regarding every variance:

1. Is the variance significant?

Management should accept variance as a rule rather than the exception. The probability that actual quantities and prices will exactly match the standard are very much remote. Also, management must decide when a particular variance has to be investigated or when variances should be ignored.

The basic criterion here is the magnitude of the variance, i.e., is a variance large enough to require investigation. For example, some managements may decide that variances under 10 per cent of standard need not be investigated.

Another criterion relates to the consistency of occurrence. A once-in-a-while variance of Rs.1,000 may not be as significant as a Rs. 500 variation that recurs frequently.

A third criterion relates to the management's ability to control the variance. If the variances are beyond the control of

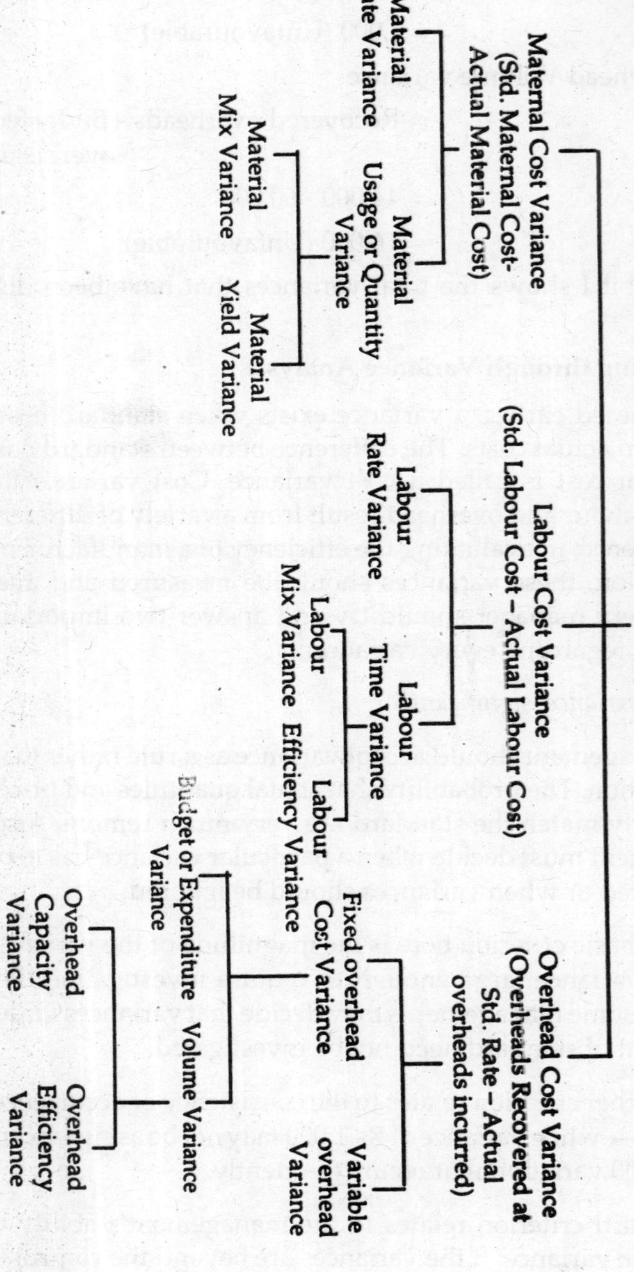
Total Cost Variance
Maternal Cost Variance (Std. Maternal Cost- Actual Material Cost)
Material Rate Variance
Material Usage or Quantity Variance
Material Mix Variance
Material Yield Variance
Labour Cost Variance (Std. Labour Cost – Actual Labour Cost)
Labour Rate Variance
Labour Time Variance
Labour Mix Variance
Labour Efficiency Variance
Overhead Cost Variance (Overheads Recovered at Std. Rate – Actual overheads incurred)
Fixed overhead Cost Variance
Variable overhead Variance
Budget or Expenditure Variance
Volume Variance
Overhead Capacity Variance
Overhead Efficiency Variance

Exhibit I

the management, the management has no choice but to forget about the variances.

Hence variances should be analyzed when the expected saving through investigation appears to be greater than the expected cost of conducting the investigation.

2. What action should be taken?

Variance analysis helps in the determination of the causes of the variance. Management should get to the causes of variances before praising or belittling managers. If variances are favourable, the causes should be found. Whether the cause is due to a loose standard or truly effective management. Similarly, unfavourable variances should be investigated. Are the causes beyond the control of the management due to certain unexpected changes, e.g., price increases, rush orders, etc.

Hence, all significant variances should be investigated and corrective action taken to find out why the variance occurred. Probably, with better control, the variance can be eliminated or reduced in the future. If the standards are unrealistic, they should be revised.

Evaluation of Cost Variance

Six separate cost variances have been computed till now for the XYZ Company for the month of October. These variances are summarized as given below:

Material Price variance	= favourable — Rs. 4,000
Material Quantity variance	= favourable — Rs. 1,000
Total material variance	= favourable — Rs. 5,000
Labour rate variance	= favourable — Rs. 90,000
Labour efficiency variance	= unfavourable — 80,000
Total Labour variance	= favourable — Rs. 10,000
Overhead spending variance	= unfavourable — Rs. (2,000)
Overhead volume variance	= unfavourable — Rs. (16,000)

Total overhead variance = unfavourable — Rs. (18,000)

Net unfavourable cost variance in October — Rs. (12,900)

The above summary of cost variances can help managers in identifying problem areas and in controlling costs in the future months. For example a favourable material price and quantity variance indicates that the purchasing and production departments are using material in a very efficient manner*.

However, the production manager has a serious problem regarding labour efficiency variance. The actual time being taken by the workers is much more than the standard time allowed to produce a given amount of product.

Unfavourable labour efficiency variances can be caused by a management decision to use poorly trained workers or poorly maintained machinery or by downtime resulting from the use of low-quality materials. In some cases, generaally bad working conditions and low employee morale may also adversely affect the efficiency of the workers. A favourable labour rate variance may signify that lower paid (or lower skilled) workers were used or that actual wage rates are below the standard labour rates.

An unfavourable overhead spending variance indicates excessive levels of expenditure. This could have resulted both from increasing prics of goods and services used and from excessive consumption of these goods and services. An unfavourable overhead volume variance indicates that the factors employed or the activity base used in costing overheads to the products has been used inefficiently.

---

* A favourable material price variance indicates that the manager responsible for material purchases paid less per unit than the price allowed by the standards. This may be a result of receiving discounts, effective bargaining or scme other factor. In some cases when a favourable price variance may be due to bulk purchases or purchase of materials of substandard quality, the manager's performance will be questioned. A favourable material quality variance may be due to factors such as less material waste than allowed by the standards, better than expected machine efficiency, more efficient use of raw materials, etc.

Review Problem

I. Good Luck Ltd. has a manufacturing division which makes a product to which the following details relate:

Per unit

Materials	5 kg. at Rs. 3/-	Rs. 15
Direct Labour	10 hours at Rs. 2/-	Rs. 20
Variable overhead	10 hours at Rs. 2/-	Rs. 10

Relevant fixed overheads are budgeted at Rs. 8,000 per month and planned output is 2,000 units per month. The selling price is Rs. 50/- per unit.

An incentive scheme is in operation in the division concerned whereby employees are paid a bonus of 10% of the standard cost of materials saved and 40% of direct labour time saved valued at standard direct labour hour rate. During a recent month when output was 1,700 units, the following actual results were recorded:

Direct materials used (8,000 kg)	24,800
Direct wages (18,000 hours @ Rs.2.20 per hour)	39,600
Variable overhead	20,000
Fixed overhead	10,000

(a) Calculate the variance which occurred during the month.

(b) Calculate the total bonus payment to the employees.

Solution: Material Variances

MCV = MPV + MQV

Material Price Variance (MPV)

AQ (SR - AR)

AQ × SR - AQ × AR

(8,000 x 3) - (24,800)

24,000 - 24,800

800 (A)

Material Quantity Variance (MQV)

SR (SQ - AQ)

3 (8,500 - 8,000)

3 (500)

1500 (F)

Material Cost Variance (MCV)

(SR × SQ) - (AR × AQ)

25,500 - 24,800

= 700 (F)

Notes:

1. AQ = 1,700 × 5 = 8,500 kg
2. SQ × SR = 8,500 × 3 = Rs. 25,500

Labour Variances

LCV = LRV + LEV

Labour Rate Variance (LRV)

AH (SR - AR)

18,000 (2 - 2.20)

3600 A

Labour Efficiency Variance (LEV)

SR (SM - AH)

2 (17,000 - 18,000)

2,000 A

Labour Cost Variance (LCV)

$(SR \times SH) - (AR \times AH)$

$(2 \times 17{,}000) - (2.20 \times 18{,}000)$

(34,000) - (39,600)

5,600 A

Notes:

1. SR = 1,700 x 10 = 17,000 hours

2. $SQ \times SR = (1{,}700 \times 10 = 17{,}000$ hours at Rs. 2 = Rs. 34,000)

Variable overhead Variancies

VOHV = VOH Exp. V + VOH Eff. V

Expenditure or Spending Variance (VOH Exp. V)

= (Standard variable overheads - Actual variable overheads)

$= (1800 \times 10) - (20{,}000)$

= 18,000 - 20,000

= 2,000 (A)

Efficiency Variance (VOH Eff. V)

= Standard Variable overhead rate per hour (AQ - SQ)

= 10 (1700 - 1800)

= 1000 (A)

Variable Overhead Variance (VOHV) = Recovered variable overheads - Actual variable overheads

= 17,000 - 20,000

= 3,000 (A)

$$\frac{\text{Actual Hrs. worked}}{\text{Std. time per unit (hrs)}} = \frac{18{,}000\text{S Q}}{10} = 1800 \text{ units}$$

Fixed overhead Variances

Fixed overhead Expenditure Variance

= Budgeted Fixed overheds - Actual Fixed overheads

= 8,000 - 10,000

= 2,000 (A)

Fixed overhead Volume Variance

= SR (Actual output - Budgeted output)

= 4 (1700 - 2,000)

= 1200 (A)

Fixed overhead Cost Variance

= Recovered Fixed overheads - Actual Fixed Overheads

= 6,800 - 10,000

= 3,200 (A)

Recovered fixed overheads = 1700 × 4 = Rs. 6,800

Std. fixed overhead rate per unit

$$= \frac{\text{Budgeted Fixed overheads}}{\text{Budgeted output}}$$

Fixed Overhead Volume Variance can be divided into two types:

1. Fixed overhead Efficiency Variance = SR (AQ - SQ)
2. Fixed overhead Capacity Variance = SR (SQ - BQ)

= 4 (2000 - 1800)

= 800 (A)

Variable overhead Variance

Variable overhead cost Variance = Standard variable overhead cost - Actual variable overhead cost

$= 1700 \times 10 - 20{,}000$

= 3,000 (A Variable overhead spending Variance = Actual Hours Std. Variable overhead rate - Actual variable overhead rate).

$= 18000 \times 1 - 20{,}000$

= 2,000 (A)

Variable overhead Efficiency Variance = Standard Variable overhead rate (Std. Hours - Actual Hours)

= 1 (17000 - 18000)

= 1,000 (A)

Bonus

Material Quantity Variance = 1,500 (F)

Bonus $1500 \times 10\% = 150$

Standard Cost of labour = 2,000 (A)

Since the labour efficiency Variance is negative, no bonus is paid to the workers.

Hence total Bonus payment to the employees = Rs. 150/-

II. The following standards have been set to manufacture a product:

Direct materials (2 kg at Rs. 4/- per unit) Rs. 8/-

Direct labour (10 hours at Rs. 8/- per hour) Rs. 80/-

In June, when 4,000 units were manufactured the following actual results were recorded:

Direct materials purchased (8,000 kg. at Rs. 4.20 per unit)

Material used 7,900 kg.

Direct Labour

(39,700 hrs at Rs. 8.10 per hour)

Calculate the variances which occurred during the month.

Solution:

Material Price Variance

AQ (SR - AR)

= 8,000 (4.00 - 4.20)

= Rs. 1,600 (A)

Material Quantity Variance

SR (SQ - AQ)

= 4.00 (8,000* - 7,900)

= Rs. 400 (F)

Labour rate Variance

AH (SR - AR)

= 39,700 (8.00 - 8.10)

= Rs. 3,970 (A)

Labour Efficiency Variance

SR (SH - AH)

= 8.00 (40,000 - 39,700)

= 2,400 (F)

Summary Statement of all the Variances

Material Price Variance	Rs. 1,600 (A)
Material Quantity Variance	400 (F)
Net Material Variance	Rs. 1,200 (A)
Labour Rate Variance	Rs. 3,970 (A)

* 4,000 units × 2 kg. per unit = 8,000

Labour Efficiency Variance	2,400 (F)
Net Labour Variance	Rs. 1,570 (A)

III. Shipco Manufacturing Company has a standard cost system and keeps all cost standards up-to-date. The standard variable costs for one unit of finished product are:

Direct Materials (3 kg. @ Rs. 12.50 per kg.)	Rs. 37.50
Direct Labour (1.2 hr. @ Rs. 9.00 hr.)	10.80
Variable overhead (1.2 hr. @ Rs. 5.00)	6.00
Standard variable cost per unit	Rs. 54.30

Normal capacity is 15,000 direct labour hours, and budgeted fixed overhead costs for the year were Rs. 54,000. During the year, the company produced and sold 12,200 units. Related transactions and actual cost data for the year were as follows:

Direct materials consisted of 37,500 kg. purchased and used; unit purchase cost was Rs. 12.40 per kg. Direct labour consisted of 15,250 direct labour hours worked at an average labour rate of Rs. 9.20 per hour. Actual factory overhead costs incurred for the period consisted of variable overhead costs of Rs. 73,200 and fixed overhead costs of Rs. 55,000.

Using the data given, compute the following:

1. Standard hours allowed.
2. Standard fixed overhead rate.
3. Direct matrerials price variance.
4. Direct materials quantity variance.
5. Direct labour rate variance.
6. Direct labour efficiency variance.
7. Overhead spending variance.
8. Overhead efficiency variance.

9. Controllable overhead variance.
10. Overhead volume variance.

Solution

1. Standard hours allowed = good units produced x standard direct labour hours per unit.

   12,200 units × 1.2 direct labour hours / unit = 14,640 hours

2. Standard fixed overhead rate = budgeted fixed overhead cost / normal capacity

   = Rs. 54,000

   15,000 direct labour hours

   = R. 3.60 per direct labour hour

3. **Direct materials price variance:**

Price difference:	Actual price paid	Rs. 12.40/kg.
	Less standard price	12.50/kg.
	Difference	Rs. .10(F)

   Direct materials price variance = (actual price - standard price) × actual quantity.

   = Rs. .10 (F) × 37,500 per kg.

   = Rs. 3,750 (F)

4. **Direct materials quantity variance:**

Quantity difference:	Actual quantity used	37,500 Kgs.
	Less standard quantity (12,200 units × 3 kgs.)	36,600 Kgs.
	Difference	900 (A)

   Direct materials quantity variance = (actual quantity - standard quantity) × standard price

   = 900 (A) × Rs. 12.50 / per kg.

   = Rs. 11,250 (A)

5. **Direct labour rate variance:**

Rate difference:	Actual labour rate	Rs. 9.20/hr.
	Less standard labour rate	9.00/hr.
	Difference	Re. .20 (U)

   Direct labour rate variance = (actual rate - standard rate) × actual hours

= Rs. .20 (A) × 15,250 hours

= Rs. 3,050 (A)

6. **Direct labour efficiency variance:**

Difference in hours: Actual hours worked 15,250 hr.

Less standard hours allowed 14,640 hr.*

Difference 610 (A)

Direct labour efficiency variance = (actual hours - standard hours allowed) × standard rate

= 610 hr. (A) × Rs. 9.00/hr.

= Rs. 5,490 (A)

*12,200 units produced × 1.2 hr. per unit = 14,640 hr.

Difference Re. .10(F)

7. **Overhead spending variance:**

Overhead costs incurred		
Variable	Rs. 73,200	
Fixed	55,000	Rs. 128,200
Less flexible budget for effort expended		
Actual hours worked × variable overhead rate		
15,250 labour hours × Rs. 5/hour		
	Rs. 76,250	
Plus budgeted fixed costs	54,000	130,250
Overhead spending variance		Rs. 2,050 (F)

8. **Overhead efficiency variance:**

Flexible budget for effort expended		
(see computation in 7 above)		Rs. 130,250
Less flexible budget at level of achieved performance		
Standard hours allowed × variable overhead rate		
14,640 labour hours × Rs. 5/hour		
	Rs. 73,200	
Plus budgeted fixed costs	54,000	127,200
Overhead efficiency variance		Rs. 3,050 (A)

9. **Controllable overhead variance:**

Actual overhead incurred		Rs. 128,200
Less budgeted factory overhead for 14,640 hours:		
Variable overhead cost		
(14,640 hr. × Rs. 5.00/direct labour hours)	Rs. 73,200	
Budgeted fixed factory overhead	54,000	
Total budgeted factory overhead		127,200
Controllable overhead variance		Rs. 1,000 (A)

10. **Overhead volume variance:**

Total budgeted factory overhead (see calculation in 9)		Rs. 127,200
(see calculation in 9)		
Less factory overhead applied:		
Variable: 14,640 hr. × Rs. 5.00 /direct labour hour	Rs. 73,200	
Fixed: 14,640 hr. x Rs. 3.60 / direct labour hour		52,704
Total factory overhead applied		125,904
Overhead volume variance		Rs. 1,296 (A)

IV. A Company presents the following variance data for the month:

	Material A	Material B	Material C
Material Price Variance	Rs. 44,000 F	Rs. 20,000 F	Rs. 24,000 F
Materiala Quantity Variance	40,000 A	30,000 A	40,000 A
Net Material Variance	Rs. 4,000 F	Rs. 10,000 A	Rs. 16,000 A
Units Produced requiring this material	50,000	90,000	160,000

Two kgs. of each kind of material are allowed for each unit of output requiring that kind of material. For material A, the average price paid was Re. 0.40 per kg. less than standard; for marterial B, Re. .10 less; for material C, Re. .06 greater. There are no opening or closing inventories of any kind of material (that is, materials are purchased and used in the same period).

For each of the three materials, calculate the following:

a. Number of kg. of material purchased.

b. Standard cost per kg. of material.

c. Total standard material cost.

Solution:

Material A:

a. Price variance = Re. .40 per kg.

Total price variance = Rs. 44,000 F.

Kg. purchased and used = Rs. 44,000 / Re. .40

= 110,000

b. Standard kg. allowed for:

50,000 units = 100,000

Used over standard = 110,000-100,000 = 10,000

Quantity variance = 40,000 (A)

Standard unit price = Rs. 40,000 / 10,000 = Rs. 4.00

c: Total standard matrerial cost:

= 100,000 kg. × Rs. 4.00 per kg. = Rs. 400,000

Material B:

a. Kg. purchased and used

$$\frac{\text{Rs. } 20{,}000}{\text{Rs. } 10} = 200{,}000$$

b. Standard unit price

= Rs. 30,000 / (200,000 -180,000)

$$= \frac{\text{Rs. } 30{,}000}{20{,}000} = \text{Rs. } 1.5$$

c. Total standard material cost:

= 180,000 kg. x Rs. 1.5 = Rs. 270,000

Material C:

a. Kg. purchased & used:

$$= \frac{\text{Rs. } 24{,}000}{\text{Re. } .06} = 400{,}000$$

b. Standard unit price = Rs. 40,000

(400,000 - 320,000)

$$= \frac{\text{Rs. } 40{,}000}{80{,}000} = \text{Re. } 0.5$$

c. Total standard material cost:

= 320,000 × Re. 0.5 x Rs. 160,000

1. Overhead Variance:

V. AK Ltd. combined fixed and variable overhead costs are as follows:

Overhead Applied	Rs. 90,000
Flexible Budget Overhead	Rs. 95,000
Actual Overhead	Rs. 97,000

a. What is the amount of under or over applied overhead, assuming that full absorption costing was used?

b. What is the production volume variance?

Solution:

Actual Cost	Flexible Budget	Overhead Applied
Rs.97,000	Rs. 95,000	Rs. 90,000
	Under applied overhead Rs. 6,000 (A)	
		Production Volume Variance Rs. 5,000 (A)

VI. Overhead Variance:

Omega Company has record the following overhead informations for the current year:

Budgeted fixed overhead Rs. 5,100

Actual overhead incurred Rs. 15,200 of which Rs. 5,500 is fixed.

Variable overhead rate per direct labour hour Rs. 2

Standard hours allowed for actual production 5,600

Actuala labour hours used 5,400 hours

Calculate:

a. the fixed overhead price variance.

b. variable overhead price or spending variance.

c. variable overhead efficiency variance.

Solution:

1. Fixed overhead price variance

= [Actual fixed overheads-Budgeted fixed overhead]

5,600-5,100 = Rs. 500 (A)

2. Variable overhead price or spending variance

= Actual variable overhead - Actual hours at standard overhead rate

[(Rs. 15,200 - 5,500) - (Rs. 2 × 5,600)]

[Rs. 9,700 - Rs. 11,200] = 1500 (F)

Variable overhead efficiency variance:

(Actual hours × standard overhead rate) - (Standard overhead rate on actual production)

(2 × 5,400) - (2 × 5,600)

10,800 - 11,200

= 400 F

VII. Following is the direct material cost for product X:

Standard price per materials unit	= Rs. 4.50
Actual quantity used	= Rs. 2,600
Standard quantity allowed for production	= Rs. 2,300
Materials price variance	= Rs. 390 F

Solution:

Materials Price Variance = Actual Quantity (Standard Price - Actual Price)

Rs. 390 = 2,600 [4.50 - Actual Price]

390 = 2,600 × 4.50 - 2,600 × AP

390 = 11,700 - 2,600 × AP

or Actual Price = Rs. 4.35

VIII. An Electronics Company's budget contains these standards for materials and direct labour for a unit of 10 boxes:

Material	2 kg.	@ Rs. 50	Re. 1.00
Direct Labour	1 hour	@ Rs. 4.40	Rs. 4.40

Although 100,000 units were budgeted for September, only 97,120 were produced. Two hundred thousand kg. of materials were purchased for Rs. 105,000. Direct labour costs were Rs. 380,000 for 95,000 hours.

a. Compute the materials price variance

b. Compute the materials efficiency variance.

c. Compute the labour price variance.

d. Compute the labour efficiency variance.

Solution:

a. Material Price Variance

= (Actual Material atg Actual Prices) - (Actual Material at Standard Prices)

$$\frac{200{,}000\ (105{,}000 - \text{Rs. }50)}{200{,}000}$$

= 200,000 [.525 - .50] = 5,000 (A)

b. Material Quantity Variance = Actual Quantity at Standard Price - Standard quantity at Standard Price

.50 [200,000 - 194,240]

= 2,880 (A)

c. Labour Rate Variance = Actual Hours at Actual rates - Actual hours at standard rates

$$95{,}000 \quad \frac{380{,}000 - 4.40}{95{,}000}$$

95,000 [4.00 - 4.40] = 38,000 F

d) Labour efficiency variance:

Actual hours at standard rates - Standard hours at standard rates

95,000 - 97,120 × 4.40

= 9,328 (F)

Presentation of Variance Analysis to Management

The benefits of any control system depend on how quickly and in what form the necesary data are presented to the management. There are no hard and fast rules for presentation of information. The following format may be considered suitable in many cases:

Comparative statement of cost

Production..... Month.....................19

A. Summary

	Element of cost	Standard Rs.	Actual Rs.	Difference Rs.
A1	Direct material cost			
A2	Direct Wages			
A3	Variable Overheads			
A4	Fixed Overheads			

B. Variance Analysis

No.	Nature of Variance	Amount Favourable Rs.	Amount Adverse Rs.	Reasons Remaraks
B1	Material Price Variance			
B2	Material usage and quantity variance			
B3	Material mix variance			
B4	Material yield variance			
B5	Labour rate variance			
B6	Labour efficiency variance			

B7	Idle time variance
B8	Variable overhead variance
B9	Fixed overhead expenditure variance
B10	Fixed overhead volume variance
B11	Fixed overhead efficiency variance
B12	Capacity variance

Date Cost Controller

Notes:	A1 = B1 + B2	A2 = B5 + B6 + B7	A4 = B9 + B10
	B2 = B3 + B4	A3 = B8	B10 = B11 + B12

Questions

1. Define and state the purpose of standard costs.
2. What is a variance? How can variance analysis help management achieve control of operation?
3. Is a standard cost an estimate cost? What is the main objective of using a standard costing system?
4. How do standards help in controlling production costs?
5. What are the causes of a favourable or unfavourable Labour Rate variance and Labour Efficiency variance. Of the two variances which is more likely to be under the control of management? Explain with examples.
6. Why does the management not investigate all unfavourable variances? Elucidiate with examples.
7. "Favourable variance should not be investigated". True or false comment.
8. "The larger the variance, the more likely management is to investigate it". Do you agree with this statement? Why or why not? Give example.
9. How would you interpret an unfavourable direct material quantity variance?
10. What are the various factors that cause labour cost variance? How can this variance be avoided?

Problems

1. The Joy Company gives the following data for the month of June, when 1,100 finished units were produced:

   Materials used: 3,600 kgs.

   Standard per finished unit: 3 kg. at Rs. 3 per kg.

   Materials purchases: 5,000 kg. at Rs. 3.25 per kg.

   Direct Labour: 2,450 hours at a total cost of Rs. 9,800.

   Standard Rs. 7.60 per finished unit, 2 hours per unit.

   Required: Calculate the various material and labour variances and comment on your result.

2. Saagar Supplies manufacture and sell plastics. During May the company produced and sold 80,000 sheets of plastics and accumulated the following cost data:

	Standard Unit Cost	Total Actual Cost
Direct Materials:		
Standard (1 kg. @ Rs. .20 per kg.)	Rs. 20	
Actual (77,000 kg. @ Rs. .22 per kg)		Rs. 16,940
Direct Labour:		
Standard (02 hr. @ Rs. 5.00 per hr.)	0.10	
Actual (1,700 hr. @ Rs. 5.05 per hr.)		8,585
Overhead		
Standard:		
Variable (Rs. 6.00 per direct labour hour)	Rs. .12	
Fixed (Rs. 12,000 for Master budget volume	.17	
of 82,000 units and 1,700 direct labour hours)	.29	
Actual	23,400	
Total	Rs. .59	Rs. 48,925

Required:

1. Compute the price and efficiency variances for direct material and direct labour.

2. Compute the various overhead variances and also the total variance.

3. Prepare a standard cost income statement to report all variance to the management. Sale price of the plasti: sheets was Rs. 2.00 each.

3. The Gemini Company has established the following standards for producing an item called compact:

   Materials: 2 units of X costing Rs. 5 per unit.

   Labour: 1 hour @ Rs. 7 per hour.

   Variable overhead: 1 hour at Rs. 3 per hour.

   Last month the firm produced 10,000 units of Company and incurred the following costs:

   Material: 16,000 units of X costing Rs. 84,000

   Labour: 8,200 hour costing Rs. 60,000.

   Variable oerhead costing: Rs. 26,000.

Required:

(a) What is the standard cost for one compact?

(b) Identify and anaylize all variances.

4. Calculate the labour variances in the following situation:

   Actual direct labour payroll

   (21,500 hours at Rs. 3.75) = Rs. 80,625

   Standard labour allowed per unit:

   4 hours at Rs. 4 = Rs. 16

   Production for month (in units) = 6,000

5. The following data relates to a manufacturing company for the second quarter of 19x1:

   Standard activity (units) 25,000

   Actual Production (units) 22,000

   Budgeted fixed overhead Rs. 16,000

   Variable overhead rate (per unit) Rs. 2.50

   Actual fixed overhead Rs.16,000

   Actual variable overhead Rs. 40,000

   Compute the overhead budget variance and the overhead volume variance.

6. NK Company uses a flexible budgeting system for controlling manufacturing overhead costs. It has established a flexible budget for overhead as follows:

   Fixed Overhead: Rs. 500,000 per month

   Variable Overhead: Rs. 2 per unit.

   Actual data for January, February and March are as follows:

	Units Produced	Total Overhead Costs
		Rs.
January	50,000	650,000
February	60,000	600,000
March	40,000	580,000

   Determine the total overhead cost variance for each month.

7. Information on MK Company's direct materials costs is as follows:

   Actual Quantities of Direct Maerials Used 20,000

Actual Costs of Direct Materials Used	Rs. 40,000
Standard Price per Unit of Direct Materials	Rs. 2.20
Flexible Budget for Direct Materials	Rs. 42,000

a. What was MK Company's direct material price variance?

b. What was the Company's direct materials efficiency variance?

8. A Company reports the following direct labour information for product M for the month of November:

   Standard Rate Rs. 6.00 per hour

   Actual Rate Paid Rs. 6.20 per hour

   Standard Hours Allowed for Actual Production 1,500 hours

   Labour Efficiency Variance Rs. 700A

   What are the actual hours worked?

9. A.V. Ltd. which uses standard costing, shows the following overhead information for the current period:

Actual Overhead incurred	Rs. 12,600 of which Rs. 4,000 is Fixed.
Budgeted Fixed Overhead	Rs. 3,500

   Variable Overhead Rate per Direct Labour Hour Rs. 3

   Standard Hours allowed for actual production 3,500

   Actual Labour Hours used 3,200

   What are the variable overhead price and efficiency variance, and the fixed overhead price variance?

10. The standard cost of a product manufactured by Ritu Ltd. is as follows:

Direct Materials (.50 kg)	Rs. 1.00
Direct Labour (10 hours)	Rs. 3.80
Variable overhead	Rs. 2.50
Fixed overhead	Rs. 1.50
Total	Rs. 8.80

The standard volume of output is 80,000 units per month. A total of 30,000 kgs of materials were purchased at Rs. 40.00 per kg. During the month of October, 90,000 units were produced with the following costs:

Direct materials used (29,000 kg. at Rs. 4.00)	Rs. 116,000
Direct Labour (50,000 hours at Rs. 5.50)	Rs. 275,000
Variable overhead	Rs. 120,000
Fixed overhead	Rs. 70,000

Calculate the material, labour and overhead variances which occurred during the month.

11. From the following data calculate and analyse all variances. Also prepare an income statement with the data given below:

Standards per unit of production

Direct materials, 5 kg. of material X at Rs. 4.

Direct Labour 8 hours at Rs. 6.

Variable overhead, R. 4 per direct labour hour.

Actual:

Sales (15,000 units at	Rs. 140)
Production (units)	15,000
Direct materials used (42,000 kg.)	172,200
Direct Labour used (60,000 hr.)	36,000

Variable overhead	275,000
Selling & Administrative expenses	150,000

Business Decision Problem

12. The President of a large company has received the following report:

Total material costs for the month of June (5,800 kg. at Rs. 3.50 per kg.)	Rs. 20,300
Unfavourable material price variance Rs. 3.50 - Rs. 3.00) x 5,800	Rs. (2,900)
Unfavourable material quantity variance (5,800 kg. - 5,200 kg.) x Rs. 3.00	Rs. (1,800)
Standard matrerials at standard price for the actual production in June	Rs. 15,600

The president has discussed the unfavourable price variance with the purchasing officer. The purchasing officer agrees that he should be held responsible for most of the unfavourable price variance. However, he does not agree to the inclusion of Rs. 300 (600 kg. of excess material used at Re. 0.50 per kg.), which he feels is the responsibility of the production department. He feels that the extra 600 kg. of material purchased is due to the efficiency in the use of the materials by the production department. The production manager does not agree with the above arguments. He argues that he is basically only responsible for the excess quantity of materials used.

But he objects to the inclusion of Rs. 300 of unfavourable price variance due to the excess materials used in the materials quantity variance. This he says is the responsibility of the purchasing officer.

The president now asks for your advice. He wants you to answer three questions:

a. Who is responsible for the Rs. 300 in dispute.

b. In case the responsibility cannot be clearly assigned, where should the accounting department include the variance? Why?

c. What can be the other plausible reason when the responsibility for material variances cannot be clearly identified? Explain.

14

Responsibility Accounting and Segmental Analysis

An accounting system designed to personalize accounting reports is termed as a responsibility accounting system. The present chapter explains the technique of a responsibility accounting system, the main purpose of which is to make the control process more effective. In this system, costs are identified with the individuals responsible for them and individual managers are accountabel for the performance of the business segments under their control. The performance reports are structured and classified according to defined responsibility areas of specific managers. In addition, an effective responsibility accounting system requires an organization strucure where the focus is on revenues and costs a manager can control. Hence, with the responsibility being localized it is possible to hold individual managers accountable for the performance of business units under their control.

Responsibility accounting focusses on the reporting and not the recording of cost and revenue data. It is a reporting function that provides each level of management with the information it needs to control costs. Managers at all levels of the organization are truly managers of cost. Managers are expected to prepare their budget or standad cost and they are responsible for all variances. These variances are then used by both the higher level managers to rate subordinate managers and also by each manager concerned as a basis for self-evaluation.

Thus, Responsibility Accounting is the process of*:

1. Designating the responsibility centres within an organization.
2. Delegating authority to the managers of the responsibility centres.
3. Preparing budgets, accumulating results, and preparing performance reports for the responsibility centres.
4. Holding the managers responsible, or accountable for their actions.

Responsibility Centres

The distinction between controllable and non-controllable costs is the key to a successful responsibility accounting and reporting system. Every rupee that a company spends should be traceable to and controllable by at least one manager. Managers are expected to identify the costs for which they will be held accountable. A responsibility accounting report contains only those items that are controllable by the responsible manager; or if both controllable and non-controllable items are included, clearly distinguishes those items that are not controllable. Under a responsibility accounting systgem, performance reports are prepared for each organizational unit. These organizational units are referred to as a responsibility centre. A responsibility centre is an area of activity within an organization, managed by an individual who has been given both authority and responsibility for the activities of that area. In an entire organization, there are many responsibility centres. If a responsibility centre only involves cost or expenditure, it is called a cost/expense centre. When the responsibility centre involves both revenues and costs, it is called a profit centre. And if the managers are evaluated on how well they use the total resources entrusted to their care, the unit is called an investment centre.

* Smith, Keith and Stephens, "Accounting Principles", McGrew Hill International Editions, 1989.

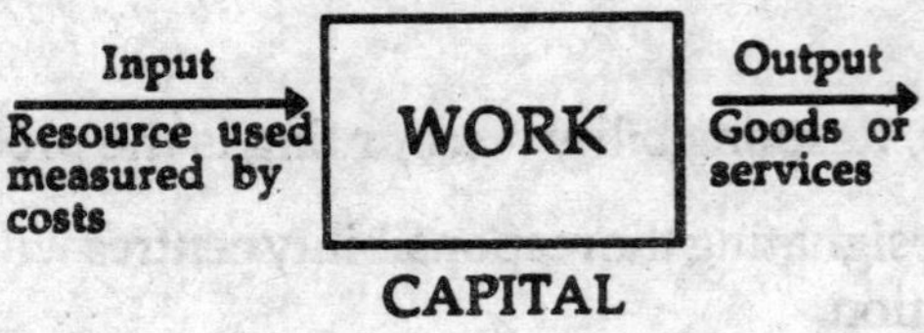

Fig. 14.1. Responsibility Centre*

The figure above shows the essence of any responsibility center. A responsibility center uses input to produce goods and services. Management is responsible for obtaining an optimum relationship between inputs and outputs. The goods and services produced by the Responsibility Center are usually in accordance with its objectives and are furnished either to another responsibility center or to the outside wold.

The cost of inputs is always measureable while outputs are more difficult to measure. In some cases inputs are directly related to outputs while in other cases there is an indirect relationship e.g. expenses on advertising research and development, employee training etc.

Efficiency and Effectiveness

Two criteria for judging the performance of a responsibility center are efficiency and effectiveness. Both these terms are generally used in a comparative sense, and not in an absolute sense.

Efficency is the ratio of output to Input and usually efficient responsibility centres are those that work with the lower consumption of resources.

Effectiveness is the relationship between a responsibility centers outputs and its objectives. A responsibility center is effective if its outputs contribute to its objectives. Effectiveness is a little difficult to measure and is usually non-quantifiable since both objectives and outputs are a little difficult to measure. Companies many times express effectiveness in judgemental

* Adapted from Management Control Systems, Text and Cases by "Authory, Dearden and Govindarajan", Seventh Edition.

and relative terms. A responsibility center should be both efficient and effective and the choice is not of choosing one or the other. As is generally said 'A responsibility center is efficient if **it does things right** and it is effective if it does the **right** things'.

Types of Responsibility Centre

I. Cost/Expenses Centre

A cost centre is responsible only for costs incurred by the centre; it has no direct influence over revenue generaion. The manager of a cost centre is accountable for the unit's action and is responsible for producing a quality product at a reasonable cost. The performance of the manager of a cost centre is evaluated on the basis of (i) their ability to control costs and (ii) the quality of the services that they provide to the organization. Examples of expense centre are service centres (e.g. the maintenance departments).

II. Profit Centre

When the manager of an organizational unit is responsible for the difference between revenues and costs, the responsibility centre is known as a profit centre. A profit centre has both revenues and expenses.

Managers of profit centres are responsible/accountable for generating revenues and incurring costs so as to maximize profits. In case of large companies, there are several departments and each department works like a mini business. It is easier to manage these mini businesses and each manager is responsible for generating a profit from sales in his department.

Consider the case of a large retail organization. It has several departments who in turn function as separate, independent profit centres. For example, a large departmental store may have several departments such as women's clothing, children's clothing, men's wear, jewellery, cosmetics, toys, etc. Each department functions independently and can be evaluated as a profit centre. Thus, a profit centre's manager has the responsibility and the authority to generate a desirable profit from that centre during a specified time.

III. Investment Centre

An investment centre is the broadest and most inclusive type of responsibility centre. A manager of an investment centre is involved in decisions to invest in plant, equipment and other capital resources and is also responsible for revenues and costs. Thus an investment centre is a segment of a company having revenues, expenses and a specified investment base.

In an investment centre analysis, the relationship between profits and assets need to be examined. Since the manager has control over the assets, he is evaluated on the basis of the effective use of those assets. The appropriate method to do so is by calculating the Return on Investment. Return on investment (also called rate of return) is computed by dividing segmental earnings by the appropriate investment base.

Criteria for Divisional Performance Measurment

Three important criteria for measuring divisional performance are -

1. The measure chosen should indicate clearly the contribution made by each division to the overall profitability of the company.

2. The measure should be independent from the performance achieved by other divisions of the company. This will be possible only if all the costs can be completely allocated to each division and overlappings are not there. Divisional managers can then be completely held accountable for the costs and profits of their divisions.

3. The measure should provide a common basis for comparing and evaluating the performance of divisions operating in different geographic and product markets. Two measures generally used to measure divisional performance measurement are Return on Investment (ROI) and Residual Income (RI).

I. Return on Investment (ROI)

Return on Investment (ROI) =

$$\frac{\text{Net Income}}{\text{Total Assets}} \text{ or } \frac{\text{Divisional Profit}}{\text{Divisional Investment}}$$

The ROI is made up of two ratios. They are:

$$\text{ROI} = \frac{\text{Net Income}}{\text{Sales}} \times \frac{\text{Sales}}{\text{Assets}}$$

The ratio of net income to sales measures the profit margin whereas the ratio of sales to assets measures the asset turnover. The ROI can be increased by increasing the profit margin and the asset turnover ratio or by some combination of both.

The Return on Investment as a measure of overall performance is conceptually easy to understand. It can be used for making comparisons between the performance of various divisions. It also encourages divisional managers to retain assets that give satisfactory return on investment and to discard assets that are not upto the mark.

Also the expanded version of ROI shows that an increase in sales, by itself, will not increase ROI because sales cancel out. But a decrease in investment/assets with other factors remaining the same, will increase ROI.

Suppose that return on sales is 15% and investment turnover is 2 times. This gives a ROI of 30% (15% x 2). If the manager now changes the product mix to items with lower margins and faster turnover, so that return to sales is 10% and investment turnover is 2½ times. ROI will now fall to 25% (10x2½). Hence the expanded version of the ROI gives clues regarding the strategies used by companies. Two companies may be having the same ROI, but by using two different strategies. One company may be operating on a high investment turnover while the other may be working towards a high return on sales.

	Co. A	Co. B
Return on Sales	12%	8%
Investment Turnover	2	3
ROI	24%	24%

II. Residual Income (RI)

Residual income is the income of a dvision produced in excess of the minmum required rate of return. Management usually establishes the minimum rate of return which is greater than the cost of capital. For different divisions, companies usually set different minimum rates of return which is in accordance with the risks associated with their business. Business which are risky will need to earn higher returns than business which are more stable. RI can be calculated as follows:

RI = Divisional Income – (Divisional investment × Target ROI)

Assume that the divisions income is Rs. 2,00,000, divisional investment is Rs. 5,00,000 and that the cost of capital is 20%. RI can now be calculated as follows:

RI = 2,00,000 – (20% × Rs. 5,00,000)
= 2,00,000 – 1,00,000
= Rs. 1,00,000

Thus, RI calculates the minimum required rupee return. If the firm earns less than the RI, the investors will want their capital to be invested elsewhere. The basic reason for using RI as a measure of divisional performance is that it measures the profits that the division provides to the firm over and above the minimum profit required from the amount invested.

RI also offers significant advantages over the ROI measure. RI is more flexible since a different percentage or rate can be applied to investments of different risks. For example, division in different lines of business may have different cost of capital; assets in the same division may be exposed to different risk classes. RI allows the managers to incorporate differences in risk-adjusted capital costs while the ROI measure accounts for no such changes.

Example:

	Required ROI is 10%		Required ROI is 20%	
	Division A	**Division B**	**Division A**	**Division B**
	Rs.	**Rs.**	**Rs.**	**Rs.**
Investment	1,00,000	8,00,000	1,00,000	8,00,000
Divisional income	25,000	1,20,000	25,000	1,20,000
Requried / minimum return (Investment × minimum return)	10,000	80,000	20,000	1,60,000
Redidual income	Rs. 15,000	Rs. 40,000	Rs. 5,000	Rs. 40,000

RI has an advantage over ROI as a measure of divisional performance. It could show that a division with a higher ROI is less valuable to the firm as a whole than with the lower ROI.

Suppose that division A produces Rs. 25,000 income on an investment of Rs. 1,00,000. This gives a ROI of 25%. Division B earns Rs. 1,20,000 on an investment of Rs. 8,00,000. This gives a ROI of 15%.

As shown in the example, consider two alternatives: (1) required ROI is 10% and (2) required ROI is 20%.

The residual income for each division are as shown in the example above.

If the minimum requried ROI is 10%, division B makes a greater contribution to the firm than does division A despite division B's lower ROI. However, if the minimum required ROI is 20%, division A is more valuable to the firm as division B makes a loss of Rs. 40,000. Hence, if the decision criteria for evaluating divisional performance is RI, the division with the highest RI will be rated highest.

ROI vs RI

ROI is the most commonly used measure for divisional performance measurement. It is easy to understand and can be used for interfirm comparisons provided that the firms whose results are being compared are in the same industry and are of nearly the same size.

However, using ROI may influence a divisional manager to select only those projects whose returns are above the minimum required rate of return. Divisional managers may turn down investment opportunities that are above the minimum acceptable rate of return but below the ROI that is currently being earned y the company. Such investments that may reduce the divisions ROI business may be rejected by the divisional manager. This may result in sub-optional decision making by the manager.

Example:

Assume that the profit of a division is Rs. 20,00,000 while the investment of the division is Rs. 50,00,000

$$\text{The divisions' ROI} = \frac{20,00,000}{50,00,000} \times 100 = 40\%$$

Now suppose that the division gets an opportunity to make an additional investment of Rs. 10,00,000 which would give a profit of Rs. 3,00,000. The ROI for the additional investment is 30%.

$$\text{ROI} = \frac{3,00,000}{10,00,000} \times 100 = 30\%$$

This investment is acceptable to the company because the minimum required ROI for this type of investment is 25%. However, the additional investment would lower the divisions' ROI to 38.33%.

$$\text{ROI} = \frac{20,00,000 + 3,00,000}{50,00,000 + 10,00,000} = 38.33\%$$

If the performance of the division and its manager is evaluated on the basis of ROI, the manager may be inclined to reject the new investment as his ROI has fallen from 40% to 38.33%. The manager, in order to preseive his ROI, may make a decision which is not optional from the view point of the entire organization.

From the firm's viewpoint, the proposed investment should be undertaken as its ROI is greater than the minimum required rate. To encourage the divisional manager to make the decisions that benefit the firm as well as the division, the residual income approach can be taken into account using RI in the example illustrated above.

	Without new project	With new project
Divisional investment	Rs. 50,00,000	Rs. 60,00,000
Minimum required ROI	25%	25%
Divisional profit	Rs. 20,00,000	Rs. 23,00,000
Less minimum required	Rs. 12,50,000	Rs. 15,00,000
Residual income	Rs. 7,50,000	Rs. 8,00,000

A divisional manager evaluated on the basis of RI will undertake this project because his performance shows an improvement with the additional project undertain. The RI criterian encourages managers to maximize the total rupee profit and also increases the wealth of the shareholder's by accepting projects which earn a rate of return in excess of the minimum required rate of return (cost of capital). Finally the RI method ensures that the decisions taken by the different division are in tune with the interests of the organizaiton as a whole.

Hence the successful operation of a responsibility accounting system depends upon the coordination of the various goals of an organization. Responsibility accounting provides the means for structuring the goals of a business organization. In addition, in responsibility accounting, the data flow is reduced, in the sense that each level of management has only that data which is needed to control those areas for which he is responsible.

Review Problem

I. The following information refers to the Modern Company which has two segments. Results of operations for 19x1 were as follows:

	Segment A	Segment B	Total
	Rs.	Rs.	Rs.
Sales	60,000	80,000	1,40,000
Variable Expenses	30,000	40,000	70,000
Fixed Expenses			
Direct	6,000	12,000	18,000
Indirect	12,000		

(a) Modern Company has total operating assets of Rs. 2,00,000 of which Rs. 1,75,000 are identified with the two segments as follows:-

	Segment A	Segment B
	Rs.	Rs.
Assets directly used by and identified with thesegment	75,000	1,00,000

(a) Prepare a statement showing segmental contribution to Indirect Expenses and the total income for the Modern Company.

(b) Determine the Return on investment for evaluating each segment and also for the entire Company.

(c) Comment on the results of (a) and (b)

Solution

Modern Company

Income Statement showing segmental contributions to Indirec Expenses for the year ended Dec. 31, 19x1.

	Segment A	Segment B	Total
	Rs.	Rs.	Rs.
Sales	60,000	80,0000	1,40,000
Less Variable Expenses	30,000	40,000	70,000
Contribution Margin	30,000	40,000	70,000
Less Direct Fixed Expenses	6,000	12,000	18,000
Contribution to Indirect Expenses	24,000	28,000	52,000
Less Indirect Expenses			12,000
Net Income			40,000

(b) Contribution to indirect expenses

		Segment A	Segment B
		Rs. 24,000	Rs. 28,000
Assets directly used by and identified with the segment		75,000	1,00,000
ROI	=	32%	28%
Net operating Income		Rs. 40,000	
Operating assets		Rs. 2,00,000	
ROI		20%	

(c) The contribution margin towards indirect expenses is higher for segment B in part (a) of the results. But in part (a) segment A shows a higher return on investment. This shows that when a segment is evaluated as an investment centre, the centre with the highest investment base will not necessary show the highest return. But when the segment is evaluated as a profit centre, the centre with the highest investment base will usually show the best results.

The return on investment for the company as a whole is lower (i.e. 20%) than for the segments individually (Segment A 32%, Segment B 28%) because of the increased investment base.

II. From the following data calculate :

(a) Turnover of Capital

(b) Net Income

(c) Net income as a percentage of Sales

Sales	Rs. 10,00,000
Invested Capital	Rs. 2,00,000
Return on Investment	15%

Solution

(a) Turnover of Capital $= \frac{10,00,000}{2,00,000}$

$= 5$ times

(b) Net income = 15% of Rs. 2,00,000
= Rs.30,000

(c) Net income as a percentage of Sales $= \frac{30,000}{10,00,000} \times 100$

= 3%

III. The following data is given:

	Division A	B	C
Invested Capital	1,00,000	1,20,000	80,000
Revenue	10,00,000	4,80,000	2,40,000
Income	10,000	14,400	14,400

(a) For each division calculate the income percentage of revenue, the capital turnover and the rate of return on Invested Capital.

(b) Which division is performing the best? Explain

(c) If the imputed rate of interest for each division is 8% on the invested capital, calculate the residual income for each division.

Solution:

(a)

	Division A	Division B	Division C
Income percentage of revenue	1%	3%	6%
Capital Turnover	10 times	4 times	3 times
ROR on invested capital	10%	12%	18%

(b) Division C performs the best as it has the highest return on invested capital as also the highest income percentage of revenue.

(c)

	A	B	C
Income	10,000	14,400	14,400
Imputed Interest	8,000	9,600	6,400
Residual Income	2,000	4,800	8,000

IV. A Company uses ROI to measure the performance of its operating divisions. A summary of the annual reports from two divisions is shown below. The company's cost of capital is 12%.

	Division A Rs.	Division B Rs.
Capital invested	2400	4000
Net Income	480	720
ROI	20%	18%

Required:

1. Which division is more profitable?
2. At what cost of capital would both divisions be considered equally profitable?
3. What performance measurement procedure would more clearly show the relative profitability of the two divisions?

Solution:

1. The question of which division is more profitable depends upon the definition of profitability. Division A has a higher ROI while Division B's net income is higher. The incremental return Company B has earned on its higher capital investment can also be calculated Division B has earned an extra Rs. 240 on an investment base of Rs. 1,600 (Rs. 4,000 - Rs. 2,400). This is a 15% incremental ROI. As this incremental return (15%) is higher than the firm's cost of capital of 12%, Division B is more profitable than Division A.
2. When the cost of Capital is 15% (B's incremental ROI), the two divisions would be equally profitable.
3. The Residual income would clearly show the relative profitability of the two divisions-

	Division A	Division B
	Rs.	Rs.
Capital invested	2,400	4,000
Net Income	480	720
Capital charge @ 12%	288	480
Residual Income	192	240

The higher RI of B of Rs. 48/- just equal the 3% incremental return on the Rs. 1,600 larger investment base.

Questions:

1. Define responsibility accounting?
2. What is a responsibility centre?
3. What role does controllability play in a responsibility accounting system?
4. Describe a profit centre, cost centre, expense centre. Give examples to illustrate your answer.
5. Describe an investmetn centre? What is the logic of using an investment centre as a basis for performance evaluation?
6. Compare and contrast an expense centre and an investment centre.
7. "It may be desirable to use a different ROI measure for evaluating the performance of a division and the performance of the divisions manages". Explain.
8. "The return on investment measure may be biased in favour of divisions with older plant and equipment". Elucidiate with examples.
9. What are the advantages of using residual income instead of ROI?
10. What is responsibility accounting and how does it facilitate the control process?

Problems

I. Ritu Corporation has three production plants (A, B and C). These plants are treated as responsibility centres. The table below summarizes the results for a particular month:

Plant	Revenue	Expenses	Investment base (gross assets)
A			
B			
C			

Required

(a) Which plant manager seems to have done the best job if (i) the plants are treated as earnings centres and (ii) the plants are treated as investment centres.

(b) Comment as to why the earnings centre analysis and investment centre analysis give different findings.

2. Return on investment is often expressed as the product of two components - capital turnover and margin on sales. You are considering investing in one of three companies, all in the same industry and are given the following information:

	COMPANY		
	A	**B**	**C**
	Rs.	Rs.	Rs.
Sales	5,00,000	2,50,000	50,00,000
Income	50,000	25,000	25,000
Capital	2,00,000	20,00,000	20,00,000

Calculate:

1. Why would you desire the breakdown of return on investment into margin on sales and turnover on capital?

2. Compute the margin on sales, turnover on capital, and return on investment for the three companies

and comment on the relative performance of the companies.

3. XYZ is a large integrated Company with operations throughout the world. The manager of one of the division has been directed to submit his proposed capital budget for 19x1 for inclusion in the company wide budget.

   The Division Manager has for consideration the following projects, all of which require an outlay of capital. All projects have equal risk.

PROJECT	INVESTMENT REQUIRED	RETURN
	Rs.	Rs.
1.	5,00,000	2,10,000
2.	3,00,000	80,000
3.	2,20,000	70,000
4.	1,15,000	55,000
5.	90,000	13,000
6.	3,25,000	1,20,000

   The division manager must decide which of the projects to take. The company has a cost of capital of 20%. An amount of Rs. 10 lakh is available to the division for investment purposes.

   1. What will be the total investment, total return, return on capital invested and residual income of the rational division manager if

      a. The company has a rule that all projects promising at least 20% or more should be taken.

      b. The division manager is evaluated on his ability to maximize his return on capital invested (assume that this is a new division with no invested capital).

      c. The division manager is expected to maximize residual income as computed by using the 15% cost of capital.

2. Which of the three approaches will induce the most effective investment policy for the company as a whole? Explain.

4. Consider the following data:

	Rs.
Sales	3,50,000
Invested Capital	2,00,000
Return on Investment	15%

Calculate:

(a) Turnover of Capital

(b) Net Income

(c) Net Income as a percentage of Sales.

5. Fill in the blanks:

	Division		
	A	B	C
Income percentage of revenue	5%	?	2%
Capital Turnover	4	5	
Rate of return on invested capital	?	50%	16%

6. You are given the following data:

	Division		
	X	Y	Z
	Rs.	Rs.	Rs.
Invested Capital	8,00,000	12,00,000	10,00,000
Revenue	24,00,000	24,00,000	30,00,000
Income	80,000	96,000	1,80,000

1. For each division calculate the income percentage of revenue, capital turnover and the rate of return on invested capital.

2. Which division is performing the best?

3. If the imputed interest rate for each division is 12% on invested capital, calculate the Residual income for each division?

7. The operating performance of the three divisions of a company are as shown below:

	Division A	Division B	Division C
	Rs.	Rs.	Rs.
Sales	25,00,000	80,000	20,00,000
Operating Profits	7,00,000	30,000	10,00,000
Investment	15,00,000	1,20,000	1,00,000

(a) Calculate the most profitable division if the criterion is (i) operating profit margin (ii) rate of return on investment.

(b) Which measure is a better indicator of overall operating performance? Give reasons to explain your answer.

8. The Suny Corporation has three operating divisions. The managers of these divisions are evaluated on their divisional Net Income Before Taxes, a figure that includes an allocation of corporate overhead proportional to the sales of each division. The operating statement for the first quarter of 19x1 appears below:

	Division			
	A	B	C	Total
	Rs.	Rs.	Rs.	Rs.
Net Sales (000)	1,200	1,200	1,600	4,800
Cost of sales	1,050	540	640	2,230
Division overhead	250	125	160	535
Division contribution	700	535	800	2,035
Corporate overhead	400	240	320	950
Net income before taxes	Rs. 300	Rs. 295	Rs. 480	Rs. 1,075

The manager of Division A is unhappy that his profitability is about the same as Division B's and much less than Division

C's even though his sales are much higher than either of these other two divisions. The manager knows that he is carrying one line of products with very low profitability. He was going to replace this line of business as soon as more profitabile product opportunities became available but has retained it until now, since the line was still marginally profitable and used facilities that would otherwise be idle. The manager now realizes, however, that the sales from this product line are attracting a fair amount of corporate overhead because of the allocation procedure and may be the line is already unprofitable for him.

This low margin line of products had the following characteristics for the quarter:

	Rs.
Net Sales (000)	Rs. 800
Cost of Sales	600
Escapable division overhead	100
Contribution	Rs. 100

Thus, the product line accounted for 40% of divisional sales but less than 15% of divisional profit.

Required:

1. Prepare the operating statement for the Sunny Corporation for the second quarter of 19x1 assuming that sales and operating results are identical to the first quarter except that the manager of Division A drops the low margin product line entirely from his product group. Is the Division A manager better off from this action? Is Sunny Corporation better off from this action?

2. Suggest improvements to the Sunny Corporation's divisional reporting and evaluation system that will improve local incentives for decision-making that is in the best interests of the firm.

15

Transfer Pricing

In an organization where there are a number of divisions or departments, the question of pricing of products from one division to another becomes important. For example, the price that one division should charge or be allowed to charge another for goods and services provided. A Transfer-price is the internal price at which goods and services are transferred from one profit or investment centre to another profit centre within the same company. Transfer pricing becomes necessary in order to determine whether organizational objectives are being achieved in each department of a company. They are also important in evaluating the divisional performance.

In this chapter, the objectives and techniques of Transfer Pricing are discussed. Examples have also been given to illustrate the concept in actual practice.

Generally, transfer prices should fulfil three objectives: **First**, it should promote goal congruence and optimal decision-making. The objectives of the various divisions or departments of a company should be consistent with the overall objectives of the company as a whole. If the divisions take independent actions,they may not be in the best interest of the organization as a whole. For example, if the buying and selling profit centres of the same company maximize their individual performance, transfer-pricing problems may be created.

Second, transfer-pricing should enable reliable performance appraisal of each independent unit of an organization. Management must properly evaluate the transfer prices of each division so that it helps them in assessing the true worth of each division, evaluates the contribution made by the division to total company profits and also helps them in decision making.

Finally, divisional managers should develop offers of transfer prices that reflect the cost structures of their divisions and also maximum divisional autonomy. For example, if the division is operating, below capacity, a transfer price that falls between incremental cost and market price is usually the best. When the division is operating at full capacity, usually a market-based transfer price is best. If divisions are free to buy and sell outside the firm, the use of market prices leads divisions to maximize the goals of an organization also.

In summary, the best transfer-pricing system is the one that helps managers to make decisions that are in the best interests of the firm as a whole. In situations where managers are free to negotiate the transfer prices, they are likely to make decisions that benefit both the division and the firm as a whole.

Transfer Pricing in Practice

Transfer price is an important factor in evaluating divisional performance measurement mainly because of the desire of the selling and buying divisions of the same company to maximize their individual performance. A great deal of intra firm buying and selling occurs in decentralized firms which necessitates the setting of transfer prices. For example, a textile mill might sell some of its cloth to outsiders and some of its cloth for further processing to divisions within the same firm.

In actual practice, transfer price of goods and service is usually subject to much controversy. The pricing method to be used, also depends upon many factors. Some of the important transfer-pricing policies are:

1. Market Price

When there is an existing market outside the firm for the

intermediate product and the market is competitive, then the use of market price as the transfer price between divisions is ideal and leads divisions to act in the manner that maximizes corporate goal congruence.

A competitive market implies the existense of buyers and sellers, such a market provides an incentive to efficient production because excessive costs cannot be passed on to buyers. Since market prices will usually be determined by the forces of demand and supply in the long run, the profit which results under this method provides a good indicator of the overall efficiency of the various units.

However, there are difficulties in implementing this policy:

(a) Outside market prices are not available for the product or service being considered.

(b) When the prices are available and the market does exist, it may not be truely representative. For example, the market price may be controlled by one or two large companies or the market may not be perfectly competitive. Also, market prices may not be the right choice as a transfer price if there is considerable excess capacity in the market or the selling division is operating below capacity.

(c) All product transfers do not necessarily have equivalent external markets. For example, a price is only strictly comparable when all features are identical.

(d) In a period of rising prices market price method is difficult to use since prices change within a short span of time.

Notwithstanding the above, market based transfer prices are generally the best and are usually used to make reliable assessments of divisional performance.

2. Full Cost with or without a Profit Mark-up

Under this svstem, transfer prices are based on full costs

with a percentage mark up on total costs in some other cases. Such a price system is commonly used because there may be no intermediate market which helps in setting a transfer price. This method gives no incentive to the selling division to keep its costs down. The selling manager is automatically given a certain level of profit with the percentage markup at full cost. Also, the selling manager makes more profit by allowing costs to increase and the cost which is calculated is only accurate at one level of output. Hence, this method suffers from the drawback that sub-optimal decision-making may occur within the firm.

3. Variable Cost Transfer Pricing

This method is best, theoretically, when the selling division has excess capacity. The manager will establish a transfer price equal to variable costs. This helps the manager to make decisions that are optimal from the organization's view point. However, variable cost based transfer policies causes the supplying division to report zero profits or a loss equal to fixed cost. Performance evaluation of the division also becomes difficult and meaningless. One possible way of partially resolving this problem is to credit the supplying division with a share of the overall profit which arises due to the transferred item.

4. Negotiated Transfer Pricing

This pricing scheme allows the supplying and buying division to negotiate with each other and then set the transfer price. This method tries to preserve divisional autonomy and is assumed to lead to optimal decision in the best interests of the firm as a whole.

However, if the buying and selling divisions do not independently agree on a price or the parties concerned do not have equal bargaining power, then negotiated transfer prices may lead to sub-optimal decisions. The existence of an arbitrator to settle disputes also reduces the autonomy of divisions. Hence, negotiated transfer prices are best when both the divisions have equal bargaining power.

In summary, firms should set transfer price at levels that

reflect the cost structures of their divisions and available alternatives. Ideally, transfer prices should be set in a manner that it meets all the criteria for inducing top management's desired decisions. Such prices should encourage managers to take actions that benefit the firm as a whole. No single transfer price is best; the best transfer price depends on the circumstances at hand.

How is Transfer Pricing Abused?

With globalisation transfer pricing became an unwanted reality. Price charged by one company in Country A to another company in Company B is reflected in the profit and loss account of both companies, either as an income or an expenditure.

Thus prices charged impact the tax paid by the two related companies. By resorting to transfer pricing related entities can reduce the global incidence of tax by transferring higher income to low tax jurisdictions or greater expenditure to those jurisdictions where the tax rate is very high.

For example, the current tax rate on domestic companies in India is 35 per cent. Company A is located in India and CompanyB in country XYZ. Both belong to the same group. If tax rate in country XYZ is 15 per cent, then Company B will transfer raw material to Company A at slightly higher prices.

This will enable Company A to show a higher expenditure and reduce its taxable profits. On the other hand slightly higher income will not harm Company B much as the tax rate in its country is very low. Thus the global group as a whole will benefit from tax savings.

How do Tax Authorities Detect Transfer Pricing?

Globally several methods of detecting transfer pricing have been set out, to check whether transactions between related parties have been at arm's length.

The transaction method relies directly or indirectly on information of prices at which similar transactions have been entered into by unrelated parties. This method is further divided into the comparable uncontrolled price (CUP) method and the cost plus (C+) method.

The transactional profit method, as the name indicates, is transfaction-specific: it examines whether or not profits from a particular deal are reasonable.

Why do transfer pricing regulations gain importance in a developing country like India?

Import of raw material, semi-finished goods for assembling and most important of all intellectual property such as know-how and technology are areas prone to transfer pricing.

Such goods or services can be sent to associate companies in India either at a higher or lower rate than prices charged to unrelated parties to secure a global tax advantage. In a high-tech age, Indian companies often rely on technology and know-how from their foreign joint venture partners: thus strict regulations are very important.

Are the regulations in India adequate to curb transfer pricing abuse?

Transfer pricing regulations are extremely stringent in developed countries such as the USA, UK, Canada, Australia and Germany.

In these countries, the tax payer has to maintain extensive records of all transactions with related parties. In the UK such disclosures have to be made in the self assessment returns filed with tax authorities.

In India, though provisions relating to transfer pricing regulations are there in the Income Tax Act, 1961, they are not very effective as tax payers are not required to maintain detailed documents or voluntarily disclosed information of related party transactions.

Example

A company has two divisions: Division A and Division B. Division A sells to Division B and to other outside customers. Division B buys from only Division A. The following unit costs were incurred by Division A for the coming year:

Direct materials	Rs. 10
Direct labour	6
Variable manufacturing	3
Overhead	
Variable selling costs	1
	Rs. 20

Suppose that for the year Division A produced 40,000 units of which 30,000 were sold to Division B for Rs. 25/- each. The outside sales were for Rs. 30/-. The fixed manufacturing costs for the year were Rs. 80,000.

After Division B receives the component from Division A, it processes it a little further and then sells it to customers. The variable unit costs of Division B are Rs. 5/- and its fixed costs for the year are Rs.50,000. Division B sells all the units received from Division A at Rs. 35/- each.

Exhibit 1 shows how transfer pricing affects each division's income statement and the company as a whole. The 30,000 units transferred from Division A to Division B is shown as Rs. 7,50,000 of internal sales for Division A and as Rs. 7,50,000 of transferred-in cost to Division B. Both these amounts are not taken into account in preparing the overall company income statement. This is done so as to provide the external users of financial statements with information relating to the economic activities of the company with outside parties and not internal transfers.

Supposed now that Division B is allowed to buy from outside suppliers. An outside supplier has offered to supply the same type of units for Rs. 22/- to Division B. Division A does not agree to reduce its price even though it has no alternative use of its production capacity.

Exhibit 2 shows that Division B increased its net income by Rs. 90,000 when it purchased from an external supplier. However, the profit of Division A and the company as a whole went down when Division B purchased from outside.

Exhibit 1

Budged Income statement for the Ddivisions and Company as a whole, Internal transfer

	Division A	Division B	Company
	Rs.	Rs.	Rs.
Sales			
External*	3,00,000	10,50,000	13,50,000
Internal**	7,50,000		
Total	10,50,000	10,50,000	13,50,000
Variable Costs			
Incurred***	8,00,000	1,50,000	9,50,000
Transferred-In****		7,50,000	-
Total	-8,00,000	-9,00,000	-9,50,000
Contribution Margin	2,50,000	1,50,000	4,00,000
Less Fixed Costs	80,000	50,000	1,30,000
Net Income	1,70,000	1,00,000	2,70,000

* 10,000 units x Rs. 30/- = Rs. 3,00,000 and 30,000 units x Rs. 35/- = Rs.10,50,000.

** 30,000 units x Rs. 25/- = Rs. 7,50,000

*** 40,000 units x 20/- = 8,00,000 and 30,000 units x Rs. 5/- = Rs. 1,50,000

**** Transferred. In costs is the same as internal sales.

Exhibit 2

Budgeted Income Statement for the Divisions and Company as a whole, External Supplies

	Division A	Division B	Company
	Rs.	Rs.	Rs.
Sales			
External*	3,00,000	10,50,000	13,50,000
Internal	-	-	-
Total	3,00,000	10,50,000	13,50,000
Variable Costs			
Incurred**	2,00,000	1,50,000	3,50,000
External purchases***	-	6,60,000	6,60,000
Total	-2,00,000	-8,10,000	-10,10,000
Contribution Margin	1,00,000	2,40,000	3,40,000
Less Fiixed costs	80,000	50,000	1,30,000
Net Income	20,000	1,90,000	2,10,000

* 10,000 Units x Rs. 30/- = Rs. 3,00,000 and 30,000 units x Rs. 35/- = Rs. 10,50,000

** 10,000 units x Rs. 20/- = Rs. 2,00,000 and 30,000 units x Rs. 5/- = Rs. 1,50,000

*** 30,000 units x Rs. 22 = Rs. 6,60,000

Exhibit 3
Budgeted Income Statement for the Divisions and Company as a whole

	Division A	Division B	Company
	Rs.	Rs.	Rs.
Sales			
External*	3,00,000	10,50,000	13,50,000
Internal**	6,60,000	-	-
Total	9,60,000	10,50,000	13,50,000
Variable Costs			
Incurred***	8,00,000	1,50,000	9,50,000
Transferred in****	-	6,60,000	-
Total	-8,00,000	-8,10,000	-9,50,000
Contribution Margin	1,60,000	2,40,000	4,00,000
Less Fixed costs	80,000	50,000	1,30,000
Net Income	80,000	1,90,000	2,70,000

* 10,000 units × Rs. 30/- = Rs. 3,00,000 and 30,000 units × Rs. 35/- = Rs. 10,50,000

** 30,000 units × Rs. 22/- = Rs. 6,60,000

*** 40,000 units × Rs. 20/- = 8,00,000 and 30,000 units × Rs. 5/- = Rs. 1,50,000

**** Transferred-in costs is the same as Internal sales.

Finally, assume that Division A is willing to negotiate a transfer price with Division B for Rs. 22/-. Exhibit 3 shows the income statements for each division and the company as a whole with the negotiated transfer price. Comparing Exhibit 1 and 3, we observe that the overall income of the company remains the same when there are internal transfers and the transfer price reduces from Rs. 25/- to Rs. 22/-. However, the profit of Division B increases and that of Division A decreases. Division B is pleased to have outside competition since its net profit increases under both the alterenatives.

Hence, transfer prics affect the profitability of both the buying and selling divisions. Performance evaluation of the divisional managers can also be done in a realistic manner. The impact of transfer prices on the company as a whole should be examined carefully to fully assess the results of the decisions involved in transfer pricing.

Illustrations

I. The XYZ Corporation has decentralized its manufacturing and marketing activities. Each function is now organized as a profit center. The output of a manufacturing division is transferred to the Marketing division at standard cost plus a 20% markup. For one of the company's largest volume products, the following flexible budget has been computed at typical output levels:

	Output (Units)		
	Rs.	Rs.	Rs.
Overhead	40,000	50,000	60,000
Indirect Materials	80,000	1,00,000	1,20,000
Indirect Labour	1,50,000	1,62,000	1,74,000
Equipment Rentals	2,00,000	2,00,000	2,50,000
Miscellaneous	1,40,000	1,45,000	1,50,000
Total Overhead	5,70,000	6,07,000	6,94,000
Direct Materials	3,20,000	4,00,000	4,80,000
Direct Labour	1,60,000	2,00,000	2,40,000
Total budgeted costs	10,50,000	12,07,000	14,14,000

The standard cost per unit is calculated at an annual volume of 50,000 units but the forecasted volume level fot the next year is 45,000 units.

Required:

(a) At what price is this product transferred from the manufacturing to the marketing division?

(b) The marketing division has uncovered an opportunity to sell 15,000 additional units to a new customer at a price of Rs. 22/- per unit. This is a special one-year contract that will not affect the pricing for current or potential customers. The manager of the marketing division has asked the manufacturing manager to supply these units at a transfer price of Rs. 20/- per unit. The manufacturing manager has emphatically declined this offer. "How can I transfer these items below my cost? Not only will I not make my standard markup on each unit, I'll lose money on every item that I produce at this transfer price. I am willing to be reasonable since business is slower than usual, but this offer is ridiculous".

Analyze the situation in an attempt to mediate this dispute.

Solution

1. If the output is 50,000 units, the average cost is

$$\frac{12,07,000}{50,000} = \text{Rs. } 24.14 \text{ per unit}$$

Adding the 20 per cent markup, yields a price of Rs. 28.97. However if only 45,000 units are sold, the cost of manufacture can be estimated to be Rs. 11,28,500. The Revenues would be 45,000 @ Rs. 28.97 = Rs. 13,03,650. The profit would therefore be Rs. 1,75,150 or 15.5 per cent over costs. The transfer price at an assumed volume of 45,000 units to yield a 20 per cent mark-up over costs would be Rs. 30.09.

2. On a full cost basis, it certainly looks that the manager

would lose money at Rs. 20/- transfer price. But, if there are no alternative uses for the unused capacity in the manufacturing division, then the incremental cost for the special contract can be compared with the incremental revenues. To produce 15,000 units, the total cost would be:

Cost @ 60,000 units	Rs. 14,14,000
Cost @ 45,000 units	Rs. 11,28,500
Incremental cost of 15,000 units	Rs. 2,85,500
Incremental cost per unit	Rs. 19.03

Thus, if the manufacturing manager receives Rs. 20/- for each unit transferred to the marketing division, he will make, not lose money, on this special contract. A transfer price of Rs. 20/- or perhaps a price of Rs. 21/- would be appropriate in this situation.

However, the manufcturing manager may still refuse to produce the additional 15,000 units at a Rs. 20/- or Rs. 21/- transfer price if :-

a) He does not understand that his incremental cost is only Rs. 19.03 per unit.

b) He has a better or more profitable use of the available capacity.

II. The ABC Corporation has three operating divisions. The managers of these divisions are evaluated on their divisional Net Income Before Taxes, a figure that includes an allocatikon of corporate overhead proportional to the sales of each division. The operating statement for the first quarter of 1999 appears below:

	Division			
	A	B	C	Total
	Rs.	Rs.	Rs.	Rs.
Net sales (000)	2,000	1,200	1,600	4,800
Cost of sales	1,050	540	640	2,230
Division overhead	250	125	160	535
Division contribution	700	535	800	2,035
Corporate overhead	400	240	320	960
Net income before taxes	300	295	480	1,075

The manager of Division A is unhappy that his profitability is about the same as Division B's and much less than Division C's, even though his sales are much higher than either of these other two divisions. The manager knows that he is carrying one line of products with very low profitability. He was going to replace this line of business as soon as more profitable product opportunities became available but has retained it until now, since the line was still marginally profitable and used facilities that would otherwise be idle. The manager now realizes, however, that the sales from this product line are attracting a fair amount of corporate overhead because of the allocation procedure and may be the line is already unprofitable for him.

This low margin line of products had the following characteristics for the quarter:

	Rs.
Net sales (000)	800
Cost of sales	600
Escapable divisional overhead	100
Contribution	100

Thus, the product line accounted for 40% of divisional sales but less than 15% of divisional profit.

Required:

1. Prepare the operating sttement for the ABC Corporation for the second quarter of 1999 assuming that sales and operating results are identical to the first quarter except that the manager of Division A drops the low margin product line entirely from his product group. Is the Division A manager better off from this action? Is the ABC Corporation better off from this action?

2. Suggest improvements to the ABC Corporation's divisional reporting and evaluation system that will improve local incentives for decision-making that is in the best interests of the firm.

Solutions

1. Without the Rs.8,00,000 is sales from the low margin product line in Division A, the second quarter operating statements will be:

	Rs.	Rs.	Rs.	Rs.
Net Sales (000)	1,200	1,200	1,600	4,000
Cost of Sales	450	540	640	1,630
Division Overhead	150	125	160	435
Division Contribution	600	535	688	1,935
Corporate Overhead	288	288	384	960
Net Income Before Taxes	312	247	416	975

The Division A manager is able to show a Rs. 12,000 higher profit because the Rs. 1,00,000 in lost contribution margin from the dropped product line is more than offset by the Rs. 1,12,000 reduction in corporate overhead. Divisional sales are now only 30 per cent of corporate sales rather than the previous 41.7 per cent of sales. The ABC Corporation is worse off because it has lost the Rs. 100,000 contribution margin from the dropped product line with no reduction in corporate overhead.

2. The easiest solution is to not allocate fixed corporate overhead to divisions. Then, the problem of dysfunctional behaviour will not arise. But central management may want the division managers to "see" the cost of corporate operations so that they will understand that the corporation as a whole is not profitable unless the combined divisions' contribution margins exceed corporate overhead. In this case, an allocation basis should be chosen that is not manipulable or under the control of division managers, and has the property that the actions of one division do not affect the allocations to other divisions (as occurred in the second quarter for the young Corporation). In general, a lump-sum allocation based on, say, budgeted net income, or budgeted assets, rather than an allocation that varies proportionately with an actual measure of activity (such as sales or

actual net income) will minimize dysfunctional behaviour. The allocation should be such that managers treat it as a fixed, unavoidable charge, rather than a charge that will vary with decisions they take.

3. The basis that should be chosen to allocate fixed corporate overhead should be such that is not under the control of divisional managers or be liable to be manipulated. It should also be sufficiently independent so that actions of one division do not affect the allocations to other divisions. The managers of the firm must realize that the organization as a whole will not be profitable unless the total contribution margin of all the divisions exceed the corporte overheads.

   The basis chosen should be such that managers treat it as a fixed unavoidable expense rather than an expense that will vary with the decisions they take.

III. A company has two Divisions: A & B. Each division has full authority on all decisions regarding sales to internal or external customers. Division A always acquires a certain component from Division B. Lately Division B has increased its price to Rs. 220/- per unit. Division A's management has thus decided to purchase the component from outside suppliers at a price of Rs. 200/-.

Division B had recently acquiraed some new equipment that was mainly used to make this component. The manager of Division B gave the high depreciation charges as the reason for the price increase to Rs. 220-. He has requested the President of the Company to instruct Division A to buy from Division B at the Rs. 220/- a unit price. The following information is given:

A's annual purchase of component	4000 units
B's variable cost per unit	Rs. 190/-
B's fixed cost per unit	Rs. 20/-

Assume there are no alternative use of the facilities of B.

Required:

1. If P buys from outside suppliers at Rs. 200/- per unit will the company as a whole benefit?

2. Assume that the selling price to outsiders drops to Rs. 185/- should A purchase from outsiders.

3. Assume that B could modify the component at an additional variable cost of Rs. 10/- per unit and sell the 4000 units to other customers for Rs. 225/-. Would the entire company thenbenefit if A purchased the 4000 components from outsiders at Rs. 200/- per unit.

Solution

This exercise illustrates the conflicts that can arise from transfer pricing.

1. B's fixed costs are apparently Rs. 80,000 per year and these costs will be unaffected by whether A purchases externally or internally. If A purchases from outside, its cash costs will be Rs. 8,00,000 per year. If A purchases internally the incremental cost to the firm is Rs. 7,60,000 per year. (4000 @ Rs. 190). Thus the firm as a whole is worse off by Rs. 40,000 if external purchases are made.

2. Cash outlay for external

   Purchases - Rs. 7,40,000 (4000 @ Rs. 185/-)

   If the selling price drops to Rs. 185/- it is more profitable to purchase externally.

3. A purchases externally at Rs. 200/-

   B modifies the component and sells at Rs. 225/-

   Net cost to the firm

A's Purchase	4000 @ 200	Rs. 8,00,000
B's Variable cost	4,000 @ (190+10)	8,00,000
B's Revenues	4,000 @ 225/-	9,00,000
Net cash cost		Rs. 7,00,000

If A purchases internally from B

Net Cash cost = 4000 @ 190

= Rs. 7,60,000

Thus, it is more profitable for both A & B to transact in the external market.

IV. The ABC division of a company produces water pumps for automobiles. It has been the sole suppliers of pumps to the automotive division and charges Rs.10/- per unit, the current market price for very large wholesale lots. The pump division also sells to outside retail outlets, at Rs. 12.50 per unit. Normally, outside sales amount to 25% of a sales volume of 2 million pumps per year. Typical combined annual data for division are as follows:

	Rs.
Sales	21,250,000
Variable costs @ Rs. 8 per pump	16,000,000
Fixed costs	2,000,000
Total costs	18,000,000
Gross margin	3,250,000

The Sure Life pump company an entirely separate entity, has offered the automotive Division comparable pumps at a firms price of Rs. 9 per unit. The ABC Division claims that it cannot possibly match this price because it could not earn any margin at Rs. 9.

Required

1. Assume that you are the manager of the automotive Division. Comment on the ABC Divisions claim. Assume that normal outside volume cannot be increased.

2. The ABC division tells that it can increase outside sales by 1.5 million pumps per year by increasing fixed costs by Rs. 2 million and variable costs by Rs. 1 per unit while reducing the selling costs to Rs.12. Assume that maximum capacity is 2 million pumps

per year. Should the division reject intra-company business and concentrate on outside sales?

Solution

1. Both the ABC division and the company as a whole will benefit if the Rs. 9/- price is met. If not, gross margin will fall to 2,50,000 as shown below:

Sales 5,00,000 @ Rs. 12.50/-		Rs.62,50,000
Variable cost @ Rs. 8/-	Rs. 4,000,000	
Fixed Cost	2,000,000	
Total cost		Rs. 6,000,000
Gross Margin		Rs. 250,000

Average cost = 18,000,000/2,000,000 = Rs. 9

If pumps are supplied internally @ Rs. 9 then

Sales	
External @ Rs.12.5	Rs. 6,250,000
Internal @ 9	13,5000,000
Total	19,750,000
Variable cost @ Rs. 8	16,000,000
Contribution Margin	3,750,000
Less: Fixed cost	2,000,000
Gross Margin	Rs. 1,750,000

(a) If the pumps are supplied at Rs. 9 internally, the profit reduces to Rs. 1,750,000 from Rs. 3,250,000, the entire profit amount coming from external sales. Though the division will not make any profit internally but still it is able to cover all its costs and earn a mark-up of Rs. 1,750,000. The manager of ABC Division, still in a profit position should be able to supply the pumps internally at Rs. 9.

(b) If the company starts buying pumps from outside the ABC Division will suffer a heavy set back as it cannot increases outside sales and there will not be any internal sales. In this case ABC Division will only be able to sell 500,000 pumps externally and 1,500,000 will be unsold with division and division will incur losses.

Sales	
External @ Rs. 12.5	Rs. 6,250,000
Internal	—
Total	6,250,000
Variable cost	16,000,000
Contribution Margin	(-) 9,750,000

The division will be unable to cover up its variable and fixed cost. Thus, it's better for the division to supply the pumps at Rs. 9 to the company.

(c) If the bargaining power of ABC Division is good in the external market it can try charge a higher price to increase profit and cover up some profit lost due to internal sales.

2. Yes, the division should reject intra-company sales and concentrate on outside sales since the gross margin would be Rs.20,00,000 whereas if the automative division business is accepted, gross margin is Rs.17,50,000.

Sales	**Rs.**
Externally @ Rs.12	24,000,000
Internal	—
Total	24,000,000
Variable cost @ Rs.9	18,000,000
Contribution Margin	6,000,000
Less : Fixed cost	4,000,000
Gross Margin (new proposal)	Rs.2,000,000
Gross Margin (accepting intra-company business)	17,50,000
Difference	250,000

Questions

1. Why are transfer prices recesary? Describe the basis for establishing transfer prices.

2. Why are market based transfer prices considered optional under many circumstances?
3. What are the limitations of market-based transfer prices?
4. What are the disadvantages of a negotiated transfer price system?
5. Briefly explain the objectives of transfer pricing with examples.

Exercises

1. Make or Buy & Transfer Pricing:

   Regal Appliance Corporation is organised into three divisions, A, B and C. One of the firm's products uses components, made by A and B, with the final assembly done by C. One unit from A and one unit from B are required.

   The following data is given:

Selling Price (Division C)	Rs. 150
Variable Costs:	
Division A	Rs. 40
Division B	Rs. 20
Division C	Rs. 15
Total variable costs	Rs. 75
Volume	·1,000 units

   For each unit supplied to Division C, Division A and B charge Rs. 45 and Rs. 25 respectively from Division C. The Manager of Division C has found an outside supplier who will sell the component, currently being purchased from Division A, at Rs. 40 per unit.

   (a) Based on current operations, calculate the contribution margin for A, B and C.

   (b) Should Division C accept the outside offer? If A meets the outside price C will continue to buy from A?

2. Dropping a segment:

A company manufactures three different products: X, Y, Z. The following information has been collected from the books of accounts:

	X Rs.	Y Rs.	Z Rs.	Total Rs.
Sales	700,000	200,000	400,00	
Variable Cost	300,000	100,000	150,000	
Contribution Margin	400,000	100,000	250,000	
Fixed Cost				
Joint	120,000	80,000	90,000	
Separable	60,000	30,000	40,000	
Net income (Loss)	220,000	(10,000)	120,000	

(a) Will you advise the company to drop product Y? Give reasons for your answer.

(b) Prepare a revised income statement assuming product Y was dropped.

(c) Assume that the sales of X will increase by 10% if Y is dropped? Will this change your answer? Why?

3. Make or Buy:

Anu Electronics Corporation produces a product X, for which the following are the unit cost and total cost. Currently it costs the company Rs. 50 to produce the product in lots of 500 units.

	Unit Cost	Total Cost
Raw Material	Rs. 15	Rs. 7,500
Direct Labour	10	5,000
Variable overhead	7	3,500
Joint fixed cost	8	4,000
Separable fixed cost	10	5,000
Total cost	Rs. 50	Rs. 25,000

Anu Electronics has been approached by another company, the Apex Company to make product X at a cost of Rs. 48 each, with no sacrifice in quality or delivery. Should Anu Electronics accept the offer? Give reasons for your answer?

4. A company has two divisions, A and B. The division A is currently operating at full capacity. It has been asked to supply its product to division B. Division A sells its product to its regular customers for Rs. 30 each. Division B (currently operating at 50% capacity) is willing to pay Rs. 20 each for the component produced by division A (this represents the full absorption cost per component at division A).

   The components will be used by division B in supplementing its main product to conform to the need of special order.

   As per the contract terms of sales, the buyer calls for reimbursement of full cost to division B plus 10%.

   Division A has a variable cost of Rs. 17 per component. The cost per unit of division B subsequent to the buying part from division A is estimated as follows:

Purchased parts — outside vendors	Rs. 95
Purchased part — division A	Rs. 15
Other variable costs	Rs. 45
Fixed overheads and administration	Rs. 45
	Rs. 200

The company uses return on investment in the measurement of division and division manager's performance.

Required:

(a) As manager of division A, would you recommend sales of your output to division B at the stipulated price of Rs. 20?

(b) Would it be in the over-all interest of the company for division A to sell its output to division B?

(c) Suggest an alternative transfer price and show how could it lead to goal congrenuence?

5. A products variable cost is Rs. 10/- and its market value is Rs. 15/- at a transfer point from Division A to Division

B. Division B's variable cost of processing the product further is Rs. 2/- and the selling price of the final product is Rs. 21/-.

(i) Prepare a tabulation of the contribution margin per unit for Division B's performance and overall performance under the two alternatives of (a) processing further and (b) selling to outsiders at the transfer point.

(ii) As the manager of Division B, which alternative would you chose and why?

6. Arjun Enterprises has two Divisions X and Y. Division X produces a component that is used in the finished product of Division Y. The variable cost of producing the component are Rs. 60/- per unit and fixed costs are Rs. 20/- per unit. The selling price of the component in the final market is Rs. 100/-. Till now, Division Y bought 50% of the output of Division X at a negotiated price of Rs. 80/- per unit. The company wants to develop a new transfer pricing method. The different alternatives being considered are: -

(i) Add 30% to the total cost when transferring to Division Y.

(ii) Make use of the variable cost of Rs. 60/- per unit in arriving at a transfer price.

In the light of the above information, determine the Gross Profit for Division Y according to the different transfer pricing methods. Additional marketing costs are Rs. 120/- per unit. The selling price of the finished product of Division Y is Rs. 250/- per unit.

16

Human Resource Accounting and Inflation Accounting

The present chapter gives a brief account of two special areas in accounting viz. Human Resource Accounting, and Inflation Accounting.

Human Resource Accounting

The term 'Human Resource Accounting' means accounting for human beings, the most important organizational resource. The accounting of it deals with the measurement of costs which are associated with recruiting, selecting, hiring, training, placing and developing the employees of an organization. It also involves measuring the present economic value of human resources to an organization. This section describes the various methods for calculating the value of human resources in an organization.

The American Accounting Association Committee on human resource accounting broadly defines it as the process of identifying and measuring data about human resource and communicating this information to the interested parties.

The primary objective of accounting for human resources is not merely to account but also to help the management in planning and controlling the contribution of people to organizations and to society at large. Human Resource Accounting is also expected to improve the quality of financial decisions made both internally as well as externally regarding the functioning of an organization. Information regarding human resources and changes thereof may provide the management with valuable aids for monitoring efficiency of employees, regulating organizational behaviour, reducing absenteeism, and improving human relations.

Thus Human Resource Accounting helps in quantifying the service potential of employees in an organization. It helps in changing the attitude of management toward their people by viewing them as assets and thereby placing a monetary valuation on the services to be rendered by them. Such a change in attitude is likely to have an impact on their decisions involving human resources.

Very few empirical studies have been made analyzing the behavioural implications of human resource accounting models on management decisions. The behavioural implications of human resource accounting can be assessed properly only if the results of experiments with human resource accounting systems in organizations are researched and published. Hence there is a need for demonstrated benefits of human resource accounting systems.

As far as India is concerned, Bharat Heavy Electricals Limited is one of the few companies which is incorporating information on human resource accounting in its published financial statement.

Methods of Human Resource Accounting

A number of different valuation models have been developed for the measurement of human assets in an organization. The various approaches may be divided into two categories : (1) Monetary measures and (II) Non-monetary measures.

Monetary Measures

1. *Replacement Costs.*

In this method, the value of an employee is estimated in terms of the cost that the organization will have to incur if it were to replace the present employee with a person of equal ability. The replacement cost here includes recruitment, training and development expenditure alongwith the opportunity cost of revenue lost during the period of training. Flamholtz who used this model has referred to two different concepts of replacement costs viz. 'individual replacement cost' and 'positional replacement cost.' For each employee, the position he might occupy in future must be identified. Secondly, the positional replacement cost of the employee should also be measured. The probability of the employees occupying the respective positions at the expected time should also be made. This positional replacement cost is defined as the cost of replacing the set of services expected to be rendered by an individual in the present and future positions.

2. *Opportunity Cost*

The value of human assets in the opportunity cost method is determined on the basis of the value of individual employees in alternative use. The guiding criteria here is that human assets have value only when there is alternative use for them, i.e., only scarce personnel represent the value of human assets. Thus, there is no opportunity cost for employees that can be hired easily. Hekiman and Jones use the opportunity costs to arrive at the worth of employees. The approach involves a competitive bidding process by the investment centre managers for scarce employees they desire. The bid price is based on the perceived value of the individual employee and only scarce employees form the asset base of the investment centre. It is argued that evaluation of human assets on this basis encourages managers to select employees more optimally and result in most efficient use of employee time.

3. *Historical costs*

This method involves capitalizing the cost of maintaining the individual in the organization to produce the service state rewards to the organization., i.e. all costs related with recruitment, training and development of the employee. Training costs are usually demortized over a shorter period than recruitment costs since training becomes outdated as new skills must be developed to meet technological change. The value is written off annually over an individual employee's expected tenure in the organization. The unexpired value is shown as investment in human resources.

This method is considered to be useful to both internal and external users of accounting data as the method is considered by researchers to be objective and facilitates comparison.

4. *EconomicValue*

This method measures the value of human assets on the assumption that an individual generates value for an organization as he occupies and moves among organizational roles and renders services to the organization. The roles he will occupy depend probabilitically upon the roles previously occupied. Thus, the valuation process involves the use of probabilities of the employees change of position and of service to be derived.

A person's expected service value may be expressed as follows:

$$(S) = \sum_{t=1}^{n} S_1 P(S_1)$$

where

(S) is the expected total service, S_1 is the service expected to be derived from each state to be occupied by the employee and $P(S_1)$ is the estimated probability of the expected service being actually derived.

The total value of expected future service is determined by multiplying the physical equivalent of services by the price of services. The total value is then discounted at the appropriate rate of return to obtain the present value of service. The present value so obtained represents the value of human assets.

5. Discounted Present Value of Future Wages & Salaries

The value of human resources is taken to be equal to the present value of future earnings of employees till retirement.

For this purpose employees may be classified into homogeneous groups according to type of assignment, nature of work, age, level of skill etc. An appropriate rate of discount like the cost of capital may be used to compute the present value of future earnings.

Non-monetary Measures

1. Discounted net present value of future earnings based on managerial behaviour, style, policies and the employees attitudes, performance and collective capabilities. The value of human resources is measured by predicting the future earnings of the employing firm, discounting the same to net present value and allocating a portion of this value to human assets. The future earnings of the firm are predicted taking into account two types of variables: casual variables like management behaviour, style, organizational structure, and Intervening like loyalties, motivation, goals and attitudes of the employees.

2. Value of employees based on attitude scores derived from their knowledge, skill etc. and their annual income. The attitude score of an employee is then multiplied by his annual salary. The difference between this value and the employee's annual earnings represent the gain or loss the firm is incurring by retaining the employee.

3. *Flamholtz model*: According to Flamholtz, an individual's value to an organization can be measured by applying personnel evaluation methods like ranking. Individuals may be evaluated by their supervisors, subordinates, peers or independent experts. The economic value of an individual to the organization can be measured in terms of their net contribution to the organization, that is, their gross value, less the compensation and other costs associated with their utilization.

Determination of Human Value

The value of an individual to an organization may be defined as the present value of the set of future service that the individual is expected to render during the period he is likely to work for the organization. The determinants of the value potentially realizable from his services (also referred to as the conditional value of an individual) consists of three variables viz. productivity, promotability and transferability. The various factors which affect these three variables are skill and motivation of the employees, individuals role in the organization, nataure of organizational rewards etc. These variables interact mutually to ultimately determine the potentially realizable value of an individual and the probability of him continuing to work in the organization.

Importance of Human Resource Accounting

Improving the quality of managerial decisions is the basic rationale for measuring and accounting for the value of human resources in an organization. Human resources data assist in the widening of the scope of internal decision-making by permitting the consideration of a number of variables and improving the basis on which such variables are considered. The case for human resource accounting stems from the basic premise that measurement of the value of human resources can assist management in recognizing and defining problems connected with manpower management in several ways. Changes in the value of human resources may be used as an indicator of the cost of employee turnover. Assigning people to various organizational roles and tasks is usually decided on the basis of efficiency of the employees, opportunity of self development and job satisfaction expected to be derived by them. Human resource accounting can help qualify the variables required to be considered in the process of allocation.

Inflation Accounting

Accounting for changing prices (Inflation Accounting) has become synonymous with accounting for inflation due to the unprecedented pressure of inflationary price rise in most countries in recent decades. In periods of sustained price rise, historical costs lose their relevance and may even become misleading as measurements of economic value. Financial statements which are prepared on the basis of historical cost records suffer from a number of shortcomings during a period of rising prices. They are:

1. Fixed assets are stated at historical costs in the balance sheet; they do not show the true current worth and are often unrealistically low.

2. Depreciation is charged on the historical cost of the assets. As a result, depreciation provision is also inadequate for financing the replacement cost of fixed assets. The firm may, therefore, have to face serious problems because of paucity of funds.

3. In a period of rising prices, there is a significant overstatement of profits since the cost of goods sold is calculated on a historical cost basis and no allowance is made for the reduction in the purchasing power of money. Also overstatement in profits results in a heavy financial strain for the company in terms of heavy dividend, heavy taxation, etc.

In June 1969, the APB of the AICPA recommended that supplementary statements should be appended to the annual accounts of companies so as to disclose the effect of general price level changes on the financial position. Inflation Accounting seeks to incorporate realism into financial statements by adjusting them, so as to reflect in a true and fair manner the financial performance and the position of an enterprise in a particular period.

The balance sheet prepared at a point of time includes some items such as cash, debtors, etc., that are stated at current purchasing power; others such as inventory, are stated in monetary units that reflect the purchasing power of the recent past; and still others such as furniture, land, plant and equipment that are stated at historical cost. When the general price level is rising rapidly, reported profits of a company which has a major proportion of its assets which are stated at historical costs is overstated. If profits are overstated, it follows that costs and expenses are under-stated. This may lead to reporting illusory profits.

Thus, accountants use the concept of Inflation Accounting so as to convert monetary units having varying purchasing power into a single monetary unit. The objective of Inflation Accounting is to adjust historical cost figures for substantive changes in the general level in the economy. The following are some of the objectives of Inflation Accounting:-

(a) to remove the various distortions with which financial statement based on historical cost suffer.

(b) to provide for more meaningful interperiod comparison.

(c) to improve the meaning and measurement of income and expenses in the face of changing purchasing power of money.

(d) to improve the decision making in the organization.

Further, Inflation-adjusted information helps the decision makers in the following ways:-

1. Allocation of capital is achieved through the pricing mechanism in capital markets. Prices based on financial information which is incomplete or misleading results in poor pricing and allocation decision. As inflation rates vary from year to year, an element of uncertainty is there in business activities. Further, even though management is aware of the need to incorporate inflation in making business decisions, it is hindered in doing so by the lack of systematic and explicit recognition of inflation's effects in financial reports. The system of inflation accounting, if introduced will help the various parties who have an interest and stake in the business viz. shareholders, employees, external users, management and government.

2. Management will be better equipped to tackle the

problems caused by inflation and in turn improve productivity in the long-run.

3. Information about the specific price changes on individual enterprises and by industry grouping will help the policy makers to analyze the impact of the differential impact of inflation on each industry. Intlation accounting will also help in giving a clearer disclosure and in turn help the government in making various policy decisions.

4. The public understanding of the business and the various effects of inflation goes up. This helps the business in being somewhat less critically viewed by the general public helps them in their continuous exercise of mobilizing funds for expansion, new investment and also to provide employment.

Methods of Accounting for Inflation

Various methods have been proposed in accounting to reflect the true changes in the purchasing power of money. However, no consensus has yet been reached on a specific solution and the professional bodies in various countries argue that the method chosen should be accurate, reasonable, effective and easy to implement. The following are the various methods, in brief, that have been put forward for inflation accounting:

I. Current Cost Accounting (CCA)

The Inflation Accounting Committee of the U.K. government set up this method in 1975. It has been extensively studied and debated and now it has been finalized by the issue of SSAP 16 (Statement of Standard Accounting Practice).

This system takes into account price changes relevant to the particular firm or industry rather than the economy as a whole. It seeks to arrive at a profit which can be safely distributed as dividend without impairing the operational capability of the firm.

The CCA method is based on the concept that a business enterprise is a going concern which is continuously replacing its assets. The method uses current dollars/rupees and values assets at their acquisition costs and hence no adjustment for inflation is done in the accounts. The financial statements are drawn up here on the assumption that the purchasing power of money is stable over time.

However, since the purchasing power of money differs in different periods of time, these statements do not ultimately measure what they seek to measure. Yet this is the oldest and the most popular method of accounting.

The salient features of this method are:

— Fixed assets are shown not at their depreciated original cost but at their net replacement value.

— Stocks are shown at their net replacement value.

— Depreciation is calculated at the current value of assets.

— Gain/loss due to the changes in the price level are shown in a separate statement.

— Inventory consumed is valued at the price at the date of consumption.

Under this approach, assets and expenses are shown in the financial statements at the current cost to replace those specific resources. Thus, profit is measured by comparing revenues with the current replacement cost of the assets consumed in the earning process.

Suitability of the Method

The current cost accounting method is suitable when the management is committed to the industry and is interested in replacing the present plant by a new one at the end of its useful life.

II. Current Purchasing Power Method (C.P.P.): (Also known as General Price-Level Accounting)

This method is recommended by the Accounting Policy Board and also the Financial Accounting Standards Board

(FASB) of USA. This method adjusts historical cost for changes in the general level of prices as measured by the general price-level index. Changes in the general level of prices represent changes in the general purchasing power of the monetary unit. Thus Inflation, in general, reduces the general purchasing power to purchase goods and services while deflation increases the general purchasing power to purchase goods and services.

Historical financial statements consist of transactions at various times and hence replacement purchasing powers at various points in time. CPP method transforms the various historical measures into current purchasing power which represents purchasing power at the same point in time. Thus CPP method makes all accounting numbers comparable in terms of general purchasing power by removing the mixed purchasing power element from historical financial statements.

This method differs from Current Cost Accounting in that, under this approach the current values of various assets is not worked out but the financial statements are stated in terms of rupees of uniform value. Hence, this method takes into account changes in price levels which are denoted by the general price index. Thus, all amounts are expressed in units of equal purchasing power. Since this method shows the effects of changes in the general price level, this method is also called General Price Level Accounting.

The CPP method makes a distinction between monetary items and non-monetary items. Monetary items are those assets and liabilities that represent a claim to receive, or an obligation to pay, a fixed amount of foreign currency. Example of monetary items include cash, accounts payable, accounts receivable, long-term debt. Monetary items are translated at the current rate while non-monetary items (such as fixed assets, stock, plant and buildings) are translated at historical rates.

During a period of rising prices, holding monetary assets results in a loss of purchasing power. Likewise, creditors tend to gain during a period of rising prices as debts are now repaid in rupees of less purchasing power that those originally borrowed.

Non-monetary items such as stocks, plants and buildings, increase in value during inflation. The lower of cost and net realizable value can be taken and then adjusted further.

The index used here could be the cost of living index or the consumers' expenditure deflates or the general index of retail prices.

Suitability of the Method

— The method may be used when the aim is maintenance of the purchasing power in general.

— To assist decision-makers in evaluating trends, when data for a series are expressed in units of constant purchasing power.

— The shareholders can keep the purchasing power of their investment intact.

Problems in Implementation

1. The critical problem in Inflation Accounting is training accountants and others in the preparation and interpretation of information, adjusted for the effects of inflation.

2. Price indices to be used for the revaluation of assets.

3. Corporate profits are watched closely by business managers, government officials and investors. Management may sometimes have a vested interest in maintaining the present level of profits and not make any adjustment to this profit. This may be due to the management wanting to maintain the present rate of taxation, rate of return on equity capital and so on.

4. Finally, labour unions also may not agree to the adjustment of financial statement for the effects of inflation, if they fear that as a result of the adjustment, profits and hence bonus will fall.

III. 'Value to the Business' Accounting (VBA): (Also known as "Deprival Value" Accounting and "Current Cost or Lower Recoverable Amount" Accounting):

SSAP 16 (UK) defines value to the Business as (a) net current replacement cost; (b) recoverable amount. Recoverable amount is the greater of the net realizable value of an asset and, where applicable, the amount recoverable from its further use.

Where an asset will normally be replaced it is shown at the net current replacement cost, and is changed on this basis in the profit and loss account. However, when the asset is not to be replaced or where replacement cost is higher than both net realizable value and present value, the higher of the net realizable value and the present value is usually used as the measurement basis. The replacement of a specific asset is normally derived from the current acquisition cost of a similar asset, new or used or of an equivalent productive capacity.

Inflation and Productivity Measurement

Productivity can be measured as a ratio of Sales Revenue to number of employees

$$\text{Productivity} = \frac{\text{Sales Revenue}}{\text{No. of Employees}}$$

If the physical output and number of employees remains the same while sales price and hence sales revenue increase by 15 per cent due to Inflation, the productivity will go up by 15 per cent despite no change in real productivity.

Intensification of Budgeting

As a result of Inflation, the preparation of budgets by the organization may need to be intensified, to achieve a more effective use of the existing resources. An additional form of the budget—the requirement budget may need to be prepared, as is presently being done by a few organizations.

Inflation and Dividend Policy

In a period of inflation, the Board of Directors must make

sure that they are mainlydistributing current earnings as dividends. During inflation, earlier costs may have been matched against revenues, with the result that net income is higher that what it would otherwise be. The Board of Directors must make sure that they are not unintentionally distributing earnings from past years.

Limitation of Inflation Accounting

Financial statements prepared on the historical cost basis do not, as a rule, depict the real state of affairs of the organization. The figures presented in the Financial Statement do not reflect present day values. Nevertheless, accounts prepared on the basis of historical cost have the following advantages over other systems of accounting:

1. It is based on actual events and data.
2. It is widely used and understood by all.
3. Comparison of figures over a period of time can be made easily.
4. It forms the basis of tax assessments.
5. Manipulation of accounting records is difficult under historical costs.

Thus, there is an imperative need for inflation-adjusted financial statements to be presented to the shareholders and other interested parties. Yet, there are a number of objections to inflation accounting. They are:

1. The financial statements lose their credibility as the objectivity concept is violated.
2. The method is not acceptabel by the tax authorities.
3. Inflation accounting may sometimes result in arbitrary profits.

Thus, the main problem with Inflation Accounting is that the method has not been able to come up with an accounting system that would satisfy all. The method has still a long way to go and the search is on for a method that would take into account inflation and still be objective and simple in its implementation.

Questions

1. What are the various methods of measuring human resource accounting? Explain with examples.
2. Briefly explain the importance of human resource accounting? Should companies adopt human resource accounting?
3. Why do companies use Inflation accounting? What are its limitations?
4. What are the methods of accounting for inflation?

17

International Accounting

The development of interest in the international aspect of accounting is a consequence of the growing internationalisation of business. International Accounting poses a global challenge to accounting researchers. In a world of growing inter-relationships of a political, social and economic nature, it has become imperative to recognise the importance of international accounting. In the global environment and cultural context, accounting at the national level is a subject of global accounting specifically due to the growing internationalisation of markets. The international dimensions of accounting are now fundamental to accounting research. Recent developments in the world of international business and finance have made it imperative to incorporate the international perspective of accounting, not as a supplement, but as an integral part of our accounting research.

The present chapter discusses the growing importance of International Accounting in the context of globalization of business. The important reasons for studying International Accounting are also discussed. Finally, the accounting practices of a few selected countries are analyzed, and suggestions for improving the accounting standardization system are given.

Accounting research is not international just because it is conducted in another country. It becomes international when it specifically considers the comparative financial accounting practices across countries, the controversy of foreign currency translation, harmonization of the international standards in different countries, financial reporting and disclosure practices across countries and so on. It attempts toidentify and analyse the specific requirements of accounting for the operations of Multinational Corporations.

The goal of accountants in the international area is to develop standards that are not necessarily uniform with other standards but are at least understandable and recognisable, i.e., to harmonize international accounting standards.

The volume and variety of accounting practices have multiplied. Specific accounting practices have often been developed by different countries. One of the key purpose of International Accounting is also to rationalize the multitude of existing accounting practices.

The more important aspect of the evolution of accounting in the international sense has been the ability of accounting to serve effectively and usefully in different social and national set-up. It is this flexibility of accounting through centuries of development that justifies the study of the international dimensions of accounting.

Based on the preceding discussion, International Accounting can be defined as[1]: "International Accounting extends general purpose, nationally oriented accounting in its broadest sense to: (1) inernational comparative analysis, (2) accounting measurement and reporting issues unique to multinational business transfactions and the business forms of the multinational enterprise, (3) accounting needs of international financial markets, and, (4) harmonization of worldwide accounting and financial reporting diversity via political, organizational, professional, and standard setting activities.

The growing importance of international accounting is an inevitable consequence of the international forces for change at work in the world today.

Why International Accounting?

I. *The Global aspect*: A multinational company engages in

business transactions all over the globe. It usually produces where costs are lowest and raises capital where it is cheapest. The MNCs also try and develop markets wherever its products and services will be bought by people.

The economies of various countries are also becoming less independent and increasingly dependent on other economies around the world[2]. A number of companies are also formally listing their common shares in stock exchanges outside their home countries. Presently there are large euro money market and still larger foreign exchange markets.

II. *Accounting Standards & MNCs*: Setting Accounting Standard is a difficult and controversial task at the national level. At the international level, setting standards becomes even more complex, problematic and multi-dimensional[3].

The various advantages of international standards are[4]:

1. Reduction in the number of different accounting practices being followed by various countries.
2. Comparability of international financial information for investors, financial analyst and credit agencies in comparing the performance and prospects of companies from different countries.
3. Time and money saved that is presently spent to consolidate different financial information.
4. Improved decision-making as a result of "universally applicable standards".

Though a variety of international organisations are involved in efforts to harmonize accounting and financial reporting across the countries, internationalization of accounting standards is an endeavour of conflicts.

Harmonization[5] of accounting is a process whereby the size and number of differences in practices between countries are reduced. It does not imply complete standardization that would require uniform and rigid rules.

Thus a greater degree of standardisation in accounting would be of particular benefit to developing countries. Standardization would simplify and unify all aspects of accounting information system. This would improve the reliability and consistency of information.

III. *Foreign currency Translation*: Foreign currency translation is one of the most controversial issue in international activity. MNCs have to prepare consolidated financial statements incorporating the result for both domestic and foreign operations.

"Standardization" means that a single standard or rule is applied to all situation operations. To prepare consolidated financial statements a single currency framework is required; financial statements cannot be prepared from accounts that are expressed in various currencies.

A parent company and its subsidiary are integral parts of a whole company. They must be analysed in unison so that a complete currency picture evolves. And for this, foreign currency translation procedures are called for.

One of the major problems in foreign currency translation is that the foreign exchange rate used to translate foreign currency balances to domestic currency equivalents is rarely stable and tends to vary. This variation in exchange rate gives rise to exchange gains and losses that complicate the evaluation of multinational operations.

Another complication arises because Multinational Corporations use a variety of methods to translate foreign currency. The different translation methods give different results.

IV. *The Comparative Aspect*: The final reason for studying International Accounting is to assess the similarities and differences in the various accounting process, rationalized and emphasized by various countries. The reaction of each country to a particular problem is a function of the economic, political and social environment, i.e. the country's culture and traditions. We can learn by observing how other countries have reacted to various accounting problems, e.g., inflation accounting, transfer pricing, etc.

Global Perspective of Accounting Practices

The extent of harmony of accounting practices at the global level has posed pressing challenge for international accounting research. There is a need for a conceptual framework that would guide the development of accounting standards and practices on a consistent and theoretically sound basis. The adoption of international standards and conventions would help to promote economic growth and development.

Developing countries specifically tend to benefit from a greater degree of standardisation in accounting practices, as they are often faced with deficient and disorganized economic and financial data and at all levels may level an effective accounting system and related administrative skills.

On a world wise basis, the International Accounting Standards Committee (IASC), the United Nations Centre on Transnational Corporations, the Organisation for Economic Cooperation and Development (OECD) and the European Community (EC) are among the bodies interested in harmonization of accounting practices to enable greater control of multinational corporations.

The following section now analyzes the standards relating to processes in several selected countries—the U.S., Candada, England, Australia, Germany, Japan, Sweden and Switzerland. The similarities and differences in the standard setting framework of each country are mainly due to the differences in their political, social and cultural aspects.

The United States

The Financial Accounting Standards Board (FASB) is the principal standard setting body in the United States since 1973, established by the American Institute of Certified Public Accountants (AICPA), the FASB[6]. These standards are recognised as authoritative by the Securities and Exchange Commission (SEC). The SEC can bar companies, who do not support the FASB standards, from trading their securities.

The objective of FASB is to provide information that is useful to present and potential investors and creditors. It develops broad accounting concepts as well as standards for financial reporting. It also provides guidance on implementation of standards. All FASB's meetings are open to the public and this openness ensures that the public interest is considered in standard setting. An explicit conceptual framework is used by the FASB for formulating new standards and evaluating existing ones.

Another significant feature of accounting standard setting in the U.S. is that financial accounting standards are set in the private sector and enforced through public sector actions. The government represented by the SEC, has an important influence in the standard-setting process, which is essentially performed in the private sector.

For each project an advisory task force is appointed and a comprehensive memorandum is prepared identifying the various issues, questions and solutions of various problems involved in the project. Research is also conducted to a significant extent on the specific aspects of the issue. The FASB then discusses the memoranda with interested parties and public hearings are held. An exposure draft is then prepared and widely circulated to the public to encourage public comment. Feedback of the members is taken once again and if the financial accounting standard now get a majority vote from the FASB members and is accepted by the SEC, it becomes binding on all financial statement and reports prepared in accordance with "generally accepted accounting principles".

Canada

In the Canada, the Canadian Institute of Chartered Accountants (CICA) Handbook deals with current accounting standards and guidelines in financial reporting. The Accounting Standards Committee (AcSC) is an arm of the CICA. Thus, while in USA, the AICPA is no longer the standard setting body, the CICA remains such in Canada. Also, the FASB is an independent standard setting body while the AcSC is an arm of CICA.

The AcSC emphasizes secrecy in its meeting and no open meetings or public hearings are held. The AcSC maintains confidentiality in its reports and does not indicate the details of the voting pattern for each accounting standard. Also, external task forces are used to a limited extent by AcSC. By contrast all FASB's meetings are open to the public and an external task force is appointed by the FASB for each project. Discussion memoranda and exposure drafts are circulated to the public by FASB while the AcSC circulates only exposure drafts to the public.

The environment in the United States is more litigious than in Canada. As a result, the Canadian standards are more judgmental, emphasize decision usefulness than the Accounting standards in the U.S. The Canadian standards greatly emphasize the "professional judgement" of standard setters, management accountant and chartered accountants[7]. Standard setting in Canada is less stringent than is the case in the United States.

In some situations, Canada tends to adopt standards only after the United States and sometimes U.K. have implemented their own standards. Canadian accounting appears to be significantly influenced by the United States. For example, Canada like the United States has also not adopted social accounting even though it has been adopted in several other European countries like France, West Germany, U.K., etc.

England

The standard setting body in U.K. is the Accounting Standards Board (ASB), which was created in 1990. This board has a paid full-time chairperson, a paid full-time director and several paid part-time members.

ASB functions more or less like the FASB in the United States. Standard setting in U.K., as in U.S. and Canada, is also conducted in a professional and legalistic manner.

Discussion papers and exposure drafts are circulated to the public after the research studies have been carried out by the consultative accountancy bodies. After a six month period, all feedback are considered and then a draft standard is issued or a new exposure draft is prepared. The draft standard, after due process becomes a final standard.

Financial reporting in U.K. is the most comprehensive.

Australia

As the Australians distrust government regulations and bureaucratic control, standard setting in Australia is disclosure oriented. The most powerful accounting agency in Australia is the Australian Accounting Research Foundation (AARF), which operates in the private sector, as the private sector dominates the Australian economic system. In 1984, the Account Standards Review Board (ASRB) was created to review and approve financial accounting standards recommended to it by AARF, or any other interested party or individual, and hence give the standards legal backing. Hence external parties are often requested by the AARF; which recommends standards to the ASRB, to prepare a discussion paper.

Exposure drafts are widely circulated to invite proper feedback. Public hearings and discussions are held to obtain the views of users, auditors, preparers and other interested parties. Once the standard has been accepted, it becomes law and it has to be followed, barring valid reasons for not doing so.

The Australian framework of accounting gives considerable emphasis to openness in the standard setting process, which is in conformity with the openness of the Australian people. Australians seem much more inclined than the British to experiment and to make changes. Also Australia seems to be taking a inductive approach than the U.S. devoting considerable effort to document the present practices.

Germany

The German accounting system is based on the premise that "government can be trusted". Standard setting in Germany has three dimensions—it is largely a governmental decision, it is a complete subordination to tax law; and statutory law governs accounting standards.

The Comprehensive Accounting Act of December 19, 1985 integrates all existing German accounting, financial reporting, disclosure and auditing requirements into a single law; this single law is specified as the "third book" of the German Commercial Code and is applicable to all business entities.[8]

The German accounting system is governed not by accounting principles, but by law. There is no FASB nor Accounting Standards Committee in Germany. Tax laws are very powerful and there is literally no difference between financial statements prepared for tax purposes and financial statements published in financial reports. Standards are the law, not pronouncements of professional accounting associations, and are enforced as such.

Thus, the "principles of proper book keeping" developed in Germany are standards prescribed by law, which are not codified, but stem from court cases brought before the Government. Germany has nothing comparable with British-American "generally accepted accounting principles".

Hence legal requirements enjoy absolute supremacy in Germany. Germany is quicker than U.K. and Canada to introduce technological changes; but in some respects it clings to traditions and is concerned with social welfare as are U.K. and Canada. In Germany, everthing has to be done in an orderly manner.

Japan

In Japan, the emphasis is on society as a whole rather than on the individual. The government is supposed "to know best" and hence standard setting in Japan is primarily a governmental function with some influence from the Japanese Institute of Certified Public Accountants (JICPA). The JICPA is organized and operates much along the lines of the American Institute of Certified Public Accountants. The main recommendations for standard setting in Japan is administered by the Ministry of Finance (MOF) which has become increasingly influential in financial reporting. The MOF has a special advisory board, the Business Accounting Deliberation Council (BADC). This

Council prepares accounting standards which are binding for publicly traded firms. The council represents a forum in which any interested group can discuss proposed changes in accounting standards though public hearings are not held. The standards set forth by the Council Constitute GAPP and the law.

To summarize, standard setting in Japan is the function of the government and a conceptual framework is not used. Research is also not conducted to any significant extent and meetings of the Council are not open to public. In many ways, Japan is a rather traditional society with strong cultural and religious beliefs. Accounting measurements are still largely influenced by national requirements even though there is an increasing tendency to adapt international standards.

Sweden

In Sweden, standard setting is conducted jointly by the public and private sector. The public sector body is the 'Accounting Standards Board' and the private organization is the 'Institute of Authorize Public Accountants'. Thus Sweden has a dual standard-setting framework. The Swedish accounting standards stem traditionally from Statutory of law (The companies Act of 1975) which is laragely generalized in nature.

Meetings of the accounting standard setting boards are not open to public. Drafts and proposed standards are publicized but comments are generally received only from members of the Institute. Also, no external task force is used.

Like Germany, Swedish accounting also broadly follows the income tax reporting. Not only does taxation dominate financial reporting, but so does company law in general. Also, Swedėn does not resist change, where change is necessary, it is made.

Switzerland

Standard setting in Switzerland is done by the "Foundation and Board for Accounting and Reporting Recommendations", an independent private organisation that establishes accounting and reporting recommendations. As the corporation law is vague and generalised, the standard-setting process performs a definite need in Switzerland. Like Japan, the Swiss also place a great deal of emphasis on consensus. Standard setting in Switzerland is very different from other countries as it is a very security-conscious country and appears to avoid taking excessive risk. Swiss standard-setting mechanism is inward-looking, very self-protective and fearful of foreigners and outsiders.

For setting the standards, the Board assigns projects to project directors. A discussion memoranda is then prepared which is not published but there is a discussion on this first draft by the executive committee. This draft is then presented to the Board for discussion and approval, and if the draft is approved, it then represents an Exposure draft. An Exposure draft is published and widely circulated for public feedback. The feedback from the public are examined and then a decision is taken whether to adopt the standard or not. External task force are sometimes used on various projects.

The International Harmonization of Accounting Standards

Attempts to harmonize accounting standards at the international level began in 1966 when accountants from the United States, Canada and the United Kingdom formed the Accountants International Study Group (AISG). Subsequently, a group of nine countries, including the member countries of AISG, constituted the International Accounting Standards Committee (IASC) in 1973. Another important institution which has played a key role in international accounting standard setting activities has been the International Federation of Accountants (IFAC), which was founded in 1977.

The thrust of the movement towards the harmonization of accounting standards has been continuing since a long time. A major problem in the international context is that the scope of standards is not always clearly specified, posing consequent potential for confusion.

Standard setting varies from country to country mainly because cultural values vary markedly from one country to another. Standard setting is conducted jointly by the private and public sectors. For most of the countries discussed here, standard setting is essentially a cross between the professional and the legalistic judgement. U.K., Canada and some Commonwealth countries emphasize the professional judgment in the standard setting process. Further, the United States in contrast to most other countries, apart from Japan, is the first to introduce technological changes and is less inclined to cling to traditions. Accounting in France and Germany is performance oriented primarily for the purpose of revenue authorities and for government. Profits from published reports and taxation purposes are the same.

Some suggestions which can be offered for improving the accounting standardization system are[9]:-

— Identify the need for standardization.

— Approach to standardization.

— Flexibility in standardization system.

— Studies of accounting changes.

— Accounting training.

Hence, efforts to establish International Standard of accounting are gaining momentum which has brought the issue to the forefront. A major problem here is that the scope of the standard is not always clearly specified, posing consequential potential for confusion. International harmonization of accounting will not come about as a result of imposition of uniform accounting practices - rather it will result from an awareness of the cultural and societal reasons for such differences as they exist in each country.

Questions

1. Briefly explain the term International Accounting. What are the important reasons for studying accounting in a global context?
2. Why do companies take into account the concept of

international accounting? Give examples to illustrate your answer.

3. Explain the difference and similarities between the two terms 'Harmonization' and 'Standardization'.

4. Briefly explain the process to harmonize accounting standards at the international level. What are the problems in this regard?

5. What suggestion can you offer for improving the process of accounting standardization?

Notes:

1. Choi, Ferederich D.S. & Mueller, Gerhard, G., "International Accounting", p. 12.

2. For example, today most companies raise the money they need from wherever conditions are most attractive—irrespective of what country that happens to be. Hence, as MNCs operate in many countries, they face different economic conditions. Accounting practices are usually not the same in different countries and what is satisfactory in one country may not be satisfactory in other countries. Thus, the need for International accounting is felt so that accounting practices are adjusted substantially upon crossing national boundaries.

3. Also, at the international level, the scope of standards is also not always clearly specified resulting in potential for confusion.

4. John N. Turner, "International Harmonization: A Professional Goal", Journal of Accountancy, Jan. 1984, pp. 58-59.5. Tendency for accounting standards throughout the world to be raised to the highest possible level and to be consistent with local economic, legal and social conditions.

5. The two terms "Harmonization" and "Standardization" have been used interchangeably here. However

the difference between the two terms is as follows: "Harmonization" implies that different standards might prevail in different countries as long they are "in harmony", i.e. they do not logically conflict.

6. "Financial Accounting Standards Board".

7. As a result, an explicit conceptual framework or constitution of objectives is not used for setting standards in Canada.

8. This is in accordance with the EEC directive on the harmonization in financial reporting, Germany, as member of the EC must respect the EEC directive.

9. Enthoven Adolf J., "Standardized accountancy and economic development", Article in Finance and Development, March 1973.

18

Accounting System and Computers

Computers are very useful and provide valuable assistance for accountants. They can be used for all forms of routine ledger keeping, calculataing and periodic production statement. Also, the ability of the computer to make decision enables the accountant to extend the scope of his analysis. The present chapter discusses the usefulness of computers in accounting.

A computerized accounting system provides valuable assistance for large organizations with diversified operations. There are also advantages of using a computerized accounting system in small organizations.

Most accounting systems are structured to provide the information needed to generate financial statements. The structure of an accounting system includes journals, ledger accounts and other financial transactions organized in a chronological order.

The Journal is known as the book of initial entry and provides the initial record of a business transaction. The ledger accounts summarize and record the transaction data from the journal and are used as Master files in a computerized system. At the end of an accounting period, ledger accounts are closed, adjustment entries made and the financial statements prepared.

A computerized accounting system uses the general ledger as the master file and uses software programs to manipulate data entry, editing, updating records and files and periodic closing electronically.

The speed and accuracy with which the computers perform the calculations make them specially useful for management accountants. For example, the variance statement prepared manually calculates the variances above a given percentage (say ± 6%) away from the standard. The computer could perform a more detailed calculation without any extra effort on the part of the accountant. The variances and their significance could be ascertained by the computer programme—and if significance variance is detected, a more detailed analysis could routinely be undertaken without any extra effort. Hence, computers leave the management accountant with more time for higher-level purposes, i.e., decision-making, planning and controlling operations.

Computers and Management Accounting

Computers have brought about a significant refinement and improvement in the various facets of management accounting. Some of the important applications of computers are in the following areas:

— Budgeting

— Variance Analysis

— Analysis of Financial Statements

— Cost Accounting.

Computers are a valuable tool for management accounting purposes mainly because of their speed, accuracy, storage, calculating and decision-making ability. Computers, like in all other fields, perform these tasks in accounting and there is a growing role for computers in accounting and finance. Computers, though not essential, can be very useful for management accountants.

Speed: Computers perform the task at a very high speed. For example, if the computer is calculating financial ratios or printing a budget statement, it would do so in a minute fraction of the time it would take manually.

Accuracy: If there are no errors in the data input or programming errors, then the computer operations ensure 100 per cent accuracy in the results obtained. Only in an unforeseen combination of circumstances of some rare cases, do computer systems produce errors. A higher speed and accuracy helps the managers to devote more time for analysis.

— On-line data entry and inquiry for faster processing and reporting more control.

— Complete audit trials for close tracking.

— Rapid and complete updating, cross-referencing and retrieval of huge volumes of data that would be virtually impossib!e using any manual system.

— Account summary and control balance that are always update.

— Complete budgeting facility.

— Complete sttistical and management reporting as financial information is always current and is available.

— Multi-Company processing and reporting capability.

Storage: Computers are used to store huge volumes of data that would otherwise be very difficult in the manual system. Cross-referencing, retrieval, repeating are some of few areas which has been made much simpler and easily accessible with the help of computers.

Decision-making ability: Computers, not only perform the calculations very accurately but also, depending on the results, take different decisions. This decision making ability of the computer, has specifically helped in making computers qualitatively different and useful to cater to the expanding needs of business and industry.

Therefore computers can be used for processing information that has the following characteristics*:

---

* T. Lucey: 'Management Accounting', ELBS with DP Publications, 1972, pp. 439-440.

(a) Speed is an important factor.

(b) A number of interacting variables.

(c) There are reasonably accurate values.

(d) Accuracy of output is important.

(e) Operations are repetitive.

(f) Large amount of data exist.

Financial Accounting Software Programme

The financial accounting system is designed to meet the requirements of an organization and provides the backbone of an organization's accounting information system. Data are collected, stored and processed into information mainly to meet the financial accounting requirement of management and external agencies. A well designed and conceived system design will, in addition, permit the cost and management accounting functions tobe supported with little expenditure of funds and effort.

The specific needs of financial accounting information software will vary widely with the size of the organization, the purpose of the organization and the degree of accountability of the organization to the public at large. Nevertheless, the accounting requirements imposed by the Financial Accounting Standards Board, the Securities and Exchange Commission, the Internal Revenue Service and other regulatory agencies have resulted in firms and agencies adopting certain minimally acceptable standards. Hence, it is possible to form some generally applicable statements about the features of a well-designed financial accounting software.

The central feature of any such accounting system is the General Ledger. In addition, most financial accounting systems include one or more of the following components:

— Accounts receivable

— Accounts payable

— Payroll

— Inventory

— Fixed Assets.

Financial Accounting software may be procured as a package or it may be specifically designed for a particular organization. It may be implemented as a single entity or in a modular fashion.

The major components of financial accounting software are as under:

(a) *General Ledger Programs*: It provides an accurate database for all required financial reports to management, shareholders and regulatory agencies.

(b) *Accounts payable programme*: It maintains records of all outstanding claims against the assets of an organization.

(c) *Accounts receivable programmes*: It maintains records of all amounts due to the organization.

(d) *Payroll programmes*: It maintains records of all amounts due to the salaried and other employees of an organization.

(e) *Fixed assets accounting programmes*: It maintains the records of the long-term assets available with the organization.

(f) *Inventory accounting programmes*: It maintains the records regarding the Minimum Level, Maximum Level, Reorder Level and the other status of the inventory being used in the organization.

The first three models are described here in a little more detail.

General Ledger

Basic characteristics of a computer based General ledger are:

- A chart of accounts flexible enough to take care of a variety of requirements.
- Provisions for adding, deleting and modifying the master file records.
- Automatic Interface during the end-of-period proceeding with other modules like Accounts Receivables, Accounts Payable, etc.
- Generation of reports like Trial Balance, Balance Sheet, Income statement, etc.
- Control procedures involving Interactive Menu System, self instruction documentation, automatic backups at the end of the month, recovery routines etc.

A typical General Ledger system and with its features is discussed briefly here.

The system starts with a global menu listing various features available.

Global Menu
General Ledger

1. Maintain Parameters
2. Maintain Ledger
3. Create/Update transactions
4. Reports
5. Utilities
6. Good Bye

Maintain Parameters (Parameter Screen): The user is asked to input the ranges of account codes for Assets, Liabilities, Income and Expenditure. Description of journals is also given in this screen. The Information entered at this stage becomes master information and is not altered. Additional journal can however be added in the future.

Ledger (chart of Accounts): This is the most important part of the General Ledger system. A complete chart of Accounts is entered with relevant classifications, sub-divisions etc. to facilitate flexible reporting.

Generally the previous 12 months balances are entered in the various ledger accounts.

The systgem provides for adding, modifying or deleting any account from the system through easy user-friendly screens.

Create/Update Transactions (Transaction Entry System): The General ledger system is now ready for use.

As and when the transactions occur they can be entered in the system. Adjustments entries in the General Ledger are also entered through the system.

Reports: The General Ledger can produce the following statements:

- Ledger (L)
- Trial Balance (T)
- Balance Sheet (B)
- Chart of Accounts (C)
- Income and Expenditure Account (V)

The reports can be monthly or yearly; comparative or non-comparative; detailed or non-detailed. These can be displayed on the terminal or a hand copy on the printer can be produced.

Utilities (General Ledger System Maintenance): Here the user is allowed various general purpose utilities. These include saving data on a floppy, restoring data from back-ups in case of requirement, checking consistency of data permanent deletion etc.

Accounts Receivable System: This system involves keeping an account of all the credit customers.

The basic data can be captured by using either a sales invoiced or a point-of-sale (POS) system. POS system are applicable in retail operations. A typical sales invoice will consist of the following informations:—

Organisation Information:

- Name
- Address
- Telephone No.

Order No.

Customer Account No.

Credit Authorization

Product Information

— Product Code

— Description

— Quantity

— Unit Price

— Discount

— Total

Freight Charges

Total Cost

Date to be Delivered

The sales invoice will create a debit entry to Accounts Receivable system and a credit to sales.

The Accounts Receivable file generally consists of the following information:

Customer Account Numbers

Name

Address

Credit Limit

Credit History

Prior Balance Due

Finance Charges

Current Activity of each Transaction

Invoice

— Number

— Date

— Amount

Product Information

— Number

— Description

Payments

Accounts Receivable system should have the following features:

— Maintenance of customer records (addition, deletion and modification).

— List of customer records

— Preparation of invoices

— Ability to query the system

— Generation of customised reports like an invoice register, age-wise schedule, payments expected during a specified period, etc.

— Automatic posting of journal entries

— Back-up and security utilities

Accounts Payable System (APS)

Accounts Payable System keeps track of payments to be made to various vendors. It consist of the following modules:

— Vendor Maintenance

— Inventory Maintenance

— Purchase Order Module

— Merchandise Received

Payments

The features of the Accounts Payable System are as given below:

Vendor File Maintenance: Through this option all modifications to the vendors file can be made. The user can also scan through the vendor status for further information about the vendor.

Inventory Maintenance: Here the different inventory items purchased from the relevant vendor can be entered into the APS. Vendor file maintains vendor information, while inventory maintenance links up inventory items with different vendors. Addition or deletion of inventory status does not have any impact on the vendor status.

The orders can be raised here and stored in the merchandise file to be used later when required.

Mercandise received: When the user receives merchandise from the vendor he has to enter the vendor code and purchase order number, against which goods are being received.

Payment transaction: This option takes care of the actual payment made to a vendor, either through cash or cheque. The files that will be affected by this option will be the vendor file invoice file and the transaction file. For example, in the vendor file the balance is decreased by the amount paid, the last payment date is updated etc.

In the invoice file the invoice record is adjusted by the payment made transaction. In the file, a transaction is created for the amount paid to be used by the General Ledger.

Accounting system for Small and Medium Organizations

An example of a computerized accounting system for small and medium sized companies is the 'Client Accounting System'. This system operates with three sets of files:

1. General Ledger Transaction Master File.
2. General Ledger Transaction Work File.
3. Year to Date General Ledger Transaction File.

With the help of these file, the Client Accounting System generates the following reports:-

1. General Ledger account list.
2. General Ledger transaction register.
3. Financial Statements.
4. Departmental Statements.
5. Schedules to Balance Sheet and Income Statements.
6. Sources and applications of funds.
7. Cash Flow Statements.
8. Comparative reporting.
9. Trial Balance.
10. Accumulative ledger.
11. Source cross reference for general ledger.

Most of the standard accounting entries are done easily and, where possible, automatically. Examples include reversing entries, closing entries, analyzing entries, preparation of work sheet, trial balance and the periodic and special purpose financial reports.

Thus the elements of most accounting systems are structured to provide the information needed to generate financial statements. The structure of an accounting system includes financial statement, ledger accounts, journals and financial transactions, organized in a hierarchical order.

The mechanism for financial control and accounting data base are provided by the Journal and Ledger accounts. The Journal is the book of original entry. The Ledger is a group of accounts and is prepared to summarize the data. The Ledger accounts are used as master files in a computerized system.

A computerized accounting system uses software programme to manipulate accounting functions through the computer. It can satisfy a wide range of user needs.

Thus this system performs the external role of collecting and processing the information to generate financial statements. The structure of an accounting system is such that the day to day activities of the organization are processed, recorded and acted upon.

Accounting System for Large Organizations

The salient features of an accounting system for a large organization are:

1. *Data base design*: The data base design allows for fast, rapid and sequential access to data. At the end of an accounting period, or any time during the cycle, financial information is immediately available for updating and reporting. Accounts are kept current throughout the accounting period.

2. *Account Master File*: This incorporates all ledger accounts and like the manual system, the ledger card records both current and last years actual. The relationship with various ledger accounts at different levels can also be easily established here. This system brings out the following information:

— Account number

— Account description

-- Beginning balance and current year actuals

— Current year budgets

— Revised budgets

— Forecasts.

3. *Quality Presentation*: Having obtained the data, the system should provide for the preparation of various reports according to the needs of the user e.g. regulatory reports for financial statements and reports for senior managers.

In addition, for a large organization, the financial reporting system should be such that the users always have access to current information. The relationship among various accounts should be established in such a manner that it helps in creating a fully responsive data base and the financial managers have a comprehensive computer aided system of account management.

Accounting software Packages in India

Computers have brought about a significant refinement and improvement in the various facets of accounting. Today, there are a number of accounting software programmes in India which allow for suitable modification and alteration of original data to give the user a lot of flexibility in the utilization of the data.

Questions

1. What are the advantages that computers offer over manual accounting?
2. Why is payroll suitable for a computerised accounting system?
3. What advantages does a computerised accounting system have?
4. Briefly explain the report the clients accounting system generates.
5. What are the salient features of an accounting system for a large organisation?
6. Briefly explain the major components of a financial accounting software.

Appendix - I

Presented in this appendix are the Profit & Loss Account and the Balance Sheet of a company, as prescribed by the Indian Companies Act, 1956. A Financial Statement Analysis of the given financial data has also been attempted.

Profit & Loss Account
For the year Ended 31st March, 19x2

		For the year ended 31st March, 19x2 (Rs. in Lakhs)	For the year ended 31st March, 19x1 (Rs. in Lakhs)
1.	**Income:**		
	Sales	42,10,91	37,40,86
	Other Income	69,21	68,81
	Total Income	42,80,12	38,09,67
II.	**Expenditure:**		
	Raw Materials etc.	13,77,16	10,66,31
	Interest	1,10,54	1,30,64
	Manufacturing, Selling and other expenses	24,16,06	23,29,84
	Depreciation on fixed assets	26,32	21,40
	Total expenditure	39,30,08	35,48,19
III.	**Profit:**		
	Profit before taxation	3,50,04	2,61,48
	Provision for taxation	1,43,72	1,06,17
	Profit after Tax	2,06,32	1,55,31
	Profit brought forward	2,00	2,00
		2,08,32	1,57,31
	Transferred to earnings reserve	11,50	10,00
	Profit available for appropriation	1,96,82	1,47,31
IV.	**Appropriations:**		
	General Reserve	93,88	69,43
	Dividend subject to deduction of tax - proposed	1,00,94	75,88
	Profit carried forward	2,00	2,00
		1,96,82	1,47,31

Balance Sheet
As on 31st March, 19x2

	31st March, 19x2 (Rs. in Lakhs)		31st March, 19x1 (Rs. in Lakhs)	
I. Sources of Funds:				
1. Shareholders funds:				
(a) Capital	1,21,23		1,16,73	
(b) Reserves and Surplus	5,99,55	7,20,78	2,96,64	4,13,37
2. Loan Funds:				
(a) Secured loans	4,75,80		4,75,45	
(b) Unsecured loans	2,10,07	6,85,87	1,53,98	6,29,43
Total		14,06,65		10,42,80
II. Application of Funds:				
1. Fixed Assets:				
(a) Gross Block	6,59,27		5,33,42	
(b) Less: Depreciation	1,81,83		1,59,07	
(c) Net Block	4,77,44		3,74,35	
(d) Capital work in progress	52,63	5,30,07	28,86	4,03,21
2. Investments	2,01,50		1,10,81	

III. Current Assets, Loans and Advances:				
(a) Inventories	4,86,66		5,01,41	
(b) Sundry Debtors	3,20,66		2,02,75	
(c) Cash & Bank Balances	18,20		22,09	
(d) Other Current Assets	44,54		43,54	
(e) Loans and Advances	2,62,82		1,68,65	
	11,32,88		9,38,44	
Less:				
IV. Current Liabilities & Provisions:				
(a) Liabilities	3,56,86		3,33,78	
(b) Provisions	1,00,94		75,88	
	4,57,80		4,09,66	
Net Current Assets		6,75,08		5,28,78
Total		14,06,65		10,42,80

Financial Statement Analysis

I. **Liquidity Ratios:**

a. Current Ratio $\dfrac{\text{Current Assets}}{\text{Current Liabilities}} = \dfrac{1132.88}{457.80}$

= 2.47

b. Acid Test Ratio $\dfrac{\text{Quick Assets}}{\text{Current Liabilities}} = \dfrac{646.22}{457.80}$

= 1.41

II. **Leverage Ratios:**

a. Total debt-Equity Ratio = $\dfrac{\text{Total Debt}}{\text{Total Equity}}$

$= \dfrac{1406.65 + 457.80}{121.23} = \dfrac{1143.67}{121.23}$

= 9.43

b. Long-term debt-Equity Ratio = $\dfrac{\text{Long-term debt}}{\text{Total Equity}}$

$\dfrac{14{,}06.05}{121.23} = 11.60$

c. Debt-Asset Ratio = $\dfrac{\text{Total Debt}}{\text{Total Assets}}$

$\dfrac{1143.67}{1864.45} = .61$

d. Interest coverage Ratio = $\dfrac{\text{EBIT}}{\text{Interest}}$

$\dfrac{239.50}{110.54} = 2.17$

III. Profitability Ratios:

a. Gross Profit Margin Ratio = $\dfrac{\text{Gross Profit} \times 100}{\text{Net Sales}}$

$$= \frac{350.04 \times 100}{4280.12} = 8.18\%$$

b. Net Profit Margin Ratio = $\frac{\text{Net Profit} \times 100}{\text{Net Sales}}$

$$= \frac{206.32 \times 100}{4280.12} = 4.82\%$$

c. Net Income to Total Assets Ratio = $\frac{\text{Net Income}}{\text{Total Assets}}$

$$= 206.32 / 1864.65$$

$$= 0.11$$

d. Return on Investment = $\frac{\text{EBIT} \times 100}{\text{Total Assets}}$

$$= \frac{239.50 \times 100}{1864.65} = 12.85\%$$

e. Return on Shareholder's Equity = $\frac{\text{Net Profit} \times 100}{\text{Shareholder's Equity}}$

$$= \frac{206.32 \times 100}{720.78} = 28.63\%$$

f. Return on Capital Employed = $\frac{\text{Net Profit} \times 100}{\text{Capital Employed}}$

$$= \frac{206.32 \times 100}{1406.65} = 14.67\%$$

g. Earnings per share (EPS) = $\frac{\text{Profit after taxes - preferred Dividends}}{\text{Number of Equity Shares}}$

$$= \frac{20632}{1212} = 17.02$$

(In this example it is assumed that the number of equity shares outstanding are 1212 Lakhs).

h. Price-Earning Ratio (PIE ratio) = Market Price of Share.

If it is assumed that the Market Price per share is Rs 350, then the PIE ratio is : $\frac{350}{17.02} = 20.56$